There Really Are Secrets About Men That You Should Know!

Find out all about:

- **The Enthusiasm Factor**—and what it can do for you

- **What you wear underneath** your everyday clothes tells more about you than you may know

- **Relationship pitfalls** that will surprise you

- **What you can and cannot do** about a man who strays

- **Verbal cues**...what to say to make him feel like an incredible lover

- **Condoms**...making them part of the turn-on

- **And lots more!**

"Besides having solutions for dealing with men's always perplexing desires and behavior, this book has everything you want to know about sex and making yourself the sexiest partner on the planet. I learned enough to make even me more dangerous."

—Baroness Sheri de Borchgrave,
author of *A Dangerous Liaison*

"Sydney Biddle Barrows certainly knows what makes men tick. If you're a woman, you need to read this book."

—Bob Berkowitz, host of CNBC's *Real Personal*

Just Between Us Girls

— Us Girls —

Secrets About Men From the Madam Who Knows

SYDNEY BIDDLE BARROWS

with JUDITH NEWMAN

St. Martin's Paperbacks

JUST BETWEEN US GIRLS

Copyright © 1996 by Sapphire Professional Resources, Inc. and Judith Newman.

Cover photograph by Marc Raboy.

Library of Congress Catalog Card Number: 95-40060

ISBN: 0-312-96047-6

Printed in the United States of America

St. Martin's Press hardcover edition published in 1996
St. Martin's Paperbacks edition/February 1997

10 9 8 7 6 5 4 3 2 1

This book is dedicated to Steven Reisner,
whose compassion and caring made it possible.
Nothing I could ever do or say could possibly convey
the thanks, appreciation, and gratitude I feel for all
you have done for me.

Contents

Acknowledgments

The best thing about my life is all of the wonderful people who are in it. Not a day goes by that I don't feel both lucky and privileged to be friends or professionally involved (and often both) with all of you.

Judith Newman, my coauthor, for all of the hard work and patience she put in over the past year. May we sell a million copies!

Russ Galen and Shawna McCarthy, our literary agents, for

putting Judith and me together and for getting us such a great deal.

Jennifer Enderlin, our editor at St. Martin's Press, for her excellent, insightful, and helpful suggestions, which made this book even better.

John Murphy, director of publicity, and Jamie Brickhouse, publicist extraordinare, for really being behind this book, as well as Sally Richardson and Roger Cooper for knowing a great book idea when they see one!

Carol de Fritsch, for all her legal work and professional advice, as well as her friendship and personal support.

Ed Callaghan and Tony Vargas, for all of their professional work and support, as well as their friendship over these many years.

Donna Sessa and Bob McBride, for their belief in me and all of the work they put in on my behalf.

Adam Monaco, Steve Garrin, Jill Belasco, and Michael Abandond for their generosity, help, advice, and friendship.

Armand Braiger, proprietor of One If By Land, Two If By Sea, surely the most thoughtful, giving, generous man on the planet. I can never thank you enough for all you have done for me.

Jim Hjelm, who came to the rescue of someone he didn't even know and made the most important day of my life so very special. Thank you for your unparalleled generosity.

Andy Egendorf, whose belief in me came just when I needed it, whose professional counsel I value, and whose friendship I prize.

David Silver, for giving me the opportunity to do something really big, and Stan Kugell for all his time and input.

Paul Kotik, for all the time and hard work and continued belief in our project and me.

Audrey Smaltz, for her personal and professional support all these years.

Marcia Cohen, for sticking her neck out and giving me the advice column at *Her NY*.

All the other people too numerous to name who have helped me professionally in so many ways, my gratitude and most heartfelt thanks.

To my many friends: There just isn't enough room to name you all here, but you know who you are. I hope you know how much I love and care for you and how very very important you are to me. You are the best friends anyone could ever hope to have and I consider myself lucky and privileged to have you in my life.

My family: I know it hasn't always been easy, and I want to thank you again for always being there for me.

And last, but not least, my beloved husband, Darnay Hoffman, whose love and specialness I will always cherish.

S.B.B.

A writer is only as good as her friends and family—where do you think we get our stories? In this arena I've been blessed, indeed. I'd like to thank my agent and provocateur, Russell Galen; my parents, Ed Newman and Dr. Frances Fiorillo; my cousin, Amy Scott; and my adorable and alarmingly talented friends: Nancy Kalish, Melinda Marshall, Noreen O'Leary, Jaclyn Lee, Robert Pini, David Galef, Peter Bouteneff, Erica Meyer, and Martha Barnette. You all gave me fresh ideas, and you all make me laugh.

Upon hearing the subject of this book, several people said to me, "Gee, your husband must be one lucky guy." In fact, the poor fellow knows better than anyone what a combination of a looming deadline and sheer, unadulterated panic can do to a wife's more tender feelings. So above all, thank you, my love, for your patience; I promise I'll be much less cranky during childbirth.

J.N.

If men knew all that women think, they would be twenty times more audacious.

ALPHONSE KARR

1

"How Did a Nice Girl Like You . . . ?"

The applause was almost overwhelming. Audience members crowded around, asking questions, requesting autographs, and wanting to shake my hand. I had just given my first legitimate business speech to a group of high-powered CEO types. As the "Mayflower Madam," I had been at the epicenter of a sensational tabloid story, a potent 1980s combination of sex, glamour, and money. But it was reassuring to discover that I was perceived not only as a madam but also as a businesswoman who had successfully marketed her company. Surely they knew much more about marketing than I did, yet they were wildly enthusiastic.

Finally I was able to escape to the powder room, feeling pretty pleased with myself. Immediately I found myself surrounded by several women who asked if they could have a word with me—privately. I assumed they were going to ask me something like, "Did you face any discrimination as a woman running your own business?" I guess I should have known better.

They all wanted to know the same thing: What did I—and my girls—know about men that they didn't?

It was the same everywhere I went. Women were always taking me aside and asking some variation on this question. Often they would also whisper, "What can I do so that my husband won't go to a call girl?"

Since men stray for so many different reasons—and most of them don't go to call girls—it was impossible to come up with a facile one- or two-line answer, although heaven knows I'd tried many times over the past several years. It was then that I realized that although my speeches about marketing and how I got into the business were popular, the women in the audience *really* were far more interested in what special secrets call girls have.

So I developed a four-hour seminar, and now this book, to tell all.

There was certainly nothing in my childhood that one could point to and say, "So *that's* why she became a madam!" I lived in the tiny town of Hopewell, New Jersey, until I was seven, and then we moved to Rumson on the coast. My parents had divorced when I was four, and it was terribly traumatic. Like most little girls, I adored my daddy, and the fact that he didn't make much effort to see me during my childhood certainly didn't help. My mother did the best she could, but when I look back and remember her trying to explain why there was no phone call for my birthday or Christmas or why there wasn't enough money for the latest rock-and-roll record, I realize it couldn't have been easy for her either.

I was an A and B student, one of those kids most people didn't notice because I kept to myself a lot.

When I was ready for high school, my grandmother Sydney decided it might be a good idea for me to go to boarding school. I was thrilled to get out of the house. My mother was fairly strict, and, like a typical teenager, my behavior reflected my frustration. So off I went to Stoneleigh Burnham, an all-girls' boarding school in Greenfield, Massachusetts. I loved Stoneleigh. I recall especially one time during my junior year thinking that I couldn't ever remember being so happy. I finally had a group of friends, I had a terrific roommate, my grades were good, I got to ride several times a week, and I had a boyfriend whom I adored. In fact, I adored him so much that in January of my senior year I sneaked away one weekend to visit him at his college in Pennsylvania, got caught, and was kicked out of Stoneleigh. And so for the first time in fourteen years I found myself living with my father and his family in Old Lyme, Connecticut, and finishing high school there.

When I was eighteen my mother's parents arranged for my cousin and me to make our debut at the annual ball of the Society of Mayflower descendants. This is a very grand party held every year for girls who can document that at least one ancestor was one of the original Pilgrims who came over to America on the *Mayflower* back in 1620 (hence the *New York Post*'s moniker for me, "Mayflower Madam"). I wore a traditional long white debutante dress; my grandfather and stepfather and all the men in the room wore white tie and tails. It was like a long, dreamy scene in a movie. Twenty-two years later, when I was still husbandless on my fortieth birthday, I would joke to my friends that it looked as if that debut would be the only time in my life I'd ever get a chance to wear a long white gown!

Before I left Stoneleigh I had been accepted by Elmira College, an all-girls' college in Upstate New York. Elmira's biggest selling point as far as I was concerned was that it didn't require you to have a specific major. You could just take an assortment of liberal arts courses.

At that point I had absolutely no idea what I was gong to do with my life. I had not grown up in an atmosphere where making my own decisions was encouraged, and I had no experience planning or setting goals for myself. I did what I was told (for the most part) and whoever was "in charge" at the time took care of me.

After I graduated from high school, my father found me a summer job as a receptionist at his office. One day in August I came home to find a letter from Elmira requesting a $3,000 tuition check. (Can you imagine? In 1970 that was one *full* year's tuition!) I handed it to my father, who read it, folded it back up, and out of the clear blue said to me, "You're a pretty girl. Some rich man will marry you. Why should I spend the money to send you to college?"

I was so stunned I didn't know what to think or say. I've often wondered what might have happened if I'd tried to defend myself or make a case for the importance of a college education. But I didn't. It was clear he hadn't given the matter one second of thought until the very moment he saw the bill, and he seemed quite taken with how clever and sensible a decision he had made. "If you really want to go to college," he added, "you can pay for it yourself."

With an opportunity I had always taken for granted so offhandedly and thoughtlessly snatched away, for the first time in my life I was faced with having to decide what to do with my life. I had no idea where to begin. Where I came from, women didn't have jobs, let alone careers. My mother didn't work, my stepmother didn't work, none of my friends' mothers worked. Not once in my life had anybody ever clued me in that I might ever have to be responsible for myself. I guess everyone just assumed that I'd get married and, once again, someone else would take care of me.

I continued to work in my father's office. (He refused to give me a raise, saying he couldn't afford it; later he hired my replacement at a considerably higher salary.) I saved as much money as I could while trying to figure out what I would do. Career opportunities were pretty limited for women back then. I wasn't interested in being a nurse or a teacher, and since I had barely squeaked through a typing course with a C–, secretarial work was out of the question. Walking through the mall one Saturday, I had a eureka moment. Clothes! I loved pretty clothes! I'd do something that had to do with clothes!

I ended up at the Fashion Institute of Technology in New York City, in their buying and merchandising program. I graduated first in my class and landed a spot in the Executive Training Program at Abraham and Straus. My first job was as an assistant buyer in the Bath Shop, and my boss was a woman whose professional style—both as a boss and a businesswoman—was so exemplary that I have tried to emulate it my entire life.

Soon after getting a promotion, I got an even better job at the May Company Corporate as an assistant buyer for accessories; a year later, I was a buyer for all women's fashion accessories at a small resident buying office. It was a wonderful job with a pitiful salary, but I loved it. To make a very long story short, I was fired after nine months. The company hired a woman I had to report to who expected me to participate in a kickback scheme. I refused and was out the door in a split second. She warned me that if I ever told anyone what had happened she would make sure I never worked in this business again. Since I was still a pretty naive twenty-six-year-old, I believed her. After all, if she was evil enough to take kickbacks, she was evil enough to blacklist me and make certain I never worked in this town again.

So there I was, two weeks before Thanksgiving (a time when it's almost impossible to get executive work in the retail industry), out of work and collecting unemployment. The first week of unemployment is wonderful: You sleep late, catch up on the soaps, reorganize your closets, and go through that magazine pile. By the third week you're so lonely and bored it's hard to get out of bed in the morning.

I struck up a friendship with a girl named Gina whom I'd met on the weekly line for my unemployment check. We got together several times a week just for something to do, and one day it was my turn to go down to her place in Greenwich Village for lunch. I trudged up the stairs to her fourth-floor apartment, climbed over several large boxes sitting in her hallway, and walked into her apartment to find her putting together a new stereo system.

Since I knew she didn't have any more money than I did, I was curious about where she'd gotten it. Gina was uncharacteristically evasive. I kept pestering her until she finally looked at me solemnly and said, "Sydney, do you swear you won't tell *anybody?*"

Intrigued, I said, "I swear." And then she told me: "I answer phones for an escort service."

"Ohhhh . . ." (My brain was doing a futile search for a definition) then: "What's an escort service?"

She started explaining, and then it dawned on me: Omigod! she's talking about call girls! Prostitutes!

I was both fascinated and horrified. Certainly I'd heard of them and seen them in the red-light district in Amsterdam, but I had never met anybody who actually *knew* one. I had to know everything and peppered her with all the same (and often dumb) questions everybody always now asks me. Finally I got around to asking her how much she made, and she answered, "Fifty dollars a night, off the books." Back in 1978, this was big bucks. (In fact, it's not such shabby pay today, just for answering a phone for a few hours.) So I said the same thing I think almost anybody in a similarly impoverished position might have said: "Hey, if they have any openings, let me know."

As the weeks passed, Gina regaled me with the exploits of all the girls and descriptions of some of the guys who used the service. Let's face it, her stories were a lot more interesting than anything happening in my life at that particular time.

At the end of January, as I was busily sending out résumés to get the most fabulous job in the history of retailing, my phone rang. Gina announced that one of the girls in the office was leaving. Was I still interested in the job?

I immediately got cold feet. I was afraid of the police, I didn't want to get involved with the Mafia. . . . So I told her no and mumbled something about getting a real job any minute. Gina said, "Look, why don't you just talk to the owner? You could work a couple of weeks until something comes through."

So I went to meet Eddie, and just so he didn't misunderstand what job I was applying for I wore very little makeup, glasses, slacks, and a bulky sweater. I looked like a junior high school librarian. I got the job.

Almost from the beginning, it was apparent to me that this man had no idea how to run a business. I'm not suggesting that four years in retailing made me into Lee Iacocca. But this man had no concept of truth in advertising, prompt delivery, repeat business, or inventory control. For example, if a gentleman called and said he wanted a tall, busty blonde, Eddie would swear he had just what he wanted—and then send over a short, flat-chested redhead. This is pretty much the escort service equivalent of ordering a Rolls-Royce and ending up with a Hyundai.

He didn't treat the girls much better. Among other things, he insisted that they work seven nights a week, *every* week. Given his unreasonable and impossible expectations, the girls would call in at the last minute with the most incredible excuses, which often meant there were nights when we had virtually no staff. So we'd end up sending any old warm body to the clients, who'd be furious and take it out on the girls. Eddie also refused to pay the girls until checks cleared, and for some reason checks took *months* to clear. Gina and I were constantly Monday-morning quarterbacking. We were convinced we knew how to run the business better.

The day finally came when I just couldn't take it anymore. A girl had received a check from a client for a call that had taken place before I even started working there. She came into the office and asked for her money. I looked in the drawer and saw that the envelope with the cash wasn't there. So I called Eddie and asked him where her money was. At that moment he reminded me of my father the day he told me he wouldn't pay for college. "Uh, tell her the check bounced."

"What?" I stage-whispered on the phone. I knew he was lying.

"You heard what I said. Tell her the check bounced."

"But Eddie! This is *Jan*." Jan was one of his best girls. I began to recite her praises, but he just hung up the phone.

What could I do? Take it out of my own pocket? I didn't have it. So I told her the check didn't go through. And she burst into tears right in front of me. Although I wasn't the one who had stolen her money, I was representing the person who had. And I felt just awful.

Right then I made a decision. It was bad enough that I had to lie to clients about what the girls really looked like and what time they'd be there. It was bad enough to have to beg the girls to be on call every night of the week. But I wasn't going to steal from them, too. So I quit.

I called Gina the next day, and we did our usual moaning and groaning. Then I heard myself say: "We're at least as smart as Eddie is. We're definitely nicer. Why don't we start our own escort service?" She thought it was a grand idea.

So we did. And we called our escort service Cachet.

How the Business Worked:
Anatomy of a "Call"

One of NY's finest private escort services is currently seeking a small number of exceptionally attractive, well-educated, articulate young ladies between the ages of 19 and 30 for part-time evening employment. Fluency in one or more foreign languages helpful but not required.

This was the help wanted ad I placed in *The Village Voice*, *Show Business*, and *The Soho Weekly News* to attract girls. It was a dramatic contrast to most of the other ads, which usually read something like:

```
        GIRLS! GIRLS! GIRLS!
          EARN LOTS OF
     $$$$$$$$$$$$$$$$$$$$$
```

Which ad would you answer? Right.

There was one concept I couldn't stress enough to the girls who worked for me: The men were paying for a *fantasy*—a beautiful, elegant, sophisticated woman with nothing on her mind other than pleasing him.

I had a strict dress code. My girls should look like the wife or daughter of the richest man in the biggest suite at the Pierre Hotel. This meant conservative but elegant and stylish suits or dresses and sleek high heels. Low-cut V-necks, thigh-high slit skirts, clingy fabrics, or anything beaded was verboten. We wanted to get as far away as possible from the stereotypical bimbo/hooker look; that was not the kind of girl our customers would feel comfortable with. Our clientele was made up of very successful Wall Street moguls, CEOs of major corporations, entrepreneurs of all sorts from the United States and abroad, diplomats and officials of foreign governments, as well as the ubiquitous sheikhs and princes from the oil-rich Middle East. These men were looking for pretty, bright, totally presentable companions for an evening, not gum-chewing "foxes" for a half-hour quickie.

In my experience, most men truly subscribe to the old adage, "A lady in the living room and a whore in the bedroom." So underneath the conservative, elegant clothing, I insisted that every girl wear matching bra, panties, garter belt, and stockings. If she wanted to go all out and be guaranteed a big tip, she could substitute a bustier for the bra.

We also encouraged the girls to wear the highest heels they could walk in without wobbling.

Each girl carried a briefcase (the better to elude hotel security), which contained a change of stockings (in case of runs), panty shields (for obvious reasons; why ruin that expensive underwear?), a mini-makeup kit for quick repairs, a shower cap, bubble bath, mints (mandatory for smokers), a small amount of money for cabs and telephone calls, and a Port-a-Print for credit cards. The girls were also advised to carry condoms, although in the early 1980s condoms were to be used only at the customer's request.

We prided ourselves on having young ladies of every shape, color, and description. If a man wanted a 5'10" redhead, that's what he got. Unlike Eddie, I believed in truth in advertising, because it was the only way to guarantee repeat customers. (The stereotypical all-American look was the most popular. If you were a tall, busty, midwestern-looking blonde under twenty-six years of age, you had more work than you could possibly handle.)

Many people ask me if the women ever dated or married the clients. It would certainly make sense: young struggling actresses or career women surrounded by wealthy, influential older men. Surprisingly, the answer is no. This was not due to lack of trying on the part of the clients, however. The girls knew that the person the client believed he'd "fallen in love with" was not who she really was at all, was not the always-cheerful, ever-accommodating glamorous woman who never had a headache, a bad day at the office, or any problems at all in her life. The women knew that once they let their hair down, it would be all over.

Occasionally a new girl figured that if she told a client her problems and elicited sympathy for all the tough times she was going through, she would get a bigger tip. This was almost invariably a mistake. Clients go to call girls to escape their *own* problems. So any personal problems a girl might be having that day—from a fight with her boss to PMS—had to be left outside the hotel room.

I tried not to hire girls who'd "worked" before; they were

nearly always so abused and mistreated by other agencies that they thought of men as little more than machines to crank money out of. So when I interviewed prospective employees, I specifically looked for women who were new to this business, women with a daytime job who just wanted to make extra money on the side but planned a life beyond the escort service. Most of my girls were students, aspiring actresses, models, dancers, singers, writers, artists, and women in low-paying entry-level positions in PR, publishing, and magazines. They had to be able to talk intelligently, and—even more important—they had to be able to listen. And just as in any profession, the best call girls were the ones who genuinely enjoyed their work.

We were quick to realize that men who were paying $200 an hour wanted more than just physical gratification. If that's all they wanted, they could get it for $20 on any street corner. Our average call lasted two to four hours and cost between $400 and $800. Of that time, only about five to ten minutes is actually spent in bed with the client. Remember, it takes a lot longer to make love to someone you care about than to have sex with someone you're paying. First of all, the guy realizes that *she* doesn't have to see fireworks, since her payoff in this transaction is money. And second, when he's having sex with somebody new, it's very exciting and almost always a lot quicker than with someone he's known for a long time. And don't underestimate the effect of the lingerie: Most men back then had never seen a woman in the flesh wearing the sexy underwear the girls all sported—although of course they'd seen it in magazines. The nude women most men saw in *Playboy* or *Penthouse* were wearing something like this. Of course, today it's common for women to wear frilly, frothy underwear; we can order it from the Victoria's Secret catalog that seems to arrive in the mail every other day. But back in the early 1980s, only *Playboy* bunnies and hookers wore this stuff. The rest of us women were all trying to dress like men. So when the girls at Cachet took off their clothes—and obviously they had better-than-average bodies—they were wearing incredible garments these guys had never seen in person, and—well, you can imagine, sex didn't take very long. A lot of the time it was over practically before it started.

So if a call lasts three or four hours, what are these men doing the rest of the time? They're talking. They're impressing the women with their magnificent exploits. They're pouring wine or champagne with a flourish. And often, they're pouring out their hearts.

That old stereotype of the hooker with the heart of gold had real meaning to us at Cachet. Many people have said to me, "C'mon. Hookers are hookers. How could these girls *not* be hardened by the business?" But you must remember: This was the late 1970s and early 1980s, when many women were already sleeping with guys on the first date—for free. They saw the business as a lucrative and temporary job opportunity. Luckily, we had very interesting clients: CEOs, diplomats, international businessmen—guys who were making a *lot* of money. Most of the girls were students in their early twenties; they had never drunk Dom Perignon in a $2,000-a-night suite in the Waldorf, eaten at a four-star restaurant, or seen New York from the back of a chauffeured limousine. They considered it a real adventure, as well as a great way to earn a good living.

During the four-hour "Everything You Ever Wanted to Know About Being a Call Girl" training session every new girl had to attend, one of the things I emphasized over and over again was the importance of being a good listener: how to draw him out without seeming to be prying, to be empathetic and understanding, not to give advice unless asked, to soothe his worries and let him know someone cares.

Not all the clients wanted a shoulder to cry on. Many were looking for intellectual stimulation: to laugh, talk, share ideas, discuss what was going on in the world, and learn something that perhaps they didn't know before. We went out of our way to find intelligent, lively young women who could hold up their end of the conversation with very bright, often overworked and overstressed men. Knowing how to give undivided attention (and, when necessary, a sympathetic ear) to men who often weren't getting it at home was every bit as important as knowing how to do a striptease. We demanded a girl who could do both.

Of course they did not spend the *entire* evening talking. Eventually they did get down to what we euphemistically called the nitty-gritty. We were very sexually conservative, however. With *very* rare exceptions, our girls were permitted to have only intercourse and oral sex. We were happy to refer a client to other agencies we knew if he was looking for anything more exotic.

Profile of a Client

Who was our "typical" client? He wasn't the desperate social misfit you might expect. In fact, quite the opposite was true. Since ours was such an expensive service, most of these fellows had a lot of money, and many of them earned that money during the business boom of the 1980s. By the time you reach the level of success our clients had attained, you pick up a lot of charm and polish along the way. And I wanted only straight, stuffy businessmen. I was not looking for guys who wanted to party the night away in major booze-and-coke fests (although, of course, I'm not saying that kind of evening never happened).

About a third of the clients were young, single Wall Street cowboys in their twenties and thirties, the kind of men who worked ridiculous hours, traveled constantly, and didn't have time for a casual girlfriend, much less a serious one. When they had some free time, they wanted a *sure thing;* they didn't want to spend most of the evening wining and dining a woman and then hear her say, "I don't know if I'm ready."

The other two-thirds were married, in their thirties and beyond. (Sometimes *way* beyond: we had clients in their seventies and eighties. Some of our older gentlemen called us because their wives were ill and could no longer make love.)

Many were on the road almost constantly and hated going back to an empty hotel room; they were lonely and looking for companionship. The *last* thing they wanted was someone who might try to contact them once they returned home!

Almost always our clients were affluent, charming men who didn't hire women for sex because they couldn't get it without paying. They hired them to ensure there would be no emotional entanglements. In other words, they hired girls to *make sure* they'd go away.

There was nothing caddish about most of these guys. Many of them, in addition to the money they gave the girls, showered them with presents. One client who manufactured ski jackets in the Far East made sure every girl who saw him walked away with a new jacket; one Italian gentleman doled out exquisite silk scarves as if they were Kleenex. Another favorite client, a wine merchant, held impromptu tastings of the finest wines and champagnes for his chosen lady for the evening. I even remember one fellow, who happened to be redecorating his apartment the day one of our girls visited, who just gave her a load of furniture. After they were finished, he called a limousine and helped her fill it with chairs, lamps, pictures, plants—everything he could cram in there. And although the madam was usually not the recipient of such largesse, one Christmas I received a large box of the most exquisite wrapping paper from a man who was in the business.

If these men could help the girls without fear of being exposed, they would go out of their way to do it. Partly, I think, the men were so generous because they sensed that our girls weren't pros. Instead of the greedy, grasping stereotypical hooker they expected to meet, they found young women who were genuinely grateful.

We weren't open during the day, because our clients were working, and we weren't open late at night, because they were the kind of businessmen who had eight A.M. breakfast meetings. In short, they were the guys that women today pay $5,000 to exclusive dating services in the hopes of meeting.

It was easier than you'd think to screen clients. You could

tell a lot simply by the way they conducted themselves over the phone. The man who calls and says, "Hi, my name is Mr. Jones. I'm staying at the Plaza, and I saw your ad in the Yellow Pages. Could you tell me something about your service?" is very different from someone who calls up and says, "Hey, whaddya got tonight?" The best calls were the men who asked first for a woman with personality, rather then emphasizing the way she looked. When you ask a prospective client what kind of a young lady he's looking for, and he says, "Well, I want someone intelligent, fun to be with, and also pretty, please," that's very different from, "Blonde with big tits." I didn't send girls to clients who were obviously focused on t-and-a. I could afford to be picky; there was a lot of business out there.

Because we were far more choosy about both the caliber of our girls and the clients they saw, I'd say that the girls who worked for me had more control over their work conditions than the average flight attendant, waitress, or member of most service professions. We offered health insurance coverage, which was unheard-of in the escort profession. Our young ladies had to give us only three nights a week, and we sent them to only the best hotels and residential areas.

We had one piece of advice for all our working girls that always seemed to hold true: The more you act like a lady, the more he'll act like a gentleman.

The New York Police closed us down in 1984, after I had been operating for five and a half years. The media frenzy about the Mayflower Madam lasted about six months. I paid a $5,000 fine, with no probation and no jail time. Although I certainly made decent money, it wasn't nearly as much as the newspapers at the time said. The sums of money exchanged were grossly overdramatized to make a good story even juicier.

And although the IRS would dispute this, I paid all my taxes. Cachet was not a cash business; what man walks around New York City with hundreds of dollars in his pockets? Cachet ran primarily on credit cards and checks, so of course we *had* to pay taxes. Officially, Cachet was a "temporary help" personnel agency—which is pretty accurate, if you think about it!

In 1986, *Mayflower Madam*, cowritten with Bill Novak, came out and was a huge success. The paperback the following year was also on the best-seller list for weeks. It was all about the girls and the business, and it was filled with wonderful stories. A pretty dismal TV movie, starring Candice Bergen (its only saving grace), was released in 1987 and supposedly based on the book. But the network wouldn't permit the producer to use the real story. In real life, everyone made a lot of money and had a lot of fun; it was glamorous and interesting; nothing bad ever happened to anyone, and no one was ever sorry. They didn't feel they could send this kind of message out to the public. So they made up their own story. Someone threw in a plot twist in which Candice Bergen, playing me, was proposed to by a cute lawyer who wanted to take her away from the escort business. And she said no! No way would I have said no to a cushy life with a gorgeous guy like Chris Sarandon, whom I was supposedly madly in love with. Such is Hollywood.

One of the most common misperceptions about the escort service business is that it's very dangerous. I think this notion comes from the fact that street girls, who constitute no more than 10 to 15 percent of the prostitution business in any community, are disproportionately victims of violence. If you're a psycho who wants to hurt a woman, you have to find one who's willing to go off to a secluded area with a stranger. The only kind of person who'll do that is a street prostitute. In addition, street girls are the only concrete image most people have of prostitutes. Whenever the news does a feature story on prostitution, the women are invariably desperate, drug-addicted girls in a precinct lockup, or streetwalkers being arrested. Assuming that all prostitutes are streetwalkers is like assuming that all restaurants are McDonald's.

I've been criticized for making sleeping with men for

money sound fun and glamorous—but the fact is, at the highest levels, it genuinely *is*. But it's also true that at the lowest levels, it can be harrowing. Most street girls are victims—of drug habits, of violent and abusive families, of educational systems that have failed them. By making prostitution illegal, we're actually encouraging the sleaziest members of the society to prey upon and take advantage of desperate, confused, and frightened young women. We're creating a caste of women who are totally disfranchised. If a pimp beats up a street girl or a "date" rapes her, whom is she going to complain to?

I think that as victims, these women deserve our sympathy and help rather than our condemnation and our calls to lock them up. They don't have the choices that the rest of us have.

The girls who worked for me *did* have choices. Most of them didn't suffer from burnout, because they stayed only six months to a year. And unlike other escort services, which make their women work seven days a week and are open twenty-four hours a day, I was open only from four P.M. to one A.M., and I asked our girls for only three nights a week. So they didn't have to *live* the call girl's life. That wouldn't have worked for the kind of girls I hired, because they had their own lives.

All of them are in other professions now—and many are wives and mothers. Wisely, most have not divulged their former "business" to their husbands. They look at it as something fun and adventurous they did when they were young, but they realize that their husbands would not welcome this news and would probably use it against them during some future argument. They also realize that, even if they asked, their men really don't want to know.

We're all entitled to our little secrets. I don't see anything wrong with not telling.

In recent years, as I've lectured around the country, I've had time to consider the escort business from the point of view of women I'd really never thought much about before: wives and girlfriends. (The fact that I myself got married—to Darnay Hoffman, a lawyer and television producer, in May 1994—also propelled me to look at the business from a different perspective!)

It was one thing for young, successful single men who didn't have a lot of time for personal relationships to use an escort service. But what about the men who went from the arms of our girls back to their own homes—complete with wife, children, dog, and manifold responsibilities? What brought these men to us? As women are constantly asking me, what did our girls know that they as wives and girlfriends didn't?

That is what *Just Between Us Girls* is about.

2

Rules of the
Beauty Game
Every Call Girl Knows

If I'm ever at dinner with a group of men and women and I want to initiate an interesting—and heated—argument, I've learned that I need mention only one topic: why men stray.

George is an interesting case in point. A well-known fashion photographer, he and his wife, Melissa, have been married for only four years. One day he and I happened to be talking about my Just Between Us Girls seminar, and the topic of why men stray came up. I watched a normally calm and contemplative man practically foam at the mouth:

"I'll tell you why! Who betrayed whom first? You shouldn't always blame the guys. My wife betrayed *me* first," George cried. I assumed he meant that his wife had had an affair with another man, but that's not what he was talking about at all. He continued: "When I married her, she was beautiful. She dressed impeccably, she always did her hair, she always looked fabulous. It was one of the things that attracted me the most to her.

"And then we get married, and we have two kids. Now she's a hundred pounds overweight, she never wears makeup anymore, she doesn't even wash her hair regularly. If I knew three years ago that this is what I would end up with, I never would have married her. So don't always blame these men. Because a lot of times it's the women who betray them first."

Like most women, my first reaction to George's tirade was, This guy's a Neanderthal. Whatever happened to those wedding vows, "For better or worse"? I certainly question the depth of his love for his wife. I mean, how many of us would be repulsed by our husbands if they lost their hair and grew beer guts (which, in fact, most of them do)? But the fact remains that none of us can control what we are—and are not—attracted to. George's reaction to his wife may have been extreme, but even husbands who genuinely adore their wives may simply not be able to be aroused by a woman whose physical appearance is so far from what appeals to him.

Men are more visually oriented than women. Let's face it: Who buys all the magazines that feature naked bodies? Either heterosexual men buy them to look at women, or gay men buy them to look at men. There are virtually no magazines for women to gaze at naked bodies because, frankly, we don't care that much. Virtually the entire adult entertainment industry is geared toward arousing men.

The average man does not look at a woman who's marginally attractive and say, "Gee, I bet she's a nice person" or "She's probably quite intelligent." Ask some men. If they look at a woman and they don't find her appealing enough to entertain the possibility of sleeping with her, they just don't care. Obviously, if he's sexually attracted to you and then meets you and doesn't like who you are, he's not going to pursue you. But if he looks at you and he's not sexually attracted, it doesn't matter how intelligent or fun you are. Which pretty much explains how CEOs of Fortune 500 companies can marry women they wouldn't trust working in their mail rooms—as long as they look spectacular in an evening gown.

At Cachet, there were different levels of "bookability" among the girls, depending on their looks. The most sought-after "fantasy" woman (generally blond, under twenty-five years old, with a big bust and great figure) could work only three evenings a week and make anywhere from $1,000 to $3,000. The pretty woman with a good figure but who was not blond, or the more average-looking woman with a great figure who also was very bright, could make between $750 and $2,000 a week. The least bookable girls (redheads, for some reason, were not sought after, nor were those over twenty-six or with short hair) made between $250 and $1,500—still not bad for three evenings' work.

I'm not suggesting you have to have perfect looks. What men might stare at in a magazine is not necessarily what they want for themselves. When faced with an absolute knockout, many men are just too intimidated; suddenly they'll flash back to those days when they were dweebs in high school being rejected by the captain of the cheerleading squad. Men even ascribe negative characteristics to a ravishingly beautiful girl: If she's gorgeous, she must also be a stupid, greedy gold digger, an unfaithful bitch, or hopelessly spoiled, with expectations they could never meet. She'd never be satisfied with a little token gift; it would have to be a diamond from Tiffany's. Some men even cling to this attitude when requesting a call girl. They all want someone attractive, but not necessarily someone blindingly beautiful.

Fortunately, too, we live in a world of aesthetic diversity, where one's man object of indifference is another man's erotic obsession. Men who love fat women, men who love skinny women, men who love women with big hips, and men who love women with small breasts—there are preferences on both ends of the physical (and emotional) spectrum. And just as Baskin-Robbins glories in its thirty-one flavors, there are some omnivorous men who glory in all of ours. Thank goodness.

Nevertheless, it's possible to pinpoint some general rules of attraction, rules that call girls know almost by instinct. Remember, a call girl is running a business in which *she* is the inventory. Try, for a moment, to think of your relationship as a business, where *you* are the only product you're offering. If you can improve that product with a bit of effort and a little marketing know-how, why not?

Physical Turn-Ons

As one wag observed, "A man falls in love through his eyes; a woman, through her ears." We may adore having sweet nothings whispered to us; a man needs bonbons that are more visual than auditory. One of the reasons men stray—although certainly not the only one or the most important—is that they no longer find their partners physically attractive.

Here are some general guidelines for overall body maintenance.

Moderate Fitness

Lesson #435 in the ongoing series, "Life Is Unfair": We may look at his hairy potbelly and think of it as a cute furry animal, or believe his love handles give us just a little something extra to hold on to, like the safety bar on a roller coaster. We may rub his balding pate for good luck. Women may sentimentalize and even romanticize a man's physical shortcomings, but men are much more realistic. They call a roll (of flab) a roll.

On the bright side, men are not looking at us with the eagle eyes with which we scrutinize ourselves. According to one study, whereas about 40 percent of women think they're overweight, only 8 percent of men think their spouses are too plump.

But men do appreciate a woman who takes care of her body. At Cachet, women under twenty-five or twenty-six were the most coveted not because they were sexier or more fun to be with, but simply because, with little effort on their part, they had good muscle tone. It was also fairly easy for us to book women in their thirties if they were athletes or dancers. (Of course, we may have fibbed about their age a little bit to the client.) In fact, most men who were given a choice of a gorgeous face and a so-so body or a great body and a so-so face opted for the great body every time.

So I made sure my girls stayed pretty close to the weight at which I first hired them; those who didn't were put on indefinite sabbatical until they shaped up.

Good Grooming

Few of us were born with the sort of startling good looks that allow us to wake up in the morning fresh, sparkling, and ready for close-ups. But simple grooming—and I stress the word *simple*—can make just about any woman attractive.

The girls who worked for me had to be, above all, radiantly *clean*, and you should be, too: shiny hair; scrubbed, glowing skin; translucent, natural-looking makeup (yes, sometimes it takes longer to look like you're wearing no makeup). I have an obsession with squeaky-clean ears—that's why God invented Q-Tips.

When brushing teeth, take your time and do it correctly, being sure to floss. (At the risk of sounding like your dentist, brush your tongue, too. You'd be amazed at how clean your mouth will feel and smell.) If your teeth are crooked, it's never too late to get braces. With new advances in the field of orthodontia, they even can be attached to the back of your teeth so no one will see them.

Choose antiperspirants that are unscented and don't leave a white residue that sticks to armpits and clothing. (I told the girls at Cachet to buy unscented personal hygiene products whenever possible; if you wear perfume, you don't want other odors clashing with the main scent you *want* people to notice. I also discouraged the girls from using personal hygiene sprays and douches, especially those that reeked of synthetic odors, like strawberry. Women should smell like *clean* women, not like produce.)

Skin

Perfectly silky, soft skin was one of the trademarks of the girls who worked for me. Clients constantly asked me where I found all these women with such satiny skin. Indeed, the softness of your skin lingers in your man's mind.

Tonight, take the "tush test": Run your hands over your buttocks and the backs of your thighs. If you don't use an exfoliator, there will be a prickly feeling. That's because the oil and sweat you secrete backs up in the pores and gets trapped—hence the little bumps.

Here's the secret to softness: exfoliators, which are essentially sandpaper for the skin to get rid of dead cells. Every women who worked for me had to use a synthetic exfoliator sponge called a Buf Puf.

At the end of your bath or shower, get your Buf Puf soaking wet and then put a glop of bath gel (I use Neutrogena Rainbath, a high-quality product at a reasonable price) on the blue, more abrasive side of the Puf. In a circular motion, gently rub it all over the rough spots for a minute or two. Make sure you also exfoliate the skin around the bikini area if you wax or shave, to prevent painful ingrown hairs. Be very careful not to overdo it, or you will exfoliate so much skin you'll end up with a big scab.

It takes six to eight weeks of doing this every other day to see results; after that, you need to do it only once a week to keep the skin smooth. Apply plenty of moisturizer afterward, for extra smoothness. Exfoliation is particularly great for women of color: Removing dead skin cells takes care of that ashy look, and your skin will glow.

About body hair removal: American men prefer women with hairless armpits and legs. Most of us shave (always use a shaving cream or gel; bathe in water long enough to soften and swell hairs). Waxing, done by a professional or at home, is the way to go if you have a fairly high tolerance for discomfort. The results last for several weeks, and repeated waxing makes hair grow back more sparsely. (There is one drawback to waxing. The hair has to be long enough for the wax to grip it. So you will have to put up with some stubble between waxings.)

And anything even vaguely resembling a mustache must go. Use bleach to camouflage regrowth until it is long enough to wax again.

Hair

Hair has always been a source of power and eroticism. When Delilah robbed Samson of his long locks, she stole his strength; and when medieval knights rode into battle, they often wore a piece of their lady's hair in a locket near their hearts.

Thomas Cash, a psychologist at Old Dominion University, recently conducted a study on hair type and what attracts men. Although the preference for Christie Brinkley look-alikes was not as overwhelming as you'd think, 38 percent of men preferred blondes (think of that number, compared with the percentage of real blondes in the country—only about 17 percent) and 52 percent preferred blue eyes. (In my business, I could never have enough blondes working for me; there was always more of a demand than a supply.)

Short hair generally does not turn men's heads. Neither

do bizarre asymmetrical cuts or wild colors. (As Fran Lebowitz once said, "Violet will become a good color for hair at just about the same time brunette becomes a good color for flowers.") Most men prefer medium to long hair, straight or wavy; if there's curl, let it be Botticellian ringlets, not head o'frizz. Girls who worked for me and got their hair permed often had to go on hiatus.

Whatever the hair type, men feel about hair spray the way roaches feel about Raid: It's a first-class repellent. And Big Hair is better suited for the clubs than for a night of *amour*.

Breasts

Notwithstanding all the attention dancers at topless clubs are getting these days (nearly all of whom have been surgically enhanced), men are not as obsessed with breast size as women think they are. Approximately half of Cachet's clients requested "around a B cup" (which is the average size), but only 10 percent were looking for a D or larger. Fully 40 percent thought bust size was so unimportant that they didn't even think to mention it. So statistically, 90 percent of our clients were perfectly happy with a B or less.

Big is less important than reasonably perky. Because breast tissue is mostly fat, no amount of exercise will either enlarge or shrink the breast. But by exercising the muscles underneath the breast (with weight training), large breasts look firmer and sit higher on the chest, while women with small breasts can achieve something approaching cleavage. (Of course, with the new Wonderbra, everyone can have cleavage.)

Legs and Buttocks

"Tha's got such a nice tail on thee," he said, in the throaty caressive dialect. "Tha's got the nicest arse of anybody. It's the neces woman's arse as it! An ivry bit of it woman, woman sure as nuts. Tha'rt not one o'them

button-arsed lasses as should be lads, are ter! Tha't got
a real sloping bottom on thee, as a man loves in 'is guts.
It's a bottom as could hold the world up, it is."

This passage from D. H. Lawrence's *Lady Chatterley's Lover*
has always been a favorite paean to a woman's posterior,
where ideal size and shape are a perennial subject of debate.
Interestingly, the buttocks are one part of the human body
where men's taste is more catholic than women's. On men,
women prefer small and hard. Men's fancy for women's buttocks runs the gamut from boyish and tight to expansive,
soft, and squeezable. Those interested in women's derrieres
consider themselves connoisseurs of such factors as shape,
proportion, and wiggle quotient.

Some therapists speculate that so-called leg men who find
legs the sexiest part of the body had mothers who tended
not to pick them up and hug them to her breast when they
were upset. Consequently, they clung to her legs, and this
became the first part of the female body they eroticized.
Whatever the case, men love them long, lean, and toned.

Unfortunately, cellulite, those little lumps of fat, are not
under our control; even liposuction won't eradicate them.
Some women with very slim legs still have cellulite, and
some very large-legged women have none. It all depends on
the way the fat cells on your legs are distributed. (Why don't
men have cellulite? Women tend to have fat cells that pro-
trude outward when they gain weight—hence those cottage-
cheese thighs—and male fat cells tend to form a horizontal,
netlike pattern.) Leg-toning exercises obviously are the best
thing you can do to keep cellulite in check.

Hands and Nails

A handshake is usually the first sensuous experience we have
with a man. And when he notices your fingernails, they
should give as good an impression visually as the positive
tactile impression of a firm handshake. Use hand lotion
every time you wash your hands to keep the skin smooth.

Fingernails: Long or short? Bitten to the quick? Rounded or square? Clear polish or color? And how much color—pale, prom-date-peach, or blood red? Traditionally, the well-groomed hand has been a mark of wealth, a sign, Susan Brownmiller writes in *Femininity*, her 1984 study of women's gender roles in America, that "manual labor lies whimsically beyond its reach."

In choosing a nail style, remember a basic design rule: As in architecture, furniture design, and nouvelle cuisine, form and function should balance. Dolly Partonesque fingernails may look interestingly ornamental, but they don't allow for much subtle, caressing handwork. At Cachet, the ladies' fingernails could be brightly colored and fairly long, but not dragon-lady long—and never with a chip. Professional manicures do seem to last longer, so for do-it-yourselfers, clear polish is more practical than colored.

Toes

I also insisted that my girls have pedicures, which give an overall sense of good grooming and keep feet smooth and silky. If you're reluctant to use bright colors on your fingernails, go wild with your toes.

The ladies had two tricks for keeping their feet petal soft: pumice stones, to scrub away dead skin, and Vaseline. At night, slather tootsies in Vaseline, put on a pair of old socks, and the next morning feel the difference. (Needless to say, the Vaseline treatment is done during nonworking hours only.) Major callus removal should be done by a professional pedicurist.

Clothing Suited to the Occasion

The male animal is a murky swamp of contradictions: What's off-putting on one occasion is a turn-on to him on another. In other words, he'll love you in a leather miniskirt when it's he—and perhaps some strangers—who is doing the admiring in, say, a nightclub; he'll hate you in that skirt at his parents' house for Sunday dinner. Use your common sense. He wants to be proud of your sexuality—and he's happy if you're proud of it, too—but only if he feels you're displaying it primarily for *his* pleasure.

But in general, even when the outfit is demure, men don't want you totally to hide your figure. The ladies at Cachet always had to wear suits or dresses with waists, never pants.

High Heels

They hurt. You can't walk in them. They're only one small step (you should pardon the pun) from footbinding. Nevertheless, men love them. (According to a survey published in *Harper's* Index, 45 percent of American women acknowledge that they wear uncomfortable shoes because they look good.) No matter how bad your legs are, high heels improve them, giving the illusion of length and thinness.

Remember that famous description of Marilyn Monroe's walk: "Jell-O on springs." It can be achieved only in high heels. A woman in high heels is feminine because she must take smaller steps and jiggle her hips in order to get anywhere.

Beware the vagaries of fashion. Heavy, clunky shoes *might* look cute on teenagers, but let's face it, if you're over twenty-five, that grunge combination of combat boots and long skirts makes you look like you got dressed in your sleep. The more slender the heel and the lower the vamp, the sexier the shoe. Don't dismiss shoes in unusual colors. I had a pair of purple spike pumps that caused men to stop me on the street and tell me how much they liked them.

Glasses

Actually, men *do* make passes at girls who wear glasses. There's something sexy about an attractive woman in serious-looking frames who can whip them off and turn into a glamorous bombshell. (I suspect lots of guys had their first crush on the school librarian.)

Incidentally, women regularly make two mistakes when trying to adjust makeup to their eyeglasses. If there's too little color, the eyes fade into oblivion; if the color's too aggressive, the woman looks as if she should be resting on a lily pad, scoping flies for dinner. Hair color and frame color should balance.

Pretty Underwear

In the late 1980s, Madonna made bustiers de rigueur in every girl's closet. When Susan Sarandon showed Kevin Costner her gams framed in black-lace garters in 1988's *Bull Durham*, sales of garters skyrocketed. And recently Lanz Nightgowns scored a coup when they marketed Victorian nightdresses modeled after the ones worn in *Little Women*. Clearly, America has an intense (if somewhat abashed) passion for beautiful underthings.

You should, too.

I can't stress enough the importance of wearing the prettiest lingerie you can find. Matching lacy bra and panties, garter belt and stockings, bustiers, G-strings, and teddies—most men can't get enough of this stuff. (Never mind that their sartorial tastes for themselves run toward baby-boy white Fruit-of-the-Loom.) Think of yourself as his favorite toy; when you're wearing gorgeous, frilly underwear, it's like he's unwrapping his favorite toy again and again.

I hear what you're saying. "Sydney, I don't want to run around with a thong bikini giving me a wedgie all day long." "Sydney, I'm too big-busted to wear those flimsy pieces of string they call bras." "Sydney, that stuff is so darn uncomfortable."

Well, let me tell you this. You don't have to wear the skimpiest of undies every day. (Although Brigitte Nielsen reportedly caught Sly Stallone's attention when she sent him a picture of herself in a LaPerla bikini. LaPerla produces the most ravishingly beautiful—and pricey—bras, panties, teddies, camisoles, nighties, bodysuits, and swimwear in the world.) There's plenty of underwear out there that's both pretty *and* comfortable. Obviously silk and nylon panties are more pleasant to the touch (to *his* touch, that is) than cotton. But cotton has also gotten much sexier. Bali, Jockey, and Victoria's Secret all make cotton panties with flowers and fripperies. But if you want the ultimate in cotton (at about $18 a pair), Hanro makes very elegant cotton undies. Utilitarian bras are a big no-no unless you're so large you have absolutely no choice. But even D cups can find beautiful—and strong—underwire bras.

I know women who save old, ratty underwear because it has good memories. Fine, save it. Press it between the pages of a book if you want to. But never, *never* wear it. As a British friend said to me, "If I see a woman with dingy drawers, I suspect the rest of her life is drab, too. Besides, I can't be too important to her if she doesn't even care enough about me to want me to like her knickers."

And remember: "matching undies" only means bra and panties should look pretty similar—a pink nylon bra with pink cotton French-cut Jockey panties is perfectly fine for every day.

Remember how your mother told you it's just as easy to fall in love with a rich man as a poor man? Well, I'm not so sure about that advice, but I do know that it's just as easy to buy pretty underwear as ugly underwear—and it's not necessarily more expensive.

No man expects you to be wearing stockings and garters all the time. But for special, intimate occasions, lose the flesh-colored pantyhose and opt for (preferably black) stockings.

Have you recently had a baby and feel a bit too . . . well, *loose* for lingerie? You might want to consider a body shaper, a new phenomenon in the lingerie category. These garments are made with 18 percent (or more) Lycra and are designed to hold in everything you want held in—without the discomfort or ugliness of a girdle. You can buy shapers for the stomach, hips, and thighs, but one of the best garments I've seen is called the Bustboosting Bodyslip, by Bodyslimmers, Inc. It hugs and smoothes every body part and even creates cleavage where none exists. One caveat: You cannot slip in and out of it gracefully (it requires a bit of tugging), so you probably shouldn't try to wear it when you want to do a slow, sensuous striptease. But it looks dandy when it's on.

Light Perfume

The girls at Cachet were instructed not to wear a scent. I hate to say it, but most of our residential clients who were married met with the girls in their own homes, and didn't want the scent to be a giveaway. Also, since a number of men have allergies to certain scents or simply don't like a certain type of perfume, it was easier and safer for the girls not to wear any.

But in real life, of course, this rule does not apply. "Nothing awakens a reminiscence like an odor," Victor Hugo once wrote. And indeed, for many of us, scent is both a repository of memory and the liquid fuel that ignites our erotic fires. Whether a smell can attract a person from across a crowded room is questionable (and of course if it can, you're wearing too much), but certainly once you love someone, his or her smell becomes an aphrodisiac.

Are you the kind of woman who wants a one-scent identity, or do you like a scent "wardrobe"? The perfume industry has been trying to convince us that women wear scent as much for their own pleasure as for a man's. But let's face it, the human animal is built to court, and scent is made for seduction. Wear scents you like on your own time; but when you're with your lover, make sure he likes what you're wearing. (According to the latest research, women who wear fragrance perceive themselves as somewhat "better" than average—more self-accepting, more confident, and, sometimes, more attractive.)

In intimate situations, perfume should be light enough to

be smelled when he's standing no more than a foot away from you. Scent should draw him, ever so gently, into your sphere.

PHYSICAL TURN-OFFS

Letting Yourself Go

Although many of us work hard to maintain our premarital appearance (a Cornell University study showed that *men* are actually more likely than women to put on weight after marriage), a number of us begin to resemble the wife in the cartoon strip *Andy Capp*: no makeup, matted hair, an extra fifty postmarital (or postpartum) pounds, chipped nail polish, a uniform of sweatshirts and sweatpants. Your attitude toward your appearance seems to be, *Well, I've caught him. Now I can relax a little bit.*

Usually when women stop paying attention to their appearance, it's not because they've stopped caring but because they care very much—about other things: the children, the job, the house. The thinking is, *I'm a wife and mother, and spending time on my looks just can't be a priority. He's not paying much attention to his looks, so why should I?*

Within a marriage, the issue of appearance can become complicated. Granted, we put far too much emphasis on appearance in this culture. But I'm not talking about aging, or having perfectly pert breasts or a straight nose. I'm concerned with our desire (and our mate's perception of our desire) to look as good as we can—as a point of pride. Losing sex appeal is a slow, insidious process. If you stop thinking of yourself as a sexy person, your husband will stop thinking of you that way, too.

Maybe you married Nature Boy, a guy who finds unshaven legs and armpits genuinely erotic. But most of us have spouses who grew up lusting after those hairless gals in *Playboy* and *Penthouse*.

I know how much effort goes into removing all that hair. But take it from me: If your husband married a woman whose legs were always smooth, he expects that hairless legs were a tacit clause in the marital contract. Ditto all those other signs of good grooming, from sweet breath to clear skin. If after the wedding you suddenly decide you just can't be bothered with mouthwash, moisturizer, hair color, and Nair—well, at the very least your husband will feel disappointed, and at worst he'll feel betrayed.

Think about it: If one of the things you found endearing about him was his brilliant smile, you wouldn't be happy if he allowed a film of moss to grow over those pearly whites, would you? It may not be grounds for divorce, but it's certainly grounds to start wondering why he has stopped caring about looking good for you.

Gray Hair

Unless you have the perfect coloring for it—tanned skin and light blue eyes—I advise against it. In an annual survey of male tastes and attitudes sponsored by *Longevity* magazine, gray hair regularly turns up as one of the top five turn-offs. Of course, women in their sixties and seventies, or even in their fifties, can look wonderful with snowy white hair (former Texas governor Ann Richards, for example), but gray hair on women in their thirties and forties generally makes them look unnecessarily aged, particularly when the hair is basically brown or black, with gray interspersed in it. So unless you're Susan Sontag, this looks says, "Sloppy."

Fashion Victimhood

Obsession with one's appearance to the exclusion of common sense is as much of a turn-off as not caring at all. The Fashion Victim makes herself into a caricature of femininity.

(Think Tammy Faye Bakker. Think drag queens.) The hair is high and sprayed stiff as cotton candy; the makeup looks like it's been applied with a paint roller; the clothing is cutting-edge trendy, regardless of how it looks. (FVs pay more attention to what suits a seventeen-year-old, 5'11", 120-pound runway model than what actually looks good on them. They don't care if their bodies resemble sausages, stuffed into that cunning black leather mini.)

Overdone equals untouchable. In fact, there's a nightmarish quality to the overdone woman. He suspects that if he kisses that face, the outer layer will come off in his hands—or worse, in his mouth—revealing a Gorgon, or Leona Helmsley. Too trendy is too much.

Shapeless, Dowdy Clothing

There was a joke on the British comedy *Absolutely Fabulous* about the kind of clothing Princess Anne wears: "It looks like she ran it up herself, dahling." The royals dress the way they do out of tradition; it's almost a British law that they remain frumpy. Fortunately, we don't have to follow their lead.

Women in shapeless clothes not only sometimes look fatter than they really are, they also give the impression that they want to hide their body (which, often, they do). You don't have to spend lots of money, be on the cutting edge of fashion, or have a perfect figure in order to be stylish. As I've said, men like to see the shape of a woman's body, even in clothing that is not overtly sexy. At Cachet, I insisted women wore clothing with a waist: no tents, no *schmatas*.

Clunky Shoes

Most women in the know realize that you need only to check out a man's shoes to tell what kind of a guy he is and how much money he makes. Men aren't savvy enough to do that with women's shoes, but they *do* notice overall appearance, and proper and flattering footwear is definitely part of the image. "Sensible" pumps do not send the same message as stylish heels. Slender heels (two inches and higher) and a low-cut vamp elongate and flatter every leg shape. And sheer hose are invariably more flattering than opaque. Style tip: Your hose should *never* be a darker shade than your shoes.

Too Much (and Too Big) Jewelry

Earrings that make the earlobes sag, rings the size of a cannonball, complicated necklaces that scream, *Look how much I spent on this!*—all these can intimidate men. Big jewelry is not only distracting in an overall visual sense, it leaves people with the impression that appearance is overly important to you. Generally, you don't want to draw attention to your accessories—in other words, you want to wear your jewelry, you don't want *it* to wear *you*.

Of course, you may *want* to wear ostentatious jewelry to convey the message: "This is what I'm accustomed to. And this is what I will expect." A certain kind of man—one who sees his woman's adornment as an extension of his own status—finds this message appealing. So if you're dripping with jewels (whether they're real or cubic zirconia), be aware that this is probably the kind of man you're going to attract. A man who's less interested in outward displays of wealth (even if he has it) will probably be turned off.

Ratty Underwear

For some reason many women assume their bras have a half-life that rivals plutonium's. They'll hold on to a favorite model through high school, college, first job . . . until the garment is gray, fuzzy from repeated washing, and with straps stretched long enough to make a slingshot. This woman is surprised when her lover takes one look at her and thinks, *Moo.*

There's also a mysterious tendency for bras to vanish and panties to reproduce; hence the average American woman's bra-to-panty ratio of 1:65. (Of course, many of those panties should have been trashed long ago. Women also have a tendency to hold on to underwear that no longer has any elastic, apparently in the hopes that elastic returns from the dead.)

Look at it this way: A bra is a relatively inexpensive accessory you can use to update your wardrobe and impress your partner. Buy lots of them. For years average-breasted women had the aesthetic edge when it came to bras: They could wear sheer little things, stretchy numbers, and confections of satin and lace. Meanwhile, the large-breasted woman had a dilemma: For her a bra had to be both a feat of engineering and a turn-on. Underwire bras were at best utilitarian. Fortunately, lingerie manufacturers have now figured out that large-breasted women still want a bit of frou-frou with their underwiring. And even very small-breasted women have been given a world of pretty brassieres to explore, which are not only delicate and feminine but also cleavage enhancing.

(When purchasing your bra wardrobe, buy bras in shapes that suit the different cuts of clothing you wear. Buy at least one that will not peek out of the armholes of your favorite sleeveless summer dress.)

Outdated Glasses

Have you looked in the mirror lately and noticed that you're still wearing the same style frames you wore in second grade, or you've been alternating between the same two pairs of glasses for the last ten years? Time to visit the optometrist.

A word to all seriously nearsighted women (like me) who've had to put up with Coke-bottle glasses: Things have changed. Eyeglass manufacturers have come up with increasingly thin glass that can correct all but the most extreme nearsightedness. Contacts, too, have become much more comfortable; you can even buy colored contacts that will let you have blue (or green or violet) eyes for the day! And you're never too old for contacts—they are now made as bifocals, too.

Dragon Lady Nails

Fingernails that can double as weapons are usually found on Fashion Victims. But even women who otherwise exercise fashion restraint go gonzo over their nails. (I think particularly of Barbra Streisand, who rather undermines the effect of her understated Donna Karan couture with those claws of hers.) They shellac them in blood reds and browns; they adorn them with jewels and tiny decals. Recently I saw a woman who'd managed to paint tiny images of her Siamese cat on each and every nail.

Most important, men find long nails frightening and repulsive. "I think of them raking over my back—and more sensitive parts—when we make love, and I'm nervous," said one friend of mine.

Heavy Perfume

Remember the popular perfumes of the 1980s—Giorgio, Obsession? I think of these as power scents: Women used them to loudly announce themselves, because a casual sniffer could detect a Giorgio woman from 100 paces.

Ask your male friends: Not too many men like them. In fact, strong scents that project across a room can be off-putting to men with sensitive noses (not to mention the fact that they could bring on an allergy attack).

Nasal, High-Pitched, or Grating Voice

At the beginning of *Funny Face*, the Fred Astaire–Audrey Hepburn movie about the world of modeling, Fred Astaire is photographing an exquisite, ethereal woman: tall, willowy, alabaster skin—utterly regal. When she opens her mouth, the voice is a fingernails-on-a-blackboard screech that becomes a running joke in the movie. Indeed, a beautiful girl with an unfortunate voice can be a complete turn-off.

After a few months of being in business I went out of my way to hire women whose voices were low and mellifluous. Many of them could have had a career on an FM radio station. I also avoided certain regional accents, (heavy New York, Southern "cracker") because, politically incorrect though this may be, these accents make you sound either vulgar or dim-witted or both.

Unfortunately, there's no quick fix for your own voice here, but there are certainly videos, audiotapes, and seminars that can help you correct an unpleasant pitch or a strong regional accent.

Being the best you can be, physically, keeps you attractive and desirable in your lover's eyes. With only a little cost in time and effort, it also enhances your own self-esteem and may even gladden your children; after all, they have a mom who takes pride in herself. Physical self-confidence also makes it that much easier for you to give yourself a "sexual tune-up"—as you'll see in the next chapter.

3

On, Off:
Flipping Your Man's
Sexual Switch

You are a wife.

You get home from a full day of work, exhausted, and you've still got another four hours of work ahead of you. As you're preparing dinner, your kids are vying for your attention; one wants to tell you what happened in school and another insists he needs the car next Saturday. Upstairs, your daughter is playing that horrendous Pearl Jam CD again. How many times do you have to tell her to shut that stuff off when you're home?

Your husband walks through the door, and dinner isn't ready yet. You'd like him to make a glaze for the ham, but he just wants to enjoy his predinner beer. He wants to talk to you for a few minutes while he relaxes. But then the phone rings, and it's your best friend in a crisis: Can you take her turn carpooling tomorrow morning? She's crying about an emergency chiropractor's appointment, your kids are rattling around demanding dinner, the dog's on the couch again. Meanwhile, your husband tries to put his arms around you. . . . How can he *always* be thinking about sex? Especially right before dinner! A moment later you feel guilty, but it's too late. He's retreated to the den, nursing his beer. Well, maybe we'll have some time together this weekend, you tell yourself. Or next weekend. At any rate, *soon*.

You are a mistress.

You are looking forward to the evening. You've had the entire day to prepare for the man who's about to walk through the door. The lights are low, Harry Connick, Jr. is on the CD player, and the delicious odor of bayberry—you remembered to buy his favorite scented candles—suffuses the room. The bedroom is spotless, and you are freshly bathed, waxed, and perfumed. The phone isn't ringing, the food has been ordered in, and there is nothing on your mind but *him*. And once he arrives, he has no obligations, no responsibilities. His job for the evening is to relax and enjoy himself.

Consider the two scenarios above. Is it any wonder so many men yearn for the freedom, the utter abandonment of responsibility, that call girls and mistresses represent?

Given the lifestyle and responsibilities of the typical wife vs. the typical call girl or mistress, can the wife *ever* compete?

Yes, she can. But, unfortunately, she can't just leave her sex life—and her relationship—to fate. She must understand her husband as well as a woman whose very livelihood depends on understanding, appreciating, and charming men. In other words, she must understand her husband's sexual needs as well as the most sophisticated call girl.

Here's my list of turn-ons that will rev his libido and turn-offs that will make it stall and sputter.

SEXUAL TURN-ONS

Enthusiasm

Although on most calls, sex was a quick and perfunctory part of the evening, I always had a few girls who loved sex for its own sake. If the chemistry was there with their "dates," they'd have a grand old time. (Interestingly, too, there was a tiny group of regular clients whom these girls always identified as "really good lovers." It surprised me that different girls always pointed to the same guys! Which means, I guess, that maybe the idea of a good lover *isn't* relative; maybe great lovers are great lovers for *everyone*!)

Although a recent study of American sexuality found that 54 percent of men think about sex daily, as compared to only 19 percent of women, I think the question was flawed. It didn't define for participants what was meant by "thinking of sex." Perhaps men think about intercourse more frequently, but women think about sexuality in toto just as frequently—everything from kissing, hugging, and hand-holding to the Act itself.

So why not let your man know what's on your mind? A woman who's enthusiastic about sex and is willing to make the first move (at least some of the time) is a godsend to her partner. After all, think how annoying it is for you *always* to be responsible for some aspect of your relationship—even if it's something you normally love to do. For a man always to have to initiate sex—always to be the one to ask the question and risk rejection—is a burden most men find onerous, even if they're been trained that it's their "job." (And that's exactly what sex can become—a job.)

Sexy sex is playful and lighthearted; it's about spontaneity, energy, and an attitude of "I think you're the sexiest man in the world." Few things are as big a turn-on to a man as a woman who loves sex as much as he does—and lets him know it.

But here, let me add one caveat: Men love women who are enthusiastic about sex *with them.* Just because you want your lover to think you are a dynamo does not mean you have to reminisce about that night with the cowboy in Montana.

Helen Gurley Brown, that master of sexual etiquette, says that no matter how many lovers you may have had, the correct number for any woman to admit to is three. Let me add to that wisdom: Even though men may ask, they don't *really* want to know. They think they want to know, but they really don't. So the best answer to the question is simply, "I don't kiss and tell."

Setting Aside Time to Play

Planning for sex is a product of enthusiasm. You need to set aside time, making sure sex isn't something that happens only when the two of you have nothing better to do (and if you're parents, the concept of having nothing better to do is a distant memory). But when you plan for it, it can be more exciting—because you look forward to it, because you want it so much with him. If you have a busy life and don't set aside time for sex, it'll rarely happen spontaneously. What's wrong with planning sex? We plan everything else, from what we'll cook for dinner tonight to where we'll vacation next year. Why should sex be any different?

Ambience

Make love at the Ritz, or do it in the No-Tell Motel? Candlelight and Johnny Mathis, or lava lamps and Nine Inch Nails? Many men have definite preferences about the sexual "environment" they thrive in, but they don't always communicate those preferences for fear of seeming a bit "feminine." After all, it's us girls who are supposed to go in for that romantic stuff. You may find, however, that he gets turned on by soft lighting, warmth, scent, music, candles, satin sheets, and a vase of roses by the bedside every bit as much as you do.

A Trim but Shapely Body

I don't suggest that you use media images of cadaverous models as your physical ideal. Still, it is a visual turn-on when you're trim and in reasonable shape. And you're more agile: You can be more sexually experimental with more positions and more vigor because you're limber. (Strong lower stomach muscles definitely make for stronger orgasms!) The better you feel about your body, the more relaxed and uninhibited you're likely to be.

So get off the couch and *move*—for the sake of your health and the sake of your marriage. You don't even have to join a health club. Here, for example, are the number of calories burned by everyday activities (per hour, based on a 130-pound woman; if you weigh more, you burn more calories):

Cleaning	225
Cycling	225
Food shopping	225
Hiking uphill	425
Running	650
Swimming, slow crawl	450
Walking, normal pace	300

Unfortunately, sex burns only around six calories per minute during the highest preorgasmic state and the stage immediately after orgasm. You'd pretty much have to be in the throes of ecstasy the rest of your life to lose a few pounds with this exercise!

Cleanliness

Ask your husband: One of the sexiest smells to any man is a woman fresh out of the shower. (Remember, too, that according to one census, the single most common sexual activity for Americans—besides actual sex—is taking a bath or a shower together.)

Sexual Self-Confidence—Women Who Enjoy Being Women

"Why Can't a Woman Be More Like a Man?" sang Henry Higgins in *My Fair Lady*. Henry, that confirmed old bachelor, was out in left field on this one. Many men would like women to think the way they do, but they're darn glad women look different. Understandably, man is aroused by woman's "otherness"—those gestures and thought processes that are utterly foreign, and therefore mysterious, to him. (One regular client at Cachet got turned on watching a girl put on makeup—something to do with the way her lips puckered when she applied lipstick.)

Be feminine and enjoy being a woman, however you define that role, rather than trying to convince your mate that you are the same as he is.

Enjoy everything that makes you feminine, from pretty nails and makeup to the softness of your breasts and hips. You've heard the French expression *Vive la différence*. French women seem to understand this concept intuitively. Which may explain why, according to one recent survey, French men and women have sex about twice as often as Americans do.

A Sense of Adventure

You don't have to be willing to climb Machu Picchu to be an adventurer (although it doesn't hurt). Adventure is less a matter of where you go or what you do than the feeling you have when you're doing it. Some women can make going to the supermarket an adventure. So try that new Thai restaurant, see the latest movie from Hungary!

That zest for the unpredictable often translates into a sense of adventure in bed. Men love:

- A woman who doesn't panic when he says "Tonight, let me tie you up."
- A woman who can tie a few good knots herself.
- A woman who doesn't shut her eyes and clench every muscle in her body when he wants to make love with the lights on (particularly when he wants to examine her private parts—lots of men get off on an up-close-and-personal examination, because they've never been allowed to *stare* at a real live woman).
- A woman who doesn't limit sexual escapades to the bedroom. Why reserve sex for beds when there are so many other rooms—not to mention the out-of-doors?
- A woman who'll try just about anything once. Even if you don't like what the two of you do, you'll be able to speak from experience.
- A woman who is open to trying new experiences of all sorts whether they involve food, people, travel, movies, or books.
- A woman who grabs a spur-of-the-moment opportunity and enjoys it.

Sexy Lingerie—Worn While Having Sex

Forget those appeals to "take it off." Men like women who buy gorgeous underwear and leave it on—or at least let *him* take it off. (What do you think all those snaps and buttons are for, anyway?) Clearly it's unrealistic to expect you always to climb into bed outfitted in stockings, garters, and high heels, but he'll love it occasionally. Black and red are generally men's favorite colors, but peaches and pinks are probably more flattering to Caucasian women, bright jewel tones to women of color.

Pornography

This is a gross generalization, but like all generalizations it contains a germ of truth: Men in this culture are more sexually literate than we are. (How can you become more sexually literate? I'll show you in Chapter 9.) They have more ideas—and desires—about the spectrum of sexual behavior because they are exposed to more in magazines and videos.

So your man's not thinking to himself *I'd like to gather my wife's hair in my hand like the reins on a horse and ride her until she drops from exhaustion and happiness* because he's so startlingly original. He's seen this scenario in movie after movie.

Women find pornography offensive for a number of reasons, some of them understandable. Erica Jong and her zipless f*** notwithstanding, most women find the idea of sex with strangers—a ubiquitous theme in adult films—disturbing. Also, the idea of sex with many partners is a turn-off to most women. We also worry that if we watch these movies with our partners, they'll want us to enact some of the scenes later on.

Well, some men *do* confuse reality with the onscreen fantasy—which suggests, for example, that the average woman can have an orgasm in twenty seconds if you simply bend her over a desk and ram it in. But the vast majority of men distinguish between videos and real life. They see X-rated films for what they are—fantasy—and enjoy them as such.

I believe pornography is cathartic for men, and necessary. Like prostitution, it almost always involves consenting adults engaged in some sexual act for a mutually agreed-on amount of money. In the vast majority of cases it does not, as today's political correctoids would have you believe, involve women's victimization and coercion. In fact, it may be one of the few industries where women are consistently paid more than men for their services. Porn is also extremely useful for giving viewers idea after idea that—with a few modifications—can be happily incorporated into real life.

(If you still find your lover's viewing of adult films off-putting, you might want to check out some of the offerings from Femme Films, which are produced for women, by women. These films actually have a plot and romance, and the sex is nonviolent.)

Sex in the Morning

Seven A.M. You're drooling on the pillow, your breath's bad enough to scare your dog, you can barely contemplate being vertical, never mind any sexual calisthenics. Yet there he is, hands fumbling for your breasts under the covers, that hard little *chin-chin* (as the Japanese put it) pressed into your thigh. You can't remember if you put your diaphragm in last night, and you don't have the energy to insist he use a condom.

You're up against that old enemy, testosterone. While you're lying there, praying for just thirty more minutes of oblivion, your partner's testicles have been busily brewing hormones all night. Consider yourself lucky that testosterone can't jump up and down on the bed, wagging its tail and barking, because that's what it would be doing if it could. Many men report being horniest in the morning, when their testosterone levels are at their highest.

Of course, you should never have sex if you're actively *averse* to the idea. But you might consider going along for the ride when you can, even if you don't feel like a femme fatale. If you're very relaxed—nay, almost comatose—sex in the morning can be very sensual, even if you don't have an orgasm. (If you're really tired, put a pillow under your hips, lie on your stomach, and go back to sleep while he amuses himself.) You'd be surprised how cheerful a guy who's been satisfied first thing in the morning can be. In my experience, this is a guy who is suddenly overcome with the desire to please you later—flowers, little notes, credit cards, whatever.

Quickies

We might like to believe that quality sex matters to our men. But quality sex (just like quality time with children) is a way of rationalizing our guilt about not giving *quantity*. The truth is that men, like children, want *quantity*: Survey after survey shows that men would choose frequent sex, even if it's not that great, over occasional marathon, mind-blowing sex.

So get used to the fact that the two of you don't have to unite in cosmic oneness every time you do it. Sometimes, in fact, he doesn't even *want* to make slow, languorous love to every nook and cranny of your body. Sometimes, he just wants to "get happy," as we said in the business.

This is probably what he uses adult magazines for (whether he admits it or not is another question): to relieve sexual tension without making too big an emotional production out of the whole thing.

Admittedly, unless you're the Bionic Two-Minute Woman, a quickie first thing in the morning won't do much to satisfy you. But maybe he'll be giving less thought to that little bimbo in accounts payable. And you can send him out the door with a bounce in his step and a song (possibly "Girls Just Want to Have Fun"?) in his heart.

A Striptease

I know what you're thinking: If you were meant to be a show-girl, you'd already be prancing around in Vegas in feathers and a G-string. But consider this: In a much-publicized 1993 University of Chicago survey of the sex lives of 3,500 Americans ages eighteen to fifty, participants were asked to rate their favorite sex acts. Almost everyone (96 percent) gave intercourse high marks. For both men and women, oral sex ranked a distant third—after an activity that many of you may not have even considered a sex act: watching one's partner undress. That gives you some idea of the erotic power of the striptease. Presumably the women undressing for their men have bodies no more perfect than your own. They've just figured out that even though nakedness is not always sexy, the process of becoming naked is.

There are a number of seminars and videos out there that can teach you the art of the striptease. And for something a bit more exotic—and maybe a bit more appropriate for the fleshier woman—you can take courses in belly dancing.

Knowing How to Undress Him

Slowly and sensually removing his clothing shows him you're not simply waiting passively for him to do all the work. The girls at Cachet knew how to undress a man as elegantly as it's done in all those James Bond flicks.

- Shirts: Start at the top and unbutton a shirt slowly, even if he's in a rush; it prolongs the excitement. After each button or two is loosened, kiss your way down his chest.
- Belts and Zippers: You should be able to undo his belt and unzip his pants without ever removing your gaze from his eyes.

    Practice belt removal by tying a belt around the back of a kitchen chair.
- Underwear: Some men love the way they look when they're hard and still wearing their underwear. When you're just beginning to get intimate, rub him through his underwear at first and let *him* decide how (and when) he's going to remove it.

Verbal Appreciation

Men love noise, lots of it. Wait, what happened to being demure and following the old English dictum, "Ladies don't move"? Forget it. Better to remember what Woody Allen said in *Everything You Always Wanted to Know About Sex*: "Sex is dirty only when it's done right."

One of my most handsome, generous clients at Cachet was captivated by a petite redhead named Angela. She was attractive, of course, but because of her coloring and size, she was one of the more difficult girls to book. Yet this guy always requested her (which was unusual, since most clients preferred a different girl every time). When I asked Angela the secret of her popularity, she just shrugged and smiled. Finally, though, the client confessed to me just what her appeal was. Her moans were like nothing he had ever heard, he said: deep, guttural, loud, and, obviously, convincing. She made him feel like the most powerful lover in the world.

Talking Dirty (in Bed)

For those who feel capable of going beyond animal-like noises in the bedroom, nothing makes a man feel more like a stud than a woman who wouldn't deign to utter a blue word outside the bedroom—but inside loses all control of herself, to the point where "I need you inside me now. Harder, do it to me harder" (the f word is optional here) comes as naturally to her lips as "Please pass the salt."

Here are a few other things your man cannot hear too often:

- "Oh my God, it's so big." (Unless it's really small; after all, these guys are not stupid.)
- "Mmmm, I love to taste you."
- "I want to watch you come."
- "I'm so sore—but let's do it one more time anyway."
- "Put it in real deep."

But notice I'm talking about using this language in the bedroom. One of the saddest consequences of no-holds-barred cursing in movies and books today is that all those good, salty Anglo-Saxon words have lost their power. One of the best ways to restore the power of dirty words is to limit them to the sexual arena. After all, that's pretty much what they were invented for.

If you're not comfortable talking dirty—or if your man truly finds such expressions distasteful, you can talk in a coy, seductive, Mae West–like manner: "There isn't going to be one inch of you that's left untouched," etc. This is especially effective when you're together in a really stuffy atmosphere—a dinner meeting, at his parents'—and you lean over and tell him what you'd like to do to him when the two of you are alone. It's not how dirty you talk, but how you *insinuate* all the naughty stuff you want to do that counts.

Women Who Enjoy Oral Sex—Giving and Taking

I asked a few friends—women who consider themselves sexually sophisticated—

> "Whoever said it tasted like a combination of plain yogurt and Drano was on target."

> "I love my boyfriend's penis, and I love putting it in my mouth. But swallowing makes me feel violated. Like the guy's saying, 'Ha! Ha! You swallowed!'"

> "The main problem is what I call 'the velocity factor.' It's scary in those last few seconds. He's really in his own world and you don't know how you'll catch your breath."

Now a few words from the guys:

> "Not that many women really like oral sex. But God, when you find one that does, it's such a turn-on."

> "I had this one girlfriend who could swallow me to the hilt. I loved it, even though it sort of seemed like a circus act."

"My wife likes to watch me come. Then she'll take my semen and spread it over her face and breasts. She tells me it's better for her skin than the most expensive moisturizer."

According to the 1993 Janus Report on Sexual Behavior, oral sex is considered "normal" by 88 percent of men and 97 percent of women. So assuming you know it's low in calories (it's protein, not fat), and assuming you've discovered that, rather than the Malibu-like wave of fluid you'd been expecting, there's only one innocuous tablespoonful—well, what's a swallow between friends?

Apparently, a lot. What's physiologically a dribble is an emotional and psychological torrent to many women. The problem is that most men, although they're too polite to insist, love it when you do. (Some even regard swallowing as a sign of seriousness of intent, the 1990s equivalent of wearing their varsity sweater.) After all, they regard semen as their *self.* How would *you* feel if your positions were reversed and he complained about the taste?

Watch a couple of adult movies, and you'll notice that the woman licks and sucks and strokes his penis with hunger and enthusiasm; she seems to think his semen is the Last Supper. (I discuss oral sex in much more detail in Chapter 9, including ways to fake swallowing if it's not a pleasant prospect to you. But keep in mind that if you can at least *seem* to bring enthusiasm and joy to fellatio, your partner will consider you a rare find.)

Cunnilingus, too, has been arousing to men pretty much since the dawn of time. (As Napoleon said in a letter to Josephine, "A thousand kisses to your neck, your breasts, and lower down, much lower down, that little black forest I love so well.") Although most of our clients were primarily interested in what our ladies could do to please *them*, a number of them loved going down on the girls, pretty much to the exclusion of anything else.

Still, despite evidence to the contrary, many women believe their husbands and boyfriends want to perform oral sex on them only out of a sense of duty. Their attitude is, I know he doesn't like it, but he doesn't want to hurt my feelings. But guess what? Nine times out of ten, that's how *you* feel about it. He finds the taste and scent of your genitals (when you're freshly washed) an incredible turn-on.

Women in this culture often make the mistake of equating "femininity" with the eradication of bodily secretions. Just as it is female to sweat after a workout (a lot of men find it erotic), it is also utterly female to taste briny and salty, not like mint. Unless we have some sort of infection or don't practice good hygiene, we are born to taste good, particularly to men. If you don't believe it, put your finger inside yourself and see how good you taste. I'm not saying it rivals, say, a piece of chocolate cheesecake, but it's a delicate, delicious taste like no other. Remember: Your attitude toward oral sex goes a long way toward influencing how he feels about it.

Climaxing on (Not Just in) You

I've said it before and I'll say it again: Men are very visual creatures. And it's not just you they enjoy watching, it's themselves as well. Maybe it's because it's such a staple scene in X-rated videos. Whatever the reason, men love to watch themselves ejaculate all over you. They're particularly pleased when you sensuously stroke the ejaculate into your skin. As in oral sex, it's a sign that you love (and not merely tolerate) their essence. Having him climax on you is also a particularly good activity when you don't feel like fussing with birth control, or when you've got your period and don't really want to have intercourse.

Shaving You

A surprising number of men like women with pubic hair in a neat little triangle, or even shaved altogether. What's more, some of them actually like to be the barber. Some feminists argue that this reflects men's sick desire for prepubescent girls, but I think it's a lot simpler and less kinky: Most men grew up looking at naked women in magazines where virtually all the models had neatly shaved pubic hair. (You didn't think it grew naturally in that Velcro strip, did you?) Plus, shaving allows them an up-close-and-personal view of your vaginal lips and clitoris—also a turn-on. (Some men out there also like you to shave them. Whatever equipment they have looks an inch larger when it's not covered with hair.)

So if he enjoys shaving you, let him try it. If, on the other hand, he just likes the effect of no hair, I recommend waxing. A day or two after shaving, you're itching like mad as the hair starts to grow back. At least with waxing, the results last a few weeks, and the itching isn't as bad when hair finally does grow back. (Warning: Waxing can be uncomfortable. Be sure your aesthetician does a small area at a time, and exfoliate gently with a Buf Puf every time you shower to prevent ingrown hairs.)

Wearing No Underwear in Public

He knows, you know, the rest of the world doesn't know—or does it? That's the pleasure at the heart of this little scenario. There's a sense that you're doing something a little naughty in front of the whole world, yet nobody knows for sure. While you're, say, shopping, he can caress your bottom, or slip his fingers underneath your dress. . . . Wearing no underwear is thus a simple way of creating a sexually charged atmosphere, even when the chances of an actual sexual encounter are pretty slim.

Two Women Together

Watching two women make love—and perhaps joining in— is one of the most common male fantasies. If your man talks about it, don't waste time worrying that he's bored with you (he's not) or is insulting you (he's not). He simply finds it tremendously exciting.

Obviously, I'm not suggesting that you immediately buy into yet another of Woody Allen's great maxims on sex ("Sex between two people is beautiful. Between *five*, it's fantastic."), since such an event can be much more emotionally loaded than you reckon on. Besides, when most men stop to consider just how *busy* a threesome is (What goes where? Who does what first?), most of them don't really want to do it. But almost all of them love to talk about it. So if it excites your lover to fantasize, why not let his imagination run free?

What if, however, your man *insists* on making his dream a reality? This, I believe, is where escort services come in.

In my business, watching two girls together was probably the most-requested fantasy. Over the phones, which we always had to assume were tapped, we referred to threesomes as "playing bridge." Our regulars would call up and say, "We need a fourth for bridge"; they got a kick out of being clued in to our code words. Many of our girls had no problem acting out this scenario. They would agree beforehand what they felt comfortable doing, and they'd choreograph the evening. These situations always were voluntary. I never asked a girl to participate in one of these scenes unless she was comfortable with it, and I made sure our clients knew that only a few of our girls liked to act them out. (The client paid extra for this fantasy as well.)

The tough call, from our point of view, came when a guy phoned and said he wanted one of our ladies to come over and play with his wife or girlfriend. Almost invariably, the wife was doing this only to please her man. Our girls certainly weren't prepared to touch another woman against her will. So usually they scoped out the situation, took the guy aside, and said gently but firmly, "Listen, you might want to rethink this. I don't think your girlfriend is interested, and I'm not comfortable doing this unless everybody's going to have a good time."

Usually, men didn't argue, and they always ended up paying the girl for her hour anyway. And if for some reason they seemed reluctant to pay, the wife or girlfriend (who by now was very grateful to be let off the hook) usually insisted.

So why compromise your personal relationship? If he's obsessed with fulfilling this fantasy, it's easier to have him hire two women to watch whom he's not going to become involved with—and with whom you don't have to be involved.

Knowing He Has Satisfied You

This is the biggest turn-on of all. There were a small number of clients who were very concerned that the girls climaxed (so of course the girls were smart enough to fake it). Maybe the guys knew, maybe they didn't; but we gave them an A for effort.

In a real relationship, I'm not suggesting you fake orgasm. It's lying, dishonest, and leads him to believe he's doing whatever it takes to satisfy you, when in fact he's not. As a result, he'll continue doing the wrong thing. And when you *have* had a good time with him in bed, tell him—not just at that moment, but the next day, and perhaps the day after that. Merely thinking about (and mentioning) good sex generally leads to more good sex.

If you love it when he performs oral sex, be especially generous with praise here. One of the reasons some men don't like doing it is because they feel they're not doing it right. The more you tell him how great he is, the more you'll get what you want.

Sexual Turn-Offs

I hate a woman who offers herself because she ought to do so,
and, cold and dry, thinks of her sewing
when she's making love.

Ovid, *The Art of Love*

Want to make a man crazy—with indifference? Here are a
few of his least favorite things, sexual turn-offs that can turn
lovemaking from a joy into a burden.

Indifference to Appearance

Remember all those classroom hygiene movies of the 1950s,
when Tom wouldn't take Janie to the malt shop because she
had B.O.? One thing guaranteed to repel a man is less than
fastidious personal cleanliness. This doesn't mean covering
up the way you smell normally; it means lots of soap and
water used in all the right places, and then enjoying the
body's natural aromas, uncontaminated by bacteria.

Obsessive Concern with Appearance

Just as slovenliness is distasteful, fanatic obsession with looks
is daunting, too. Do you:

- Check your hair and makeup every ten minutes?
- Dress in the latest fashion, even if it doesn't suit
  you?
- Sport an elaborate hairdo that needs constant up-
  keep and attention?
- Wear heavy face cream, sticky thigh cream,
  rollers, obvious zit medicine that makes you kind
  of scary at night?
- Ask him if you look fat five or ten times a day?

If any of the above sounds familiar to you, your concentration on your looks is probably driving him away, or at least driving him crazy. The message you're giving is not one of self-confidence and pride but inaccessibility ("Don't mess my hair!") and galloping insecurity.

Garments That Remind Men of Their Mothers

These include loose underwear with chewed elastic, girdles, full slips, utilitarian bras, industrial-strength support hose, and fuzzy slippers. Flannel nightgowns are iffy: If they're feminine and frilly, some men actually find them as cute as you do. But stay away from those plaid L. L. Bean numbers that make you look like a lady lumberjack.

Obsessive Attachment to Pets

It's one thing to love your pet; it's another to talk baby-talk to it, dress it in outfits that match yours, and insist it sleep in bed with you. It's amazing how many otherwise fastidious women think nothing of bedding down for the night with Fluffy or Bowzer, and are appalled at the heartlessness of a partner who doesn't appreciate a face full of cat fur at four A.M. or doggy breath first thing in the morning that *actually belongs* to a dog.

Dirty Sheets, Crumbs

Enough said.

Faking It

We all remember our first time. No the *other* first time, the night we faked one of those theatrical, peel-me-off-the-walls orgasms that would have put Meg Ryan in *When Harry Met Sally* to shame.

Women fake it for pretty much the same reason: We're nervous or uncomfortable or just plain tired, but we still want to please. It's a form of social politeness akin to complimenting a really ugly tie. You'll do it only with someone you're not sure can handle the truth.

And therein lies the problem. Occasionally, we're all but forced to fake it, particularly if we're with a man who just won't stop until he's sure you've climaxed. But faking it regularly with someone you should be able to tell the truth to (like, say, your husband) cheats both of you. It trains your mate to believe that orgasm *has* to happen or the lovemaking has been a failure, when women know that there are times we'd like to make love but don't necessarily want to climax.

There's another difficulty. If you're often unsatisfied sexually, you'll end up resenting him in all sorts of little ways. Suddenly, his inability to remember to put the toilet seat down becomes a much bigger deal than it actually is. And if he figures out you've been faking it, he'll be hurt and anxious but probably too scared to bring the subject up with you. (Yes, men really *do* worry about being with a woman who fakes it. Why else would *How to Make Love to a Woman* be a best-seller?) A lie perpetuated between two people creates a yawning chasm.

Sexual Indiscretion

I'm not sure whether it's worse to wax nostalgic about your last boyfriend in front of your current one, or to denigrate him. Either way, you're asking for trouble. Taboo subjects: your last lover's penis size, your previous partner's amazing endurance, kinky habits or unusual proclivities of previous partners. In other words, your current lover can live without the knowledge that his predecessor liked to kiss your feet (particularly if your current lover *also* likes to kiss your feet, and he thinks of himself and your activities together as unique and daring).

After all, if you talk about other men, you'll talk about him, and that's a big turn-off that plays on all of a man's many insecurities.

Ghostly Silence

Why is it that women who think nothing of yakking it up all day on the phone with their girlfriends suddenly fall silent as monks when making love? As my friend Ted told me about his uncommunicative wife, "That quiet makes me so self-conscious. As I'm touching her, my mind is constantly racing with the question, *What's Going On?* Maybe she's fantasizing about someone else. Maybe she's suffused with passion, and she's speechless. Or maybe she's thinking about her income tax returns. I haven't a clue.

"There's another horrible possibility," Ted adds. "Maybe she's quietly observing *me* making all the noise. When she's totally quiet, I feel like a clown."

Many of us who make love silently aren't even aware we're doing it. Perhaps we're afraid the kids will hear us, or we simply think noise is "unladylike." But silence creates self-consciousness and squeamishness, which have no place between two intimate partners.

Nonstop Chatter

Ideally, lovemaking isn't a quiet endeavor, but neither is it the time to make like Bill Buckley on *Crossfire.* Some women don't know when to shut up. Or they ask questions that require a more complicated response than a grunt or a yes or no. Questions directed to a partner should be simple, along the lines of, "Does this feel good?" or "How about if I . . . ?" This is not the time for, "I read a study recently that claimed 68 percent of all men have nipples that are very sensitive, but they're afraid to tell their partners. What do you think about that?"

Sexual Martyrdom

According to a five-city survey in one of the news sources I value most highly—*The National Enquirer*—three out of four women say they prefer a good piece of chocolate to sex. As one respondent put it, "[Chocolate] is a lot more satisfying, there are no risks involved, and you can always find it when you need it." I don't know whether these women are serious, but I'll bet this negativity has poisoned their lovemaking.

In fact, men whose partners "just closed their eyes and thought of England" were men who frequented my escort service. This was the kind of scenario my girls heard all the time: "My wife seems like such a generous person. She's the first to volunteer for the school bake sale, the last to leave a party after helping the hostess clean up. On the face of it, she does whatever I want in bed, but there's no *joy* there. She's not a participant in lovemaking. She gives me the impression that sex is an obligation that comes with the territory."

Sexual martyrdom can be a form of passive-aggression. Subtly, without saying a word, you make your partner feel guilty about his own desires. The message is: "I will do anything for you, as long as you understand that what you ask for is a burden to me." This attitude pretty much guarantees discord. Eventually your husband may stop asking you for sex—but he won't stop wanting to find it elsewhere. After all, a call girl never pushes away his hands or acts like she's doing him a favor.

No Spontaneity

There are women who approach sex as if they're staging a Busby Berkeley musical: The lighting has to be right, he has to take shower, she has to take shower, the right sheets must be on the bed, the music's got to be Sade, or Enya. Everything must be *just so*. There's no room for creativity or spontaneity. If the poor guy says, "I want you now," her response is, "You mean, right *now*?" or "Can't we wait until after Letterman?"

Women Who Never Initiate Sex and Women Who Always Initiate Sex

If he's always initiating, that means he's the one always risking your brush-off and he's the one for whom sex quickly becomes another in an endless series of duties. On the other hand, the Peg Bundys among us who are *always* the first to make aggressive sexual overtures are also a turn-off.

My friend Andrew, who admits that his wife catered to his every whim, would complain, "It's so annoying sometimes. She always beats me to the punch. She never gives me a chance to approach her for sex, because she's always *there*, always anticipating what I want. She doesn't wait for me to warm up to her." And if you're the one always asking for sex, you're probably seething with resentment, thinking that, if you didn't ask, you'd *never* make love. You feel you have to do all the "work" in the relationship.

Nevertheless, a woman is not like the U.S. Marines: She doesn't need to be in a constant state of readiness. This is particularly true at the beginning of a relationship. I know this isn't going to win me any points with feminists, but I still believe men need to exercise their aggressive, hunting natures by chasing a little bit. Would the lion yearn for that delectable morsel of gazelle if it came bounding over to him, ready to be eaten? (Okay, this isn't the best metaphor for male/female relationships, but you get my drift.)

Same Old, Same Old

Comedian Rita Rudner has a joke in her act that always reminds me of the perils of sexual boredom. "My sister just had a baby, and she was in labor for twenty-four hours." Pause. "I wouldn't want to do anything I *enjoyed* for twenty-four hours."

No matter how wonderful that one sexual position may be, you've got to try others. Client after client described his sexual relationship with his wife with mind-numbing precision:

"Every two or three weeks, when the kids aren't around, we climb into bed and kiss for about thirty seconds. She's usually sneaking glances at the clock. I play with her breasts, reach my hands down lower, play with her there a little while, and then she tells me the kids will be home soon. So I get on top and do my business. That's what she calls it—'doing my business.'"

Thus sex becomes a vicious cycle: When he sees how bored you are, he becomes more rushed and perfunctory. The more perfunctory he becomes, the more you're bored.

Trying Too Hard

He's tired. You pout. He's already had an orgasm and doesn't want another. You insist on making him hard again, working over his penis like you were a four-star Michelin chef and your entire reputation depended on making that soufflé rise.

The woman who tries too hard in bed usually sees sex as *the* emotional bond, and she feels overly responsible for creating and maintaining that bond. For her, the entire sexual experience is about pleasing her partner. First, it's her way of increasing her self-esteem (by pleasing her lover, she feels good about herself). Second, she worries incessantly that if she doesn't send her partner into paroxysms of ecstasy every single time, he's going to be angry or disappointed.

Any woman who needs to be the perfectly tuned sex machine twenty-four hours a day is bound to feel insecure and unhappy with her performance, and, more important, make her partner anxious about *his* performance.

The Sexual Trader

This woman links her sexual favors to some charitable act on his part. Her modus operandi is: I will have sex with you if you:

A. Take me out to dinner
B. Make the kids breakfast
C. Clean the gerbil cage
D. Are nice to my mother
E. All of the above

(Interestingly, I've always found that the women who most look down their noses at call girls are the same ones who tend to barter their sexual favors for some form of currency in their marriage.)

It's impossible to feel generous and sexy all the time. We all get angry and resentful, and our anger prevents us from being amorous. But bartering sexual favors makes your lover believe that sex is not mutual, that you are doing it only to accommodate him. Ideally, sexual intimacy is one area of the relationship that is for the benefit both of you—and where there are no strings attached.

Sex is not like U.S. policy in Iraq: It should not be linked to concessions.

Clinginess and Public Displays of Affection

In *Broadcast News*, the neurotic reporter Albert Brooks, who's constantly striking out with women, opines to fellow reporter Holly Hunter: "Wouldn't this be a great world if insecurity and desperation made us more attractive, if needy were a turn-on?"

Needless to say, it's not. The woman who persistently whines that "I can't keep my hands off you" can be embarrassing, if not a little irritating. Of course, some men don't mind hearing this and in fact enjoy being caressed and fussed over. But many more feel like my friend Tony: "I like holding hands in public, and the occasional kiss is fine. But I'd go to a party with my wife, and she'd be constantly petting me, snuggling up to me. And she liked to pick lint off my jacket, which I think is the universal sign of female ownership."

This is why an overly touchy-feely woman can be such a turn-off. Men interpret it, quite rightly, as the woman's attempt to stake out her territory. It also gives others the impression that you're starved for affection in private, which is often not the case. "I'm *very* cuddly privately," Andrew adds. "It's just that I don't feel I have to prove my manhood by slobbering all over my wife in public."

It's one thing to give your lover plenty of attention; it's quite another to lavish that attention publicly because of your own insecurity.

The Talking Map

You know how men are notoriously reluctant to ask for directions. When they're lost, they can't bear to let anyone else know they've screwed up.

Much the same can be said in the bedroom. Once you have given your mate a general idea of what you enjoy, you should give him a little room to figure things out for himself before correcting him. Some women cannot stop themselves from barking directions: "A little to the left, a little to the right. No, not like *that*." The guy ends up constantly worrying that he's going to take a wrong turn instead of being able to rev up and enjoy the ride.

There are more subtle and effective ways to give him directions. As I've said before, noise = enthusiasm. When you like what he does, moan. When you're not so happy, be silent. He'll get the idea.

The Critic, #1: His Body

In a Hyundai TV commercial that aired last year, two women are chatting. A Lamborghini cruises by, and one friend turns to the other and says the driver "must be overcompensating for a shortcoming." Her friend replies, "He obviously has feelings of inadequacy." When the driver of a Hyundai pulls up, one of the women says, wistfully, "I wonder what *he's* got under the hood."

Funny as the ad is, it plays on a common worry (one might call it abject fear) of all men: the sneaking suspicion that the main conversation of women, when they're alone, is male penis size.

We all know that isn't true. Nevertheless, the myth persists. Men also fear we're belittling their height, their bald spot, their puny chests, their flabby abs, and so on. In short, particularly at the beginning of a relationship, they can be as sensitive about their bodies as we are about ours.

The Critic, #2: His Performance

Many of us who would never think of being rude to the checkout girl in the grocery store nevertheless turn to our beloved and say the most hurtful things during or right after sex: "It was better last week." "Why can't you wait a little longer?" "You don't feel as big inside me as you used to."

One regular Cachet client (who was, not surprisingly, going through a divorce) told us about his travails with a sexually critical wife. She wanted sex one way, and one way only. She'd tell him: "Look, sex has always worked for me in the missionary position, and that's the way I want it. Real men would be happy to have someone who could come like that. But you always want to *change* things." When this guy began having erectile problems because of some medication he was taking, she actually giggled at his efforts to give her an orgasm through his hands and tongue.

We lost this gentleman's business when he found a second wife—who apparently thought his "fumbling," as the first wife called it, was just dandy.

No one should ever have to put up with a sexual oaf, the guy who just can't seem to learn some basic lessons of human anatomy. But there's a learning curve for sex, and even a tender, experienced lover may not always know exactly what *you* want. So while you should let your man know how to please you, timing and tact are everything. Wait for the right time and place. Choose a quiet time in a neutral place (not the bedroom) and stress what you *do* like, not the things he's doing that you don't like.

Sexual Humorlessness

Whatever else can be said about sex, it cannot be called a dignified performance.

HELEN LAWRENSON

Let's face it, real sex just doesn't happen the way it does in the movies. In real life both of you sweat, the hook on your bra gets caught on his sweater, your jaw starts aching, and, in what's meant to be a romantic postcoital moment, he puts his arm around you and inadvertently pulls your hair out by the roots. If you can't laugh at the less well-choreographed moments of lovemaking, a cloud of awkwardness and embarrassment will descend over your liaisons—not exactly the way to light his fire.

Women Who Dislike Oral Sex

And not only dislike it, but *show* their distaste by treating their lover's penis as if it were some slimy amphibian that just crawled out from under a rock. Either that, or they demonstrate their indifference by ignoring their partner's instructions on treating the penis with TLC.

THE SPITTERS There's a memorable scene in *The Draughtsman's Contract*, where a woman has to provide oral sex to the draughtsman on a regular basis. But she hates him so much she refuses to swallow, and you see her running to spit everything into the sink. (Later he's blinded, probably by people she's hired.) Not the most romantic of movie scenarios.

As I've said, swallowing semen is not necessary; different

men *do* taste different, and a man's diet can determine whether swallowing is a pleasant or unpleasant experience. (Garlic and liquor can taint the taste of semen.) But gagging, running to the sink to spit, or moving away abruptly and saying "Aaarrrgh" all make him feel bad about his own body. If your main problem in oral sex is swallowing, see Chapter 8 for a popular call girl technique.

THE MUTES There's something about a woman who's performing oral sex in silence that says to a man: "You know I'm doing this only for your benefit, don't you? Today's a busy day. Do you plan on coming sometime before the kids graduate college? I'm going to be ten minutes late for my therapist appointment. . . ."

Silence can be all too eloquent. Obviously you can't talk with your mouth full, but you can moan appreciatively, or breathe heavily, or stop a moment and tell him how much you love what you're doing.

Bad Oral Sex Technique

Being incompetent is almost as bad as actively disliking it:

THE TEETHERS I don't care how many romance novels you've read where a woman "nibbled" on her man. Very few men actually want to be nibbled on, and most are actively afraid of your teeth even grazing his most precious commodity. Watch those chompers.

THE HOOVERS Some women think that "sucking" a penis means working their mouths like little vacuum cleaners. They dutifully suck away until the poor guy begs them to stop. (And I won't even talk about those who take the word "blow" literally.)

THE AVENGING EAGLE Younger men might not mind a woman who just dives down there and starts pumping away. But to perform oral sex without any prelude at all can be offensive.

THE ENERGIZER BUNNY Someone who just keeps going . . . and going . . . and going—up and down, up and down, with no variation at all, right from the very beginning. (Don't get me wrong: Rhythm is very important, but only right before climax.)

Making a Man Feel Dirty or Ashamed of His Desires

I think I've figured out what many of the sexual scandals of recent years have in common. Almost invariably they involve a sexually sophisticated woman who gives some old geezer a taste of sexual freedom for the first time in his life. When Leona Helmsley wrested Harry away from his meek Quaker wife, she reportedly gave him an entirely new sexual repertoire. As the saga of New York State Supreme Court Justice Sol Wachtler unfolded (he ended up in prison for threatening and harassing his ex-mistress), it become evident that the mistress had driven the sexually backward Wachtler to obsession by showing him what a good time *really* is.

Making a man feel guilty or ashamed of his fantasies (no matter how odd they may seem to you) is a guaranteed road to discord. I'm not saying you should indulge in any activities you find distasteful, but your lover should be able to *talk* to you about anything, without fear of reprisal.

Now that you have a general idea of what turns him on and off physically and sexually, it's time to consider the main reasons your man strays—and what you can do about them.

4

The Big Itch:
Why Men Stray

I say I don't sleep with married men, but what I mean is that I don't sleep with happily married men.

BRITT EKLAND

The United States is marriage-happy. By the time they turn forty-four, only 9 percent of Americans have never married. For those forty-five and older, the proportion dips to 5 percent. We have just about the highest rate of marriage in the world.

Unfortunately, our rates of divorce also top the charts. In 1990, 2.4 million wedding ceremonies were performed, and 1.2 million divorces were filed. One of the most heavily trafficked roads leading to divorce court? Infidelity.

In her book *The Anatomy of Love*, anthropologist Helen Fisher confirms what call girls already know about marriage and monogamy. Dr. Fisher examined the habits of courtship and sexuality in sixty-two cultures and discovered that in *all* of them, divorce rate was highest for people in their twenties. She calls it "The Four Year Itch": that time when infatuation is over and a couple has to decide if they really, truly *like* each other. She believes that infidelity might once have had evolutionary advantages. Men who were good providers and presumably looked cute in a loincloth were more likely to have success spreading their seed and producing more successful offspring. There was also an advantage for women who had more than one father—and hence more than one gene pool—for their children: If there was a problem with one set of genes, the child from the next gene mix might survive.

Today, any number of social factors have conspired to loosen the ties that bind: no-fault divorce laws, the proliferation of financially independent women in the workforce who don't need husbands to survive, a more casual attitude toward commitment, and less societal stigma attached to divorce. There's also the problem of our inflated expectations. One study at the University of Texas at Austin found that the enormous leaps in divorce levels since the 1960s may have to do with our increasing selfishness.

We expect our men to be the alpha and omega of our lives. They've got to be tough and brawny yet sensitive to our feelings. They've got to know how to fix the toilet yet be equally adept at fixing our psyches. They've got to know how to cook, be supportive of our careers, yet relentlessly pursue substantial, lucrative careers of their own. Men's expectations for us are equally unreasonable. As one friend said to me about the "perfect mate" he was looking for: "I'm looking for a cross between Sharon Stone and Diane Sawyer."

What do **we ex**pect to give in return? Increasingly, not much. In our value system, where individualism takes precedence over teamwork, the sacrifice necessary for working together in the union of marriage is often overlooked.

The changes in attitude to marriage, researchers say, have had a generally depressing effect on our levels of self-worth. Generally, the happiest, most productive people are those in successful marriages, and the unhappily married people are the least happy. Which means that being in a good marriage is ideal, but being in a bad marriage is worse than being in no marriage at all.

Perhaps the worst effect of this country's divorce rate is the part it plays in a self-fulfilling prophecy. Lifelong commitments are still ideals, but everywhere we look, they're no longer realities. So married people come to believe that they have more freedom of choice, and that freedom breeds insecurity. We ask ourselves: *Is he or she the best I can do? Is there someone better for me out there?* Maybe we invest a little less time, energy, and love; maybe we don't want to put all our eggs in one basket. We are a nation of couples with one foot out the door, and this very fact alone may contribute to the downfall of many marriages.

I'm not saying that Americans are giving up on the institution of marriage; in fact, the opposite is true. People may be rejecting particular marriages that are unhappy or unfulfilling, but most divorcees want to remarry, and about three-fourths of them do.

To put a positive spin on the divorce phenomenon: Our high rates of divorce and remarriage say we're interested in keeping ourselves happy. And we still believe that marriage brings happiness.

Almost all women, even those with the most loving partners, worry about the possibility that he'll cheat. To understand what we can do to keep him faithful, we've got to understand what sends him into another woman's bed.

Common wisdom says men take infidelity much less seriously than women, because, unlike women, they can enjoy sex for its own sake, without feeling the slightest emotional attachment. As the actress Joan Fontaine once said: "The main problem in marriage is that, for a man, sex is a hunger—like eating. If a man is hungry and can't get to a fancy French restaurant, he'll go to a hot dog stand. For a woman, what's important is love and romance."

But in fact, sexual hunger is only one of the many reasons men stray, and not even the #1 reason. The most common reason a man cheats is to keep his marriage *together*.

Sounds demented, doesn't it? But if you'd talked to as many men as I have about the subject, you'd begin to understand. Most men cheat because they're trying to fill needs not being met in the marriage. Men look at marriage in part as a business transaction, a deal they made in good faith. They said "I do" in front of everyone in the world who matters to them. They don't want to turn around and say "I don't." They'd prefer to keep their end of the bargain. But they also have needs that are so important to them that they cannot deal with the frustration, unhappiness, and anxiety that not having these needs met produces. So rather than leave you—rather than walk out on a deal they've made—they will seek to have their needs met elsewhere, thus enabling them to stay in the relationship.

Reasons for Straying
You Have Some Control Over

Companionship

"My wife works as an emergency room nurse on the night shift, and I work all day. We get to kiss each other good morning and good night. We're more like roommates than husband and wife."

"When Ginny and I are at home together, there are a thousand distractions. Someone's always calling or sending us a fax. And then there's the computer, where Ginny spends a lot of time on-line. I haven't even mentioned our sons. . . ."

"When we first got married, I worked and she was home most of the time with our daughter. She was always there, waiting to greet me. After our daughter started kindergarten, she got this job where she travels seventy-five percent of the time. I spend most nights alone."

These are the kinds of complaints call girls hear every day. Since families where both partners are working have become the norm, I know an inordinate number of couples who barely see each other during the week, and then they have to divide their weekend time between doing chores and spending time with the kids. What's missing in these relationships is, simply, friendship.

After marriage, most women tend to hold onto their network of girlfriends, but men often let their friendships with men drop (if they had any in the first place). A guy thinks his wife is going to be his buddy, his sounding board, the one person who's attentive to him and interested in everything that's going on in his life. Then he discovers, to his dismay, that he is far down on her daily list of priorities. (1. Organize baby-sitter for Saturday. 2. Aerobics class. 3. Supervise PTA rummage sale. 4. Call Mom. 5. Pay electric bill. 6. Make dinner. 7. Daughter's hockey game. 8. Food shopping. 9. Laundry. 10. Sex.)

These guys are lonely. Their companionship needs aren't being met. They don't feel they're getting the understanding and support they need, let alone want. So when they go out and seek the company of another woman, paradoxically they're looking for a best friend, a buddy. (If this buddy also happens to have pouting lips and succulent breasts, so much the better.)

A lot of you are sitting there saying, "I'd be happy to be a better companion to him! I'd be thrilled to do that! If he would just *ask* to spend more time with me, I'd be delighted!" But what we don't realize is that often we inadvertently make it difficult for men to talk to us.

Women have a God-given, X-chromosome-linked talent

to perform many tasks at the same time. We can talk on the phone and make dinner, talk on the phone and do our income taxes, talk on the phone and translate the *Iliad*. Men, on the other hand, are linear. If they are alphabetizing their collection of Motown CDs, that is the *only* thing they are doing, and any interruption will result in Aretha Franklin being filed next to Martha and the Vandellas. Therefore, since they're capable of performing only one task at a time, they believe that unless you're sitting down and making eye contact, staring at them like an Irish setter (or Nancy Reagan), *you are not listening*. You do not care what they're saying, and clearly you don't care enough to spend the time to know what's really going on in their lives. I know this sounds ridiculous, but that's the way a lot of them feel.

And this, of course, is what a call girl or mistress does best: She pays attention. When he comes over, there is *nothing* on her mind but him. She is not thinking about the laundry, or her friends, or the children, or the promotion she's going to be screwed out of if she doesn't finish that big report by next week. There's him and only him.

It certainly seems unfair to expect you, who have lots of other responsibilities—who have, we hope, a *life*—to drop everything the moment your man walks in the door. But people are not always reasonable when it comes to their emotions or their feelings. A man may know he is being unreasonable yet want what he wants when he wants it. A friend of mine told me her former boyfriend once said something that is, to me, rather revealing about the male psyche: "I'm the kind of man who deserves to have women I don't deserve."

That pretty much sums up male reasoning on the subject of relationships.

Someone to Make Him Feel Special

It probably started the first time his mother praised him a little too effusively for using the potty. Since that moment, the average man wants to look at everything that emanates from his being as special and wonderful.

Women have long recognized this little boy quality in even the biggest brute. And before you got married, chances are you unconsciously played to your man's desire for approval. C'mon, admit it: Even the most feminist among us has, at one time or another, turned to a man we were in bed with, squeezed his biceps, and said, "Oooh, that's so *hard.*" And even the most enlightened SNAG (Sensitive New Age Guy) enjoyed it.

But let's face it, it's not realistic for them to expect you to keep up that level of praise and girlish infatuation forever— just as they don't feel it's realistic for them to keep saying "I love you" every twenty minutes. Their attitude is, *Hey, I married you, didn't I? I come home every night, I bring you my paycheck. Why do I have to keep telling you how much I love you all the time?*

And we say much the same thing to ourselves: *I do all the laundry, I make the meals, I take care of the kids. How could he not understand I think he's special?* It's a matter of miscommunication.

The truth is, you can never tell them often enough how wonderful they are, how special they are, how whatever they just did was the most fabulous thing anyone has ever done for you. (As Marlene Dietrich once said, "The average man is more interested in a woman who is interested in him than he is in a woman with beautiful legs." She should know.) After all, how do you think that old cliché about most men preferring dogs and women preferring cats got started? Women prefer to be loved by an animal that is independent and—not to get too anthropomorphic about it—discerning. A cat picks you as its special companion, but it doesn't fawn or grovel. Men, however, want unconditional love and gratitude, wherever they can find it. And they're not as skeptical as we are about the sincerity and depth of that love. They accept it as their due, with few questions asked.

Boredom

His life has become so predictable and so routine he feels like he's dying a slow death. Work all day, dinner at six, TV until eleven. On weekends, work on the house or the yard, Sunday dinner at Mom's, watch sports on television, and maybe go to a movie on Saturday night. Week after week, month after month, year after year.

At some point he just can't bear it anymore and goes out looking for something, anything, to make him feel alive again. If you're lucky, he'll take up bungee jumping. If you're not, he'll take up with another woman. There should always be a little something new, a little adventure in your lives—it will be good for both of you.

Intellectual Fulfillment

Silence spreads in a thick, moist fog over the dinner table. The clock ticks. Somewhere, a bell rings. A sentence is begun and quickly trails off into meaninglessness.

The beginning of a Harold Pinter play, or a day in your life?

If you and your husband find yourself discussing nothing more scintillating than what little Jason did today in kindergarten or what happened on last week's episode of *Melrose Place*, watch out. Men stray when they feel they no longer have very much to say to their wives. Usually, when someone craves intellectual stimulation, the affair starts innocently. This isn't the guy who goes out and hires a call girl. He isn't looking for anyone, but one day he meets someone at work or at the health club, and they start talking. The next time he runs into her he remembers how much he enjoyed talking to her the last time and asks her out for lunch or a drink. He has no conscious intention to take it any further, but he finds himself spending more and more time with her because she's so interesting. Since the primary sex organ in both men and women is the brain, it shouldn't surprise you that they eventually wind up in bed together, especially if your relationship isn't particularly strong.

This kind of affair is one of the most threatening to a marriage, since he's developed both an intellectual/emotional and physical/sexual bond with this woman.

He's Lost a Sense of Himself

My friend Hugh explained his affair to me this way: "My wife is the kind of woman who thinks a husband and wife should share everything, and I mean *everything*. We never went anywhere without each other, we never had a hobby or interest that the other one didn't share. When, for example, I wanted to take a fishing vacation with a buddy of mine, Gina professed this sudden desire to learn all about fishing. One day I was lying in bed, looking at Gina and thinking how attractive she was—but it was an *intellectual* kind of appreciation, you know? I didn't *feel* it. We had become so much the same person that making love to her was like making love to my own foot. She was *too much* a part of me. I felt lost. I didn't know where I began and she ended."

There's intimacy, and then there's *suffocation*, but many women don't perceive the difference. Most humans were simply not meant to be joined at the hip. A man who is losing his sense of identity, his selfhood, within a relationship is a man who's in danger of finding it again through an affair.

The Rules of the (Marriage) Game Have Changed

When you married him, you assured him you wanted nothing more than for him to pursue his career as a novelist. No, you didn't need your own home; renting was fine. No, children weren't on your agenda for a long time. No, you would never impose your religious beliefs on him.

But now, a few years into the marriage, you find that your needs have changed, and you're astounded, and perhaps resentful, that his needs haven't changed with yours. You want children *now*, and children cost more than an aspiring novelist earns. You want a home and a car, which you can't provide on your income alone. Why doesn't he see how critical it is for him to get a real job? And while you're thinking about it, would it kill him to come to church with you every once in a while?

Your demands and desires may be perfectly justified. The problem is your husband thought you both were in agreement about all of this when he married you, and now it looks to him as if you are unilaterally changing the rules of the game midstream. It's *you*, not him, who's broken the bargain. You are not playing fair. Furthermore, it's becoming clear in a myriad of ways that you don't really accept him the way he is.

All of this strife and tension make it easy to understand why he might seek out another woman who is supportive of who he is and his goals in life—just as you once were.

Career Meltdown

A man who's just lost his job or been passed over for a promotion is a man ripe for an affair. Why? Remember, to most men, they *are* their jobs. So if he's lost the job, he's lost himself. He's feeling deeply insecure and probably like a failure. What's worse, he sees his own failure reflected in your eyes, particularly if you're not shy about letting him know just how concerned you are.

What he craves more than anything else is a new start with someone who doesn't know his shortcomings. With a new woman (often, a new, *young* woman), he can be the hero again, the hero he once was to you.

Unanticipated Success

It's not only failure that can make a man stray. Sudden great fortune can also be a problem. Often a first wife will have seen her ambitious, struggling young husband through years of school or hardship while he clawed his way up the professional ladder. She may have helped support him financially, too. She knows all his failings and his petty scheming, as well as his triumphs. When he finally makes it, he may feel compelled to shed all the baggage of his past struggles—and that "baggage" may include his family. Additionally, he may feel the need to upgrade all of his "accessories," so he'll get a new wardrobe, a new home, and a new trophy wife.

Think about it: How many middle-aged doctors, lawyers, and CEOs have you heard of who are still married to their first wives?

Sexual Boredom

Remember the first time you and your husband made love? Your knees buckled as soon as he kissed you; every touch sent chills up your spine; you couldn't wait for him to be inside you, and he was so eager he probably lasted about twenty seconds. Then, a half hour later, he could do it again.

Now think about sex recently—if you've been having it at all. Have you made excuses for not doing it? Or have you consented to have sex but were so obviously just doing it to accommodate him that you practically had a stopwatch next to the bed?

Sexual boredom is epidemic in this country. Where there's no enthusiasm, no spontaneity, and no passion, there will likely be an affair.

I know, you're tired of hearing this. You argue, quite reasonably, that after you've had a long day at work or at home, after making dinner and making sure the kids do their homework, the last thing you feel like doing at eleven P.M. is making love. Then you begin to feel guilty. If you beg off four days in a row, on the fifth night you feel obligated. And he *knows* you're having sex only to accommodate him, so he rushes through it so he won't inconvenience you too much. The whole experience is a bit distasteful, so the next time around you're even less eager, and—well, you can see how easily the vicious cycle develops.

Sexual boredom is difficult to talk about. Women's magazines constantly tell us how we need to open the lines of communication with our mates—and they're right. But have you ever actually *tried* doing it? How do you tell someone you love: "Honey, I've been doing a lot of thinking lately, and our sex life is Dullsville. In fact, I would just as soon not bother anymore if you're going to rush through it like you can't wait to get on to your next little task. I think we need to work on our sex life." This is not what your man wants to hear.

So a lot of times what he does so that he doesn't bother you—and so that he can be with someone who doesn't regard the whole experience as a chore—is find someone else.

When a woman finds sex a snooze, she *may* go out and find a lover. More likely, however, she'll assume that's just the way life is and start reading a few more romance novels. But men who are sexually bored often go out and pay for sex. Their needs are very clear-cut: They don't necessarily want to get involved with someone else; they just want sex with someone who at least *seems* to enjoy it—and them.

Unfulfilled Sexual Needs

A lot of women say, "Hey, our sex life is pretty good. We do it a few times a week, and we give sex the time and attention it deserves." That may be true. But I'm reminded of that age-old comment teachers write on final exam papers when they've given you a B or a B+: "Very good, *as far as it goes*."

You might not realize he has sexual needs that he's too embarrassed to tell you about, things he believes you would find dirty or shocking. (And maybe you would.) Sometimes, these acts are as seemingly mundane as oral sex. (Even back in the relatively liberated 1980s, when I was running my business, it was not uncommon to come across a client who had never had oral sex.) Or perhaps you enjoy sex in one or two positions and therefore don't see the point of trying out anything else.

Then, of course, there are lots of men out there who want to do what professionals call "fantasies," and which you probably call the "weird stuff." I prefer to be less judgmental and use the term "non-mainstream sexual activity," which might include bondage, dominance, cross-dressing, foot worship, fetish wear, fantasy role playing, and S&M activities.

Most men need to maintain their macho image with their spouse. So for this kind of fun and games, they'd rather go to a call girl and pay for it. They'll rarely ask a girlfriend for this kind of activity, for the essence of fantasy is to keep an air of unreality about the proceedings, and a call girl, entirely removed from his workaday life, can heighten the thrill of the scenario.

Need to Feel Independent—and Single—Again

As a man grows older, he is defined by more and more roles: He is someone's husband, father, son, boss, employee. In some men, there is a profound urge to shake off these roles—which inevitably entail obligations—and recapture a time when the dad/husband/employee was merely "a man," unfettered and unleashed. (This urge for independence is often precipitated by his having a close buddy who's going through a divorce. On the one hand, there's sadness for the guy, but there's also a sense of envy, born of the [usually false] perception that the divorced man can recapture his adolescent freedom.)

Naturally, with a call girl, a man can be anything or anyone he wants to be. If in his real life he feels whipped and defeated, in his life with the call girl (or mistress), he can be masterful; if in real life he is always the one to make decisions and bear responsibilities, in his "alternative" life with the call girl he can leave all the decisions to her.

The more a man who's dissatisfied with his own life believes a call girl or mistress can "transform" him, the greater the chances that he'll seek out her company.

Sexual Inexperience

This is frequently the reason a man who marries his high school sweetheart (or the girl he went out with throughout college) strays. Perhaps he's had only you or, at most, one or two other lovers. Typically, when this guy reaches his forties or early fifties, he's past his peak in his career, the kids he had when *he* was hardly more than a kid are out of the home, and when he looks at magazines and television everyone seems to be having a lot more fun than he is, with a revolving door of new and scintillating sexual partners. He thinks, *Is this all there is? What have I been missing?* If the sex at home has become somewhat routine after years with one partner, he now may want to try everything and anything new sexually. This man will almost invariably crawl back to his wife, but not before he's gone on the chase.

He Needs More Sex

There was an unforgettable scene in *Annie Hall*. Alvie Singer (Woody Allen) and Annie (Diane Keaton) are discussing their sex life with their respective therapists. Allen's therapist asks him how often he has sex with Keaton, and Allen responds: "Never. About three times a week." Keaton's therapist asks her how often, and she shoots back: "Always. About three times a week."

This "desire discrepancy" is one of the most common problems therapists (and call girls) see. Maybe you're having sex with him two or three times a week, when what he needs and feels entitled to is once—or (if he's really young) twice—a day. This guy doesn't want to ruin what he has with you; he likes sex with you very much. But he knows that if he's constantly pushing for more, you're going to resent him.

There are also men out there whose wives are ill and simply not able to have sex with them. We had several clients at Cachet whose wives had Alzheimer's or multiple sclerosis, or whose wives couldn't have sex during pregnancy. These men paid for sex because they weren't interested in a relationship, and they wanted to keep the woman at arms' length.

He No Longer Finds You Sexually Attractive

When I think about men who stray because they're not physically turned on to their wives anymore, I always think about Humbert Humbert and his reaction to his first wife in Nabokov's *Lolita*. Desperate to keep his pedophilic impulses at bay, Humbert takes a wife who does a fairly good impression of a fluffy, frolicsome, curl-tossing, lash-batting gamine. But by the end of the honeymoon,

> The bleached curl revealed its melanic root; the down turned to prickles on a shaved shin; the mobile moist mouth, no matter how I stuffed it with love, disclosed ignominiously its resemblance to the corresponding part in a treasured portrait of her toadlike dead mama; and presently, instead of a pale little gutter girl, Humbert Humbert had on his hands a large, puffy, short-legged, big breasted and practically brainless *baba*.

An excruciating—but apt—depiction of sexual disillusionment.

So you've gained some weight, you've stopped wearing makeup, your hair doesn't fall in any discernible style. When a woman no longer is fastidious about her appearance, it's said that she has "let herself go"—a curious phrase, when you think about it. On one level, it implies a certain level of freedom, of liberation: I don't give a damn what anyone thinks of me. I don't have to pay obeisance to the God of Appearance anymore. On another level, it's terrifying: We have lost control over an important part of ourselves and can't seem to get it back.

A man has yet another way of looking at your lack of interest in your appearance: If you don't care how you look anymore, you don't care about looking good for him, and therefore you don't care about him very much at all.

Incidentally, becoming sexually attractive to your husband again does not mean getting a face-lift and a new wardrobe. Real men have realistic expectations. You don't have to look like a glamour queen, and you certainly don't have to look as young as you did the day you married. (This, I believe, is why God makes us myopic as we age—so we don't notice every wrinkle and sag on the faces of our beloved.) You simply have to *make an effort*. Paradoxically, a little vanity on your part proves to him that you care—about him, about yourself, and about your relationship.

He's Looking for Someone Who Shares His Interests

It never ceases to amaze me what women will pretend to enjoy in the name of love. A friend of mine, a New York City attorney who actively dislikes animals, fell madly in love with a veterinarian and started spending all her time with him and his four Labrador retrievers. Another friend, who could never even get it together to separate the glass, plastic, and newspapers from the rest of the garbage in her own home, got the hots for an environmental activist—and the next thing I knew, she had a mulch pile in her backyard and was volunteering at a local recycling center.

Eventually, however, we all revert to type, and this is where the trouble lies. A man who begins a relationship with you believing, in good faith, that you really *do* share his fascination with seashells is going to be mightily disappointed when he discovers the only kind of shellfish you really like is lobster at $16 a pound.

Last year, after one of my seminars, a woman came up to me and said, "I'm really glad I came here today. It made me realize I don't do the kind of things with my husband that we used to do before we got married. For instance, he's a soft-ball fanatic. I used to go to all his games. I'd bring sand-wiches, and I'd sit in the stands and cheer for his team. Now that I'm married, I don't feel I need to do this anymore. I have better things to do than watch my husband perfect his curve ball. But he's been making such a big deal about it lately, and I never understood why. Now it makes sense to me."

A former boyfriend whom I've remained friends with re-cently left the woman he had been seeing for several years. The reason? "I always thought we shared this passion for photography," he told me. He likes to go to photography ex-hibits and to go on shoots over the weekend. For the first couple of years she went with him. But this wasn't quite the passion she'd led him to believe, and she started begging off. So while he was off taking photos by himself, he met a single woman who was doing the same thing. So guess what happened? At first, he'd invite the woman to come with him just because he wanted companionship. But they spent more and more time together, and they had a great time. It was very easy for him to see her as more of a partner than his girlfriend.

So if you swore to him that you had mutual interests, and suddenly those interests vanish once he's "caught," he'll feel you deceived him. And he has a point.

He Wants Someone Who Doesn't Take Life So Seriously

Lots of men confessed to my girls that they were there be-cause, just for a little while, they needed to escape with someone whose conversation didn't revolve around duties and obligations: the kids, the bills, Father Murphy's sermon this week at church. They just wanted to *laugh* for a while. Life had become far too serious.

With these guys, affairs tend to start innocently. They

discover that a conversation with a woman they meet is refreshingly devoid of angst. It's just talking; it doesn't require them to *do* anything. Because there are no children, household issues, or other shared burdens, they're free to discuss trivia—local politics, a joke they just heard over the Internet. He's just having a good time with a woman who finds him amusing. The next thing you know, he's entangled.

Men who stray because they're looking for a little levity in their lives don't have affairs that last very long. Sooner or later (usually sooner), the affair becomes yet another aspect of life with an aura of High Seriousness. So these guys often turn to professional girls for a little no-strings-attached fun.

Marriage Has Become One Long Test

When your mate says to you, "You look great in that dress today," do you find yourself thinking something like: *What does he mean? Didn't I look great yesterday, too? Or does he mean he likes this dress on me* today, *but it didn't look so good on me the last time I wore it? Or is he trying to imply he likes* this *dress but the rest of my wardrobe should be donated to the Juliette Lewis Fund for Fashion Victims? Just what is he trying to tell me?*

Many women are so insecure about the relationship—and so insistent on making it the focal point of their lives—that they're constantly demanding proof that he loves them. These women constantly stage little tests of affection, making the relationship a minefield: "Do I look fat?" "Am I more intelligent than your last girlfriend?" Every one of us, including me, has had a relationship like this at one time or another. So you know the kind of harm it can do.

Maybe he's a workaholic and devoting very little time to you. Or maybe you have good reason to feel insecure, because you've caught him cheating in the past. But even if you're absolutely justified, your sense of desperation about the relationship will probably drive him away. An obsessive need for reassurance and closeness can make men panicky. They feel that whatever they do, however they answer your questions, it's not enough. Consequently, they are drawn to someone who's not interested in dissecting the relationship twenty-four hours a day.

Reasons for Straying
You Can Do Nothing About

I don't want to suggest for a moment that every time a man cheats it is somehow your fault, that if it weren't for some horrible shortcoming of yours, your relationship would be idyllic. But there are some reasons for straying that you can do absolutely nothing about. And I do mean *nothing*—no matter how beautiful and terrific you are, no matter how many times you show up at the front door swathed in Saran Wrap. So if you discover your husband's cheating for any of these reasons, you should be thinking seriously about moving on with your life.

Just for Fun

These guys have affairs just because they enjoy it. It's difficult for most women to understand this impulse, because when we have affairs, it's usually for a reason: We feel neglected, sex is boring or unpleasant with our husbands, we've fallen out of love. A man can love his wife just fine, thank you (or at least, love her according to *his* definition), but still want to screw around. He doesn't believe in monogamy. He likes variety, he likes women, and he doesn't take his marriage vows too seriously. (Fun Poster Boys: Ted Kennedy, Jimmy Swaggart, Mick Jagger, Michael Douglas.)

Ego Satisfaction

If he equates his manhood primarily with what's in his shorts, nothing will stop him from cheating. Sex is the only way he can prop up his shaky identity. The chase, the conquest, the *achievement* of seduction make him feel alive. A lot of times these are the guys who are having only one-night stands. It's not the relationship they're looking for; they just need to know they're attractive enough to get a constant stream of new women into bed.

The Desire for Quick, Uncomplicated, "Dirty" Sex

I'm now calling this the Hugh Grant Syndrome. A young actor who seemed to have everything—a close family, a stunning girlfriend, a top-flight career—got caught *in his car*, with his pants down, engaging in a "lewd act" with a street prostitute. As Jay Leno said, famously, "What the hell were you thinking?"

He probably wasn't thinking much at all. And, in fact, his behavior probably has nothing to do with whether or not he loves his girlfriend. But Grant, like many men, just has an inordinate desire for quick sex with no strings attached (not even the need to make small talk, as he would do with a sophisticated call girl) and an element of danger. For some men, there is something thrilling about sex that, in their minds, is demeaning—both to themselves and the woman involved.

For Chills and Thrills

These men are similar to those who want cheap, uncomplicated sex. It's not just the hunt, or the new body—it's the possibility of getting caught that fuels their need to stray. They actively leave clues about what they're doing—the lipstick on the collar, the Visa bill with the unexplained charges to hotels.

Thrill-seekers often come from sexually repressive backgrounds. Remember Rev. Jimmy Swaggart's debacle? He, too, did not *need* to pick up a girl on a street corner and pay her to masturbate. He had enough money to act out his fantasies in an expensive hotel. But on some level, he may have wanted to be caught and punished for his "sins."

Like men who want no-strings-attached liaisons, thrill-seekers often frequent massage parlors, peep shows, and street girls.

For One-Upmanship

This is the guy who just enjoys getting away with things. He cheats on his tax returns, shoplifts candy from the mom-and-pop grocery on the corner, tries to weasel out of paying a bill if he suddenly decides it's too high. For him, everyday events in life are a matter of winning or losing, and people themselves are divided into winners and losers. Winners are not subject to the rules and regulations the losers play by. A man like this has a strong need to feel superior to "the little people" around him—including you. (Not surprisingly, this kind of man is often maniacal about *your* fidelity, no matter how flagrant his own behavior. A winner's wife doesn't cheat on *him*.)

Inability to Curb Sexual Impulses

Virtually every married person feels powerfully attracted to someone other than his spouse at one time or another. Most of us, however, immediately understand the consequences of acting on that impulse. We don't do it, because we want to keep our honor, our sanity, and our house.

But there are some who can't control their sexual impulses. Perhaps their behavior is some sort of holdover from high school, when sex was so desired and so difficult to obtain that they still don't feel they have the right to turn it down. In their more extreme forms, we call them sex addicts (although perhaps in a less sympathetic era we'd call them cads). But just as I always ask a waiter not to bring bread and butter to the table—because I can't not put it in my mouth if it's there—so there are guys who are incapable of turning down a woman who shows the slightest shred of interest in them.

The Unplanned and Spontaneous Event

Many men say that an affair "just happened," but few couplings are really that spontaneous. There are, however, instances when a man is on a business trip. He looks around, sees that no one's paying any attention, and realizes he can get away with it. He'll never see this woman again, and here she is, offering herself to him.

In one famous episode of *M.A.S.H.*, Colonel Potter (Harry Morgan), the most uxorious of husbands, confessed just such a one-time transgression to Hawkeye (Alan Alda). The show was memorable and moving, because the man was wracked with guilt over a one-time event that had happened thirty years earlier. We should all be so lucky: to have a husband who did something wrong once, felt awful about it, didn't burden us with the knowledge, and never did it again.

Out of Anger

Perhaps you've taken a job where you're away from home a lot, you're making more money than he is, or he's not pleased about how much of *his* money you're spending. Maybe he thinks you're lavishing too much attention on the children, your best friend, your pachysandra patches. Whatever the situation, this guy is furious, and the best revenge his petty little mind can come up with is sleeping with another woman. This man is a scorekeeper: He doesn't discuss his anger with his wife; instead, he rationalizes his affair by telling himself he's been wronged and his cheating is just "balancing the scale" of the marriage. He reacts passive-aggressively by sneaking around behind your back; his attitude is "I'll show her."

If you're lucky, this guy will choose a call girl rather than a girlfriend or mistress and work out his anger in a situation that doesn't involve emotional entanglements.

He Wants Out of the Marriage but Doesn't Want to Leave Until He Has Somebody Else

At some point in our lives—usually when we're young—virtually all of us have done this. It's frightening to be alone. For a man who's accustomed to the constant companionship of marriage (even a *bad* marriage), having a girlfriend or mistress mitigates the terror.

He's Having a Midlife Crisis

This often is the guy who got married when he was young, and then spent his twenties and thirties immersed in work and child-rearing. All of a sudden he finds himself with kids in college and thinks, *Jeez, I'm only forty-five years old. My kids are gone, and I'm alone in the house with my wife—and I really don't know her that well anymore. Is this what I want for the rest of my life?*

By now this man has risen in his career. Younger women see his power and affluence, yet his wife still sees him as the same dweeby, insecure guy she knew in college. He desperately needs to find out if he's still attractive to other women. He's questioning both his mortality and his sexual functioning.

You've heard that old adage: "Fear is the first time you discover you can't do it a second time. And panic is the second time you can't do it a first time." Well, men take this sort of thing *very* seriously. With age, he's experiencing occasional bouts of impotence, or perhaps he's just taking longer to achieve orgasm, which is a natural part of the aging process. Alarmed by these changes, he quickly foists the blame onto his partner and then feels compelled to "prove" his potency with another woman.

(If you're not sure if your man is having a midlife crisis, ask yourself: Is he over twenty-two and owns a Corvette? If so, he's having one. Not because it's a sexy car, but because it's a sexy and *bad* car—all style, no substance. Common sense has been obliterated by testosterone anxiety.)

If the marriage is essentially solid, this guy will simply go out and get himself involved in some sort of commercial sex venture, because he doesn't really want to leave his wife or break up the family. He just wants to know what he's been missing for the last twenty years.

Fear of Aging

This is a step beyond midlife crisis. A man who's terrified of aging is compelled to go out with a woman who could be his daughter, because he somehow feels that being with a younger woman gives him a second lease on life. And of course, the messages the media sends us about men and aging confirm this concept. For every older Hollywood couple you see that's approximately the same age (Paul Newman and Joanne Woodward), there are dozens of screen couples with huge age discrepancies. And while we almost never see an older woman with a young man, fifty-fiveish men and twenty-fiveish women are regularly paired together on-screen.

A sixty-year-old thrice-divorced man with a twenty-five-year-old girlfriend explained the appeal: "Sometimes I ask myself what I have to talk about with this girl. She wasn't even born when Kennedy was shot. But the only time I ever feel like I'm sixty is when I look in the mirror. When I'm around her and her friends, I feel like I'm her age. It really makes me feel like I'm having a second life."

He No Longer Believes He's in Love

Some men don't have realistic expectations about passion. They believe that because the longing and electricity that were there in the beginning of a relationship have dimmed a bit, there is something deeply wrong with the union. Therefore, they decide they're not "in love" anymore, failing utterly to comprehend that the feelings in a relationship change and mature.

He's Secretly Bisexual or Homosexual

It's still difficult to be gay or bisexual in this culture, so it shouldn't surprise you that a substantial portion of these men marry at some point in their lives. If you discover you're married to one of them, *do not for a second think you could have done something to change his behavior.* Homosexuality is as natural—and irresistible—to him as heterosexuality is to you. Of course you may feel (justifiably) furious to learn that your partner has been lying to you about his essential nature. But do not waste one moment of your life, or his, in blame or recrimination. Undoubtedly he wanted desperately to be heterosexual, or else he wouldn't have married you. Undoubtedly, too, he cared for you very much.

Fortunately there are a growing number of support groups for women who discover their husbands are gay. You might want to contact a local gay organization in your area for more information.

What can you do if your husband has already strayed? That's the subject of our next chapter.

5

Cheating Men—
and Cheating Fate:
What You Can Do

Unfortunately, this world is full of people who are ready to think the worst when they see a man sneaking out of the wrong bedroom in the middle of the night.

WILL CUPPY

Recently I posed a question to ten of my happily married girlfriends: Would you rather find out your husband was having an affair, or that he was dead? Eight out of ten opted for early widowhood.

"Look," said my friend Abigail, "if he's dead, there's pain, loss, maybe even anger at being left. But you never have to face the big question every woman confronts when her husband's having an affair: What's wrong with me?"

I'm not sure if my friends are a representative group, or even if, given the choice in real life, they mean what they say. But I do know that sexual infidelity is one of our biggest fears. We may know intellectually that our partners still love us. We may know they're cheating for any number of reasons, ranging from sexual incompatibility (an incompatibility we've been blithely ignoring) to personal insecurity, to the thrill of the chase (they need to hunt and conquer).

For women, fidelity means only one thing: *sexual* faithfulness. But, hard as it is for women to comprehend, sexual fidelity is only one kind of fidelity to a man and often not the most important measure of his feelings. Remember, if he's having an affair, it's possible that he's doing it so he can get all his needs met *and still stay married to you*. In his mind, he's still faithful because he's giving you his money, he spends most of his free time with the children, and he considers his life and his future linked to yours. It's possible that in his mind, he's made a bargain by marrying you, and he's trying to live up to his end of the bargain—most of it, anyway.

Still, whatever our intellect tells us about his motives, our hearts and egos are ripped to shreds. We've been betrayed. That bond of trust—the ability to look a man in the eyes and know he's *yours*—is broken.

But is it broken irrevocably? That, of course, depends on many factors. Is he cheating with a call girl, a mistress, or a girlfriend? Is it a momentary lapse he feels deeply guilty about, or a pattern of deception he has little remorse over? Does he want to repair the relationship with you? And, most important, do you want to stay with him?.

I'm the last person to say a relationship should be saved at all costs. Quite the contrary: I've always firmly believed in (and practiced) monogamy, but I also believe that the notion "till death do us part" is responsible for a great deal of misery. It may be that the human animal is simply not meant to mate with one partner forever. After all, the lover who is your ideal at twenty is rarely your ideal at thirty, never mind at forty, fifty, or sixty.

Change is the only constant in our lives. What are the chances that two people whose needs and desires are changing will change together? What are the chances they'll change in ways that draw them apart?

So I'm not saying your marriage can, or should, survive betrayal. I *am* saying that if you decide to hang in there, I'll give you the tools to do it.

Is He or Isn't He? Top Signs That He's Having an Affair

Recently I had the privilege of talking with one of New York City's leading private investigators. He has two specialties: surveillance/countersurveillance and catching cheating spouses. This is what he told me: "About 10 percent of people who think they're bugged, are bugged. On the other hand, about 90 percent of people who suspect their mate is having an affair are right."

Usually, affairs don't just happen. There is a cause. Chances are your partner is not intentionally trying to hurt you. Yet there are things about your relationship he's afraid to confront you with.

So what are the signs to look for? It's not just one or two little things; it's an *overall pattern* of change in his usual behavior. It may not be in your best interests immediately to go for the jugular if you notice one or two of these signs. Usually a cheating man exhibits more than one or two. If you're going to confront him, it's better to wait until you've accumulated sufficient, irrefutable evidence. If you leap at the first whiff of suspicious behavior, he may become much cagier in covering his tracks.

Here's a list of subtle (and not so subtle) tip-offs. It's easier to recognize the signs if you're the one in charge of the family finances. But even if you're not, a man who's having an affair is rarely able to keep it a secret for very long, unless his partner chooses to close her eyes and ignore the "evidence."

Unexplained Absences

This, of course, is the most obvious clue. Sudden disappearances on the weekends for a few hours, late nights at the office when you can never reach him ("I'm sorry, I was using someone else's computer terminal"). Does he go away on more business trips than he used to, or are you no longer invited to accompany him?

Calling Patterns

Is there a sudden change in his calling habits—either he stops phoning as often, or he calls you a lot, in a feeble attempt to allay your suspicions?

Or has the time he calls you changed? For example, when he went away on business, he used to ring you late at night, just before he went to bed. Now he calls you as soon as he arrives at his hotel and always has an excuse as to why he can't talk to you later.

Is he not where he says he is, or is he always "unreachable" when you call him where he's supposed to be? Perhaps you call him at the office late, and no one answers—but then, mysteriously, a few minutes later he calls back and says he just "stepped out" for a few minutes. (If there is someone in his office whom he doesn't want to overhear him, he may be calling from another phone.) Does this sort of thing happen with increasing frequency?

Money Disappears

Strange. There used to be $1,000 a month deposited in your joint checking account for household expenses; now there's only $500. What happened to the rest of that money? What happened to the cash in his sock drawer he was putting away for a vacation fund? Despite the fact that he just got a small raise and your expenses haven't risen, is he complaining that money doesn't go as far as it used to and you have to cut back?

Your partner's extracurricular activities are likely to cost money, and if he's keeping a mistress, maybe *lots* of money. If you notice a drain on your finances that wasn't there before, somebody is bound to be getting the extra cash. It could be the racetrack, the local bartender—or her. It may be time to look carefully at credit card and phone bills for expenses that seem unconnected to your life.

The Paper Trail

Unfamiliar credit card bills, numbers you don't recognize on phone bills, a notice to renew a post office box you didn't know he had, correspondence that pertains to assets you didn't know he had—this is often how a man gets caught frequenting a call girl. His wife sees an unfamiliar charge on the credit card, tracks down the company, and discovers that Cachet Temporary Personnel offers temporary help of a different sort!

Are there checks being written to cash more often than before? Are checks being regularly written to persons or a business unfamiliar to you? Are there hotel bills from hotels *near your home*? Numerous phone calls to one or maybe two particular numbers at odd hours? One woman of my acquaintance found out about her husband's mistress when she stumbled on some correspondence from a bank about a mortgage on an apartment her husband had secretly bought for his paramour.

Secrecy

Does he get off the phone quickly when you enter the room? Or when the phone rings, does he leap up and run to another room to answer it? Did he recently purchase a beeper, despite the fact that he's neither a doctor nor a drug dealer? (If he's carried a beeper for a while, he may get an extra number that he doesn't give you.) Perhaps he spends hours on the computer, and when you come near him while he's typing he quickly exits to the Screen Saver, so you don't see what he's writing. (E-mail has become a friend to cheaters everywhere: no telltale love letters left around.)

Elaborate Explanations of His Itinerary

He used to give you a cheery, rudimentary rundown of his day; now he gives you a moment-by-moment account of his activities. By explaining his absences and unavailability in great detail, is he perhaps trying to preempt your suspicions?

Phone Follies

If you answer, there's a click or breathing on the line. Or the phone ring is some sort of signal (say, one ring, silence, and then the phone rings again). After getting such a phone call, does he suddenly need to walk the dog or go out for the paper?

Smell Signals

Another woman's perfume (or worse, her more intimate scent) is an obvious tip-off. But if he showers as soon as he gets home, or seems freshly soaped and showered many days when he comes home from work (and you note that since he's not in better shape, he's probably not showering at the gym), you may also want to take notice.

He Blows Hot and Cold

Once mild mannered, your husband now seems to be on an emotional roller coaster that has nothing to do with your life together. Guilty, anxious, and perhaps unable to take out his feelings on you for fear of being that much more obvious, he alternately screams at the children for trivial infractions and smothers them with attention and presents. He could try to overcompensate by spending more time than usual with them, or a lot less time because he's too anxious to cope.

Changes in His Eating or Sleeping Habits

There are very few people who can lead a double life without showing signs of emotional and physical strain.

Does he no longer eat dinner as often at home? (He could be dining with her.) Does he eat foods he never liked before? Does he seem to know a lot about sushi, but the two of you never go to Japanese restaurants together?

If he's anxious, he may have insomnia. Or he may use sleep as an escape, snoozing for twelve hours at a stretch. He loses his appetite and seems to be living on Maalox, or he eats compulsively. If he gets even the slightest cold, he makes a big deal about it and wants you to mother him, to see if you'll rescue him when he's down. It's both a test of how much you care and a way of seeing for himself what he'd be giving up if he left you.

He Gets a Makeover

All of a sudden, the man you'd have to nag to get a haircut or get out of his undershorts on Saturdays is looking snazzy. The hair is neat, he's got many new additions to his wardrobe, and he's working off his love handles with the Nordic Track you bought him three years ago. Perhaps there's a profusion of male beauty products (hair gel, Armani for Men cologne, skin moisturizer) on the bathroom shelf. He can't pass a mirror without checking himself out.

The Car

This sudden interest in appearance may extend to his wheels. Has he always been content with the Volvo station wagon, and now he's talking about buying a Pontiac Firebird? Or perhaps you look at the odometer and notice he's driving a lot more miles than usual. Check the glove compartment and door storage areas and under the seat for signs of her. Is the radio tuned to an unfamiliar station? Is the passenger seat often not in the position you left it? Is the seat belt on your side tighter or looser? Has he started having his car phone bill sent to his office instead of home?

Guilt Gifts

George Burns tells a wonderful story about the one time in his life (so he says) he cheated on his beloved Gracie. He was so disgusted and ashamed of himself that he went out and bought her the most beautiful diamond necklace he could find. Gracie was pretty sure she knew what was wrong, but she accepted the necklace and said nothing. Several years passed. One night, she and George were out to dinner and an acquaintance complimented her on her lovely necklace. As George stood there, aghast, she replied, "Thank you. I wish George would cheat on me again so I could get the matching earrings."

Men have to assuage their guilt somehow, and many men figure that the least they can do is pay for their bad "habit"— with jewelry, vacations, shopping sprees, new cars, and so on. Somehow, they rationalize, they are fulfilling at least one important part of their husbandly duty, even while they're neglecting another. As American humorist Molly McGee put it, "When a man brings his wife flowers for no reason, there's a reason."

Changes in Sexual Habits

So there he is, down there, performing oral sex on you, and something is . . . different. Maybe it's something subtle, like the change of the pressure of his tongue, or maybe it's something really obvious—like, for the first time, *he's doing it right.* Or he may seem newly interested in experimenting sexually with you, or introducing new sexual techniques into your routine. (Call girls rarely show men how to be better lovers—remember, her pleasure isn't the point—but it's possible that she demonstrated a position he hadn't thought of before and now he wants to do it with you.) Whatever it is, you know that something has changed and you had nothing to do with it.

As far as sexual frequency goes, a man who's cheating might either have much less sex with you or much more. He doesn't want to get caught by neglecting you, or maybe the thrill of adultery has revved up his libido. Either way, there is almost always some change in your sexual patterns.

(A warning: Don't leap to the conclusion that a man who's trying to get you out of your sexual doldrums is cheating. Maybe you lost ten pounds and are looking sexy. The desire to experiment sexually, in the absence of other signs, is not proof of infidelity!)

You Contract a Sexually Transmitted Disease

This one is pretty obvious. If you suddenly get, say, trichomoniasis, and you haven't been sleeping with someone else, the infection almost always comes from a third party. But see your doctor before you see a divorce lawyer. Some medications can cause vaginal disturbances, and occasionally yeast "just happens."

Public Behavior

When you go out, does he seem to be avoiding places you used to go together? Or, worse, has he stopped going out with you at all? (If he's been doing the town with his lady friend, he doesn't want to be showing up with a "new" woman on his arm.) At public events he's either overly affectionate (guilt, again), or acts like you're a complete stranger.

His Friends Start Acting Strangely or Avoiding You

If they know something you don't, they may be disgusted with him and sympathetic to you, but their own embarrassment *(What do I say to her? What if she asks me?)* will keep them away from you. The wives of his friends may be sworn to silence but drop little hints or act peculiarly. Are your conversations with them more stilted and superficial? If you bring up your husband in conversation, does the friend try to change the subject? Adding to their awkwardness are the questions they're inevitably asking themselves: *Whose friend am I? If I were Sally, wouldn't I want someone to tell me?*

He Seems Disconnected or Isolated

He seems to be listening to you less than he normally does. He avoids going to bed at the same time you do. You sense a sadness, even a *loneliness*, in him. (He has a foreboding about the end of his marriage, and it's eating him up inside.) As he practices more deceptions to keep the affair alive, he feels more and more cut off from you and perhaps from the children. And since he's probably not being entirely honest with his girlfriend or mistress either—having an affair inevitably involves some lying to her as well as to you—he may be overwhelmed by the sense that nobody understands or fully *knows* him. (I don't want to make you feel too sorry for him here. After all, this is a problem of his own making.)

Again, I want to emphasize: Don't panic if you notice one or two changes in your spouse's behavior. We *all* change at certain points in our lives. Instead, look at the big picture. If it adds up to a significant change in overall behavior, you may have a problem on your hands.

IDENTIFYING THE ENEMY:
GIRLFRIEND, MISTRESS, OR CALL GIRL?

Sometimes I think women who've been married act like boa constrictors who've just swallowed a sheep: They land one really terrific meal, and now they can afford just to lie in the sun and digest their dinner for a good long time. No wonder it's so easy to catch them unawares. Their rivals—the girlfriend, mistress, or call girl—are alert and hungry. And they are intent on attracting their prey—namely, your husband.

When men decide to cheat, who is available is often more of a criterion then finding the perfect woman. When a woman discovers that her husband has a mistress or girlfriend, she's often startled to find this woman is not a goddess. I've had lots of women say to me, "You know, Sydney, she was kind of unattractive and *dumpy*," as if choosing a woman less physically alluring than them somehow added insult to injury. (An even more unsettling phenomenon: Many mistresses look like a younger version of the wife. Marla Maples is a perfect example.)

Let's say you're certain he's involved in an extracurricular activity. Before confronting him, give some thought to whom he's cheating with. Is it a girlfriend, mistress, or call girl? Knowing the species of woman he's with offers guidelines on how best to proceed.

The Girlfriend

Although she may get some generous presents from him here and there, she's not in it for the money; she's in it for the *man*. Therefore, she is your most serious problem. The girlfriend waits by the phone, sneaks away with him on business trips, and cries when he's with you on Christmas and Thanksgiving. Frequently she tells herself how much happier he'd be with her (and probably *he* tells her this, too). After all, she could turn his life around, because she's the one who truly understands him.

If she's read Oscar Wilde, she'll have this quote from *A Woman of No Importance* tucked away somewhere in her diary: "Men always want to be a woman's first love. That is their clumsy vanity. We women have a more subtle instinct about things. What we like is to be a man's last romance."

Indeed, a man who has a girlfriend is not interested only in sex or a new young body. This man wants romance, conversation, attention, fun, adventure—in short, whatever he feels he's no longer getting with you. And the girlfriend is delighted to give it. She may be one of the legions of women out there who really don't feel a man is off-limits just because he happens to be married. She knows that her ability to focus her attention on him like a heat-seeking missile is something that a wife, with all of the distractions of a *real* life with her husband, often can't do.

Some women who prefer married men have problems with commitment. A married man is unavailable and therefore safer. Or perhaps they haven't the interest or the free time for a full-fledged relationship, and a married man isn't likely to make too many demands.

But most girlfriends don't find married men preferable. Most just fall in love and are as unhappy about the situation as you are. She wants an exclusive relationship with him, a relationship with a future, and very often she's just as miserable about his deceptions as you are. (Yes, it's true: Most men who have girlfriends swear on their mother's life that they *never* sleep with their wives anymore. Often the girlfriend clings to this information as proof that what she's doing isn't all that bad.)

The Mistress

> Off the Wall Street Journal's *incredibly exhaustive survey of 18,845 exhausted mistresses showed that fully 75 per cent are subject to the same kind of stress, tension, and high vulnerability to heart attacks, cancer, and suicide suffered by the high-level executives who keep them—as well as amexophobia, the fear of abrupt credit cancellation. Surprisingly, more than 3/4 of the mistresses surveyed say they find the mistress-executive relationship to be stimulating, honest, emotionally gratifying, financially rewarding, and in all ways preferable to marriage, although if the executive offered to marry them they'd grab it in a second.*

> OFF THE WALL STREET JOURNAL, *1982*

She may or may not be in love with your man, and she may or may not be truly sexually satisfied with him. But whatever the situation, money is involved in this relationship. It may not be a lot of money; for every stereotypical mistress lounging in a penthouse suite, bedecked in jewels and furs, there are a hundred girls who are just getting a little help with the rent.

If your husband is helping to keep a woman, he is primarily interested in two things: status and control. Even though he may feel guilty about his relationship with another woman, depending on the culture he was raised in, he may think that a mistress is something that every successful man must have, like a gold Rolex or a corner office. His ability to support more than one woman at a time is a testament to his virility, just as surely (and illogically) as being able to knock up a girl when he was eighteen told him he was a man.

It's not only married men who keep mistresses. You wouldn't believe how many *single* men also "keep" a woman. This way, they feel much more in control. Some single men prefer this arrangement because, once she accepts it, her ability to criticize or demand attention is severely compromised. It is also more convenient for him. If he's paying, she must always make him her priority; when he's available, she must be too. Paying someone also helps keep talk of "the future" at a minimum; it's generally understood that a future together is unlikely.

(For most mistresses, a married man is far preferable. She knows that she'll probably profit, much more generously, from his guilt over having an affair.)

So, to varying degrees (depending on the amount of financial support she's receiving), a mistress is beholden to her keeper. He may not have very much time for her, but when he's ready, she'd better be ready, too. And if she's smart, she is waiting with the martini at the door, the candlelight, the music, the dose of bittersweet romance wedged into your man's busy schedule. Sexually, too, a good mistress is always receptive. She is usually very well groomed, toned, and well dressed, and has the time for waxing, manicures, and facials. Given all the effort she puts into body maintenance, you can bet she's going to put it to good use. She also has the advantage of rarity: Even if she's not the most beautiful and exotic creature in the world (and she may very well not be), because sex with her is relatively infrequent, it's that much more exciting.

Without the responsibilities of home and children, a mistress usually has the time and energy to devote to romantic scenarios that you don't. And even if she is, say, a divorcee with her own home and children, they are usually somewhere in the background. She doesn't introduce them into the life she shares with your man, because her role is to be an escape from reality, not another version of it.

Although the mistress may be emotionally involved, she is probably more distant than the girlfriend, because she understands that what her lover cannot supply in time or lavish displays of emotion he supplies in cash. But even if she's not as threatening to your marriage as the girlfriend, she is still there, still draining your man's emotions and money, which are rightfully yours.

The Call Girl

No woman wants to find out that her mate is cheating. But if you discover he's seeing call girls, consider yourself somewhat luckier than women whose husbands have girlfriends or mistresses. Whatever his reasons for stepping out, clearly he is not looking for any kind of emotional attachment. In having sex with a professional, he probably even feels he isn't *really* cheating. In the minds of most men, if you pay for it, it's not cheating. It's more of a business transaction. There are no feelings, no danger to the relationship, particularly since he's unlikely to see the same girl twice. (Men go to call girls for variety; seeing the same girl on a regular basis is rare.)

Men go to call girls because they don't want to deal with anything real. They're guaranteed she's not going to demand more of them than they feel like giving. The way they get that guarantee is by paying for it. A wife or a girlfriend feels entitled to know where he's been, what he's been doing, and how he feels about her. Someone who's being paid has bartered away her right to make those demands. So the call girl adores everything the guy does—at least for those few hours he's with her. She's perfectly coiffed, beautifully attired, ready to do anything he wants (including ordering him to lick her boots, if that's what he *really* wants.) She is there for one thing, and one thing only: to please.

Men understand that this is fantasy. That's what they want. Most of them don't feel too badly about it—and neither should you. Of course you're upset if you discover your husband is frequenting call girls. But realize that this is the least emotionally complicated way of cheating.

At the Crossroads:
Do You Want to
Stay in the Relationship?

If you have good reason to believe your husband is cheating, you'll have to ask yourself: Do I want to stay in this relationship or do I want to get out? It isn't an easy question to answer and you might need help from a marriage counselor or therapist in order to come to a conclusion. You may also want to pick up a copy of Barry Lubetkin and Elena Oumano's *Bailing Out: The Sane Way to Get Out of a Doomed Relationship and Survive with Hope and Self-Respect*. This excellent book will help you look at many of the issues facing you during a relationship crisis.

Of course, even after a discovery of infidelity, you may still want to hold your marriage together. As I discussed earlier, there are a myriad of reasons a man strays, and if it's obvious that trust and love are not completely broken *and* your man is keenly motivated to make the marriage work again, you should do everything in your power to save your marriage.

Let me just say this up front: I think if a woman discovers her man is seeing call girls, she should almost never choose to end the relationship. (Provided, of course, the man has been safeguarding your health by wearing condoms, which he has if he's seeing a call girl. No working girl these days will let a man go condomless.)

Yes, he is cheating. But by hiring his sex partners, this fellow has made a conscious decision not to threaten the emotional relationship he has with you. Maybe he hasn't felt he could tell you what he needs sexually, or maybe he's felt your emotional absence recently. Whatever the case, he still wants you in his life. If he didn't, he'd be out looking for someone he could have a real relationship with.

In any case, whether he's gotten himself a call girl, mistress, or girlfriend, *you must confront him about his infidelity.*

What happens if you don't? Even if this particular affair ends, there will likely be another, and another. The two of you will never resolve what drove him to have an affair in the first place. And on some level, he wants to be confronted, because the pressure of leading a double life is putting him under tremendous strain. If there's no confrontation, the two of you are living with each other in a state of fear.

How you confront him has great bearing on what happens. Threatening divorce is entirely counterproductive if your real wish is to stay together. It's not facing what's really wrong in your marriage.

Countering with an affair of your own is also a lame idea. It just gives him a rationale for his own bad behavior.

Ultimatums are also useless, for two reasons. First, he may panic—"Omigod, I won't have a home anymore"—giving the other woman a chance to be understanding and take him in. Second, if he doesn't make up his mind between you and the other woman in the time you've allotted him, and then (like so many women) you cave in and give him an "extension" because you're so desperate to keep him, he'll never take your ultimatums seriously again.

Instead, you must make it possible for the two of you to discuss, without hysterics, what he's done, *and why*. No matter how painful it is at the time, honesty at this juncture is absolutely necessary. And of course, the best arena for this kind of discussion is a marital therapist.

How to Create a Shared History

When faced with a crisis in a marriage, a lot of women dismiss the most powerful weapon they have in keeping the relationship together: a shared history. You both stayed up all night when the kid was barfing his guts out with the flu. He was there for those vacations to Disney World and those early-in-the-marriage twenty-four-hour sex marathons. You have lived the same life—whether or not that life has been happy—and saying good-bye to a piece of one's life is tremendously difficult.

Most men don't leave a long-term committed relationship easily. Even if they're really unhappy in the marriage, they've still grown comfortable with you and your lifestyle, home, and routine. And of course they love their children. Remember, men don't like change, and you are the known quantity. Whatever else is out there might be exciting, but it's also scary.

There's another factor at work here. When men make a formal commitment to marriage, they feel obliged to stick with that commitment—unless things are so bad they can't stand it anymore. A lot of the men who came to see my girls told us that they were in unhappy marriages. But they wouldn't leave, because they made a deal. Your spouse made a commitment not only to you but also to your children and your families.

So if you feel your relationship is rocky right now, remember that, for the most part, you have to *work* to drive him away from you. Most men will stay with what they know, rather than venture into foreign territory.

(Those of you who've been the mistress of a married man who keeps telling you he's going to leave his wife once the kids graduate from high school or once his wife gets a job . . . well, men rarely do. Less than 20 percent of men leave their marriage partner for their affair partner.)

It's up to you continually to build a shared history. You probably do this already, without even thinking about it. Maybe all the relatives come to your house for Thanksgiving. Maybe your Fourth of July barbecue is an annual tradition among your friends and neighbors. You work together as a team; if he likes to plan your trips, you're the one who remembers to bring the camera and read up on the history of the place. Create rituals, even if they're as simple as insisting that every Friday night everyone in the family sits down and has supper together.

The important thing here is, as far as possible, to make sure you and your husband have an ever-growing inventory of shared events you remember with fondness. Take lots of photos and keep an album of pictures on your coffee table. If a guest asks you about a souvenir or objet d'art you brought home from one of your trips, tell a brief story of your journey, making sure to include the object and your partner in your tale. You might also want to give him a few frames and pictures of you and the kids to keep in his office. Keep little tokens of your life together (the ashtray your daughter made at camp, the trophy your son's basketball team won this year) on display at all times.

All these things (even reminiscing about sad events) reinforce the idea of you two as a couple. So when a rough patch comes along and he's thinking, *God, get me outta here*, he's got to stop and think: I'm not just walking out on a marriage. I'm walking out on a *life*.

An Ounce of Prevention Is Worth a Pound of Cure

You are pretty certain your man isn't straying but you don't want to take any chances. Or you think he might be and you are determined to do something about it. As we discussed in Chapter 4, there are numerous reasons why a man strays that you have some control over if he's looking for something he isn't getting from you in his primary relationship. Let's talk about what some of these needs are and how you can keep your man happy, satisfied, and home with you.

Problem: He's tempted to stray because he's bored.
Solution: Create a spirit of adventure.

One of the most common complaints my girls heard from clients: "Once I got married, our lives became so predictable and boring." Just because men whine about how humdrum they feel life has become doesn't mean they're good at doing something to liven it up. It usually falls to you to keep freshness and a spirit of adventure in your relationship.

I'm not suggesting you turn to your husband in bed one night and say, "Honey, don't you think it's about time we learned how to cliff dive?" Adventure doesn't have to be death-defying to qualify as fun. All it takes is a little sense of mischief. Here are a few things you might try.

THE DEEP POCKETS ADVENTURE You can play at being rich with no financial sacrifice. Visit a boat show and price the most expensive yacht. The next time your husband looks longingly at a Ferrari, suggest that the two of you go to a Ferrari dealer and take a test-drive. Find the toniest manse that's on the market in your neighborhood and pretend you're seriously considering buying (real estate agents will hate me for this one). Go to Tiffany's and make a fuss over your husband as he appears to be seriously mulling over whether to buy you the $300,000 emerald and diamond choker or the $400,000 flawless ruby ring. (Okay, maybe this last one is *your* fantasy, but with a little luck he could enjoy it, too.)

THE TRAVEL ADVENTURE So you can't afford the Galápagos Islands. How about a weekend away that *you* plan but you keep him in the dark until you get there? Many luxury hotels in large cities have special weekend rates. Or maybe he prefers a No-Tell Motel dirty weekend of X-rated movies and bubble baths in a heart-shaped Jacuzzi! If he's got a gambling streak, you might plan a weekend at Atlantic City or Las Vegas, or simply visit your local racetrack. Maybe his "inner child" needs a holiday at Disney World. Then again, maybe his inner cowboy needs a weekend at a dude ranch. (Old West Dude Ranch Vacations is part of a larger adventure-holiday organization you might want to learn about; call 1-800-444-DUDE.) Romantic bed-and-breakfasts, local agricultural fairs, a quickie road trip to Graceland—you're limited only by your imagination. Even if it's an afternoon at the local firemen's fair or a drive to the next county to try out a new ice cream shop, the important thing is to get out of your rut and do something different.

Problem: He's tempted to stray because he doesn't feel he gets enough appreciation.
Solution: Lavish attention on him.

I can hear you saying, "Sydney, the guy is forty-five years old. He's big enough not to need me fussing over him all the time." WRONG. This gets back to the idea that all men are little boys inside who need to feel special, just the way Mom made them feel. I don't care if he's seventy years old: Just as we never tire of hearing how pretty we look, he never tires of hearing how terrific he is.

I'm not suggesting you go out of your way to lie, or praise him for attributes he just doesn't have. But there must be some things you find special about him—you're with him, aren't you? Try to find the things you now take for granted and make something of them. Even if your praise is not quite as sincere as it was twenty years ago, it's very unlikely he'll notice.

Not only do men need to be appreciated for what they do for you, they also need to be appreciated for what they do for themselves. You appreciate it when he's worked overtime so you can afford to fix the roof or go on a nice vacation. You do appreciate that, and you should let him know. But there are other things he does that you don't act grateful for, because, frankly, you couldn't care less. Let's say he spent three hours last Saturday washing the car and polishing and vacuuming the interior. He comes inside, proudly, to tell you about the car, and you say, offhandedly, "That's nice, dear. Can you go to the corner and get a pizza for dinner?"

He's *crushed*. He's just spent three hours of his valuable time giving you the shiniest hubcaps in the neighborhood, and you don't even appreciate him for it!

So you might want to look at the things he spends time on—things that are apparently very important to him, however trivial they seem to you—and praise him for them. My friend Melanie's husband would come home on the weekend and ignore the fact that the sliding screen door onto the deck was off its track. Instead, he'd spend five hours helping his son glue together his model helicopter. Melanie used to rail against his lack of priorities, until one day it occurred to her that she was being foolish. She could hire someone to fix the screen door, but she couldn't hire someone to be a father. So she began praising him for it: "I can't believe how you fit all those tiny pieces together so perfectly. . . ."

"And," Melanie told me, "Ken would just *beam*."

The more you go out of your way to appreciate him, the greater the chance you will get some of that appreciation back.

In addition, try to determine which activities make him feel especially close to you. A friend's boyfriend loves her to go out on his boat. The truth is, she hates going out on the damn boat; she'd rather be stripping some furniture or browsing the sale racks at Macy's. But a few times each summer, she goes out and spends a night on the wretched thing, behaving as if she truly enjoyed it. He looks forward to these outings all year long; she does it for *him*.

So maybe your partner wants to share something really special to him that you put off doing because you just aren't crazy about it. It won't kill you to do it every once in a while, just to please him. It will also give you a little leverage when you need to persuade him to do something with you that *he's* not so fond of.

Appreciation doesn't mean mindless approval of everything he says and does. If you disagree with him or have a problem with the way he handled something, of course you should let him know—but not in public.

I'm not suggesting you refrain from disagreeing with him about politics or other nonpersonal issues. But don't disagree or criticize him about more personal things. If he's telling some tall tale about how he one-upped Tom in marketing, don't pipe up, "Yes, but I thought you told me the boss thought Tom was right." There's no bigger betrayal in the world for a partner, either man or woman, than to be criticized publicly. Always be his biggest fan, his rowdiest cheerleader, in public. He may not blow his own horn, but he'll be thrilled if you do.

Problem: He's tempted to stray because he's looking for a best friend, a companion who shares his outside interests.
Solution: Spend more time together.

It's tough for a two-career couple to find time to spend together, especially if they are parents, too. If you can't manage one evening a week, you must find at least one evening a month for just the two of you. If you're on roughly the same schedule, why not set aside half an hour before bedtime as your special time together. I cannot stress strongly enough how vital it is that you spend time together as a couple and relate to each other as a couple. If your schedules do not permit much time together, set aside five to ten minutes each day to talk on the phone. Try to talk about personal things: how you feel about what is going on in your lives right now, how you feel about your partner. Try to save what I call "information exchange" for another time and keep focused on the two of you.

When you have very little time to spend with each other as it is, there's often no time to share outside interests and hobbies. But you can encourage him to talk about them, to share his experiences with you during your "couple time." While you may not be able to (or want to) participate, you can still be involved by showing your interest and keeping up with things in his life that are important to him.

Problem: He's tempted to stray because he's looking for intellectual fulfillment.
Solution: Learn to fire his neurons.

Consider this: When a man goes to a call girl, the average call is two to four hours, and yet they spend only about five minutes having sex. A number of friends who've been mistresses told me that plenty of times their boyfriends came over and they didn't even sleep together. They just sat around and talked. So don't think the reason men cheat is mainly because they're not getting enough sex at home. Much of the time, that has nothing to do with why they're cheating. About 65 percent of men cheat because they don't find spending time with their partner particularly interesting.

It sounds so obvious, but I can't stress this enough: It's important to have something to say and to be well informed about the world around you. I don't mean just keeping up with what's happening with Ricki Lake's guests today, or the latest celebrity divorce scandal. (Although, don't get me wrong, many men like getting dish from *The National Enquirer* as much as we do.) You also have to have at least some idea of what's going on in the world.

One of the hard-and-fast rules I had for the women who worked for me was that they read *Newsweek* or *Time* every week, watch *60 Minutes*, and watch the news on television as much as possible. This is a *minimum*. If you can't watch the news during the week, at least tune in to the Sunday morning talking-head shows: *David Brinkley, The McLaughlin Group, Meet the Press.*

Men like to talk about *stuff*, not just what the kids are doing and whether the pool man came and vacuumed the scum off the bottom today. And if he has friends with intellectual interests, it's a bit embarrassing to him if, say, you all go out to dinner and you can't keep up your end of the conversation. (Of course, many women have the opposite problem: *They're* the ones desperate to talk to their husbands about something more intellectually challenging than, "How 'bout them Bears?")

When you have interesting things to talk about and share with him, you're also doing him a favor by giving *him* a wealth of information and insight to share with his friends. Every time you amuse him with a story you saw on CNN or bring him up to date on the latest sports star scandal, it gives him something to spice up his conversation with his boss or the guys at work. You'll be surprised how much he'll come to rely on you.

Remember: If you ever feel you've run out of subjects to talk about with your mate, you've got one sure-fire backup subject that never ceases to entertain: him, his ideas, his interests, his job. Almost invariably he is a source of unceasing interest to himself.

Problem: He's tempted to stray because he's no longer attracted to you.
Solution: Makeover time.

I don't want to make women even more neurotic about their appearance than they already are. Chances are you are much more critical of the way you look than your mate is. Although *you* may be obsessed by every lump and bump on your body, your husband probably doesn't even notice them. (It also helps, I think, to have a spouse who is seriously myopic.)

But if there's been some serious disintegration of your appearance over the last few years—a significant weight gain or slovenliness creeping into your grooming habits—get up off your butt and start doing something about it, *now.* Join a gym, join a local intramural sports team, or simply join a buddy and speed-walk around your neighborhood for a half hour every other day. (In addition to the fact that exercise helps you lose weight and gain muscle tone, recent studies also show it makes you more easily orgasmic!)

I won't lecture you about eating, either—you know what's necessary to get your weight to where you want it. Meanwhile, while you're working on getting fit, you may want to take a look at your wardrobe: When was the last time you greeted him in something other than sweats?

I certainly couldn't totter around the house in stiletto slippers trimmed in maribou and the clingy chiffon gown actresses in the 1940s always wore in drawing room comedies either. But think of some substitutes for those tentlike muumuus or the stained terry-cloth bathrobe. Think clingy (but comfy) leggings; think moisturizer and just a touch of sheer blush and translucent lipstick, instead of none at all. Tiny stud earrings you can wear and ignore might suffice for jewelry. If you look good in caps and bandannas, keep a collection of them around for bad hair days.

And underwear? Throw out anything that looks like a chew toy for your dog.

Above all, think cleanliness: clean hair, sweet breath,

scrubbed nails, and dewy skin, perhaps with a trace of body lotion in his favorite scent.

Problem:　He's tempted to stray because he feels you have changed or because his life has changed.
Solution:　Communication.

There are very few guarantees in life, but one you can always count on is change. Most change is healthy; it shows that you are growing as a person and using your knowledge and experience to direct yourself toward a more fulfilling and satisfying life. Problems arise when you and your partner grow in such different directions that your expectations and goals are mutually exclusive and there is little common ground on which to build a future. This is the primary reason for the breakdown of young marriages and relationships.

If our partner's developing sense of self and purpose is so incompatible with our own that no amount of compromise can be mutually acceptable, then perhaps it is time to part amicably. But in the vast majority of cases, an open line of communication, a strong commitment to the relationship, and the ability to compromise *can* keep a couple together. The trick is to stay on top of your feelings and changing needs and share them as they become clear to you. Pay careful attention to your partner's reaction and response and respect his point of view, even if it is painful and not necessarily what you want to hear. And, of course, you need to encourage him to talk to you about the changes going on inside himself as well.

Sometimes outside influences can really rock a relationship: loss of income, a child's illness or death, a natural disaster, even something as exciting as a big promotion or financial success. At critical times like this, it is vital for you to be his number one confidante. If you're not there for him or if he feels you don't understand or appreciate what he's going through, he may look for someone who does. And for those of you who feel you don't know how to deal with these life changes on your own, or if your partner doesn't find it easy to talk, please don't hesitate to involve your pastor or a professional counselor.

Problem: He's tempted to stray because he feels his identity is being subsumed by yours.
Solution: Let his own identity shine through.

Encourage him to take up a hobby or get involved in a sport and let him do it on his own! You can show interest and be there to cheer him on at the big game, but let him have some interests and activities that are his alone.

Maybe all he needs to recapture a sense of self is a room in the house that is entirely *his*, where he can put his beer on the table without worrying about making a water ring. Or maybe you've been choosing his clothes for him. Let him wear his lucky madras shorts on the golf course, even if they look ridiculous. Get him more involved in making decisions for the household. Not that you have to consult him every time you buy a refrigerator magnet, but at least let him know you care about his taste in domestic matters. And if it's you who's always deciding what the kids eat, or whether they get to watch television that night, cede a bit of control to him. This may be all he needs to feel he's master of his own domain again.

Problem: He's tempted to stray because he claims you're too smothering.
Solution: Get a life!

A lot of women feel insecure when men have interests that do not include them. This is a mistake. (It also doesn't make sense. Do you want him tagging along when you're shopping or getting your nails done?) Of course you want to have shared areas of interest, but it's very important to have your own interests and activities, and let him have his. It's important that you both do things on your own.

I once went out with a man who had very few male

friends. (Unfortunately, it's a fairly common situation. Studies show that most men say their partner is their best friend, while not many women pay the same compliment to *their* mates.) When I went out with my girlfriends, he would sit at home and wait for me, making me feel guilty for leaving him all to his lonesome. Why didn't *he* get a life?

There are many men who feel as I did about their women. Because when the proverbial shoe is on the other foot, a woman who makes a man feel guilty about his evenings out with the boys doesn't believe she's being unreasonable. We rationalize that since we and loverboy are both working and don't have much free time, when the weekend comes we ought to do everything together.

I'm not saying you shouldn't do things together—of course you should—but you can't expect him to do everything with you. If you can face up to and conquer your fear of independence, I guarantee that no matter what happens in your relationship, you'll have a feeling of liberation you've never before experienced. You'll still occasionally be lonely, and you'll still have problems with your partner. But you'll be living *your* life, not his.

6

A Little

Sex Education

Goes a Long Way

One of the most pervasive myths in our culture is that sex is always fun and spontaneous. In truth, good sex is a lot like going on vacation. Vacations are fun—provided you plan ahead: make plane and hotel reservations, rent a car, stop the mail and newspaper delivery, all those little chores that enable you to leave with a clear conscience. With sex and vacations, you benefit most when you explore and take small risks. And with sex and vacations, you have to withstand the occasional disappointment with good humor: Sometimes you get to paradise, and it rains!

In other words, fun (be it a long, languorous afternoon in bed or on the beach) requires a certain amount of work, particularly in long-term relationships.

I am not going to kid you here. To say that sex with a partner you've been with for years, whom you've seen in every state of decrepitude, who is as familiar to you as your own body, is going to be as exciting and spontaneous as it was the first year you were together is unrealistic. Similarly, your partner may not be able to recapture *exactly* the same excitement as he had with you the first time the two of you kissed. (In general, women seem better able to understand and accept this fact than men. Some men stray because they don't have the maturity to understand that sexual mellowing is inevitable. They think there's something wrong, and they're out there looking to recapture that sexual "high," whatever the cost.)

But settling down doesn't mean settling for less. The sex you have together can be adventurous, passionate, playful, loving, and deeply satisfying—much more so, in fact, than anything you can achieve with someone you barely know. You just must work harder than you would in a new relationship to make that kind of passionate sex a reality. (The next few chapters give you the tools to do that work.)

Before we address your partner's sexual needs, it's necessary for you to give some thought to your own. Sexual self-awareness is *the most important factor* in being a superb lover.

DISCOVERING YOUR SEXUAL PERSONALITY

The reason the Mayflower Madam became such a sensational news story, I think, was because I looked more like a carpool mom from Greenwich, Connecticut, than a flashy, overtly sexy, tough-talking madam. In the intervening years I've often wondered how often our outward personae and our sexual "personalities" coincide.

Most of us, at one time or another, have felt boxed in by the external images that we've established for ourselves, images that do not necessarily reflect our sexual selves. Cultural mores do not allow us to reveal our sexual natures to anyone but our partners, or maybe a few close friends. And even though we spend an inordinate amount of time analyzing other aspects of the self—everything from sense of style to religious beliefs to political ideology—few women stop to consider who they are sexually.

Our sexual nature is one aspect of our entire personality; it's a role we play. A personality comprises many roles: mother, daughter, wife, boss, employee, friend. Each role makes different demands on the individual. The problem for many women is that there are few *realistic* role models for sexuality. Italy and France have an innate appreciation of the sensuousness of wives and mothers—in fact, a woman's sexuality is often more celebrated after these rites of passage. But in American culture, in addition to maintaining the gravity-defying body of the girls on MTV videos, a sexy woman must project the mystique that she is somehow untouched by cares and responsibility. A mother is by definition not sexy—she's got more "important" things to worry about. The women we hold up as most sexy are the fantasy women: available, always in the mood, with buns (and other body parts) of steel. We worship what does not exist.

So when we become wives and mothers, many of us put our sexual selves on the shelf. We slip into traditional roles: "You're the daddy, I'm the mommy." We have sex, certainly, but it often becomes just another comforting routine among many. With everything else we have to concern ourselves with, it just can't be central to our lives. When you have a million responsibilities, when your energy is scattered in dozens of different places, it's hard to harness the energy to be purely sexual, even if it's just for an hour. You'd rather put on the comfy T-shirt at the end of the day, not the lingerie.

But even with all the other roles you've got to play, ignoring (or slighting) your sexual personality can be destructive. You have to be a lover as much as you're a wife and a mom. One reason for cheating I've heard from literally hundreds of men: "My girlfriend will do stuff with me my wife won't do anymore."

You've got to take the time to get in touch with your sexual self. Ask yourself: What does sex mean to me? What role does sexual intimacy play in my relationships? Am I comfortable with that? Do I feel free to express my sexuality or do I hold back? Why? What makes me feel most desirable, most alive? *That's* the essence of sexual personality.

There are three components to sexual personality.

Sexual Beliefs and Attitudes

Our ideas about sex, and about our own sexuality, start to form almost from the moment we're born. From the moment we can focus our eyes, we observe our parents. How do they behave toward each other? How do they seem to feel about each other's bodies? Do they kiss and hug in public? Or do they barely touch each other? These early experiences can determine whether we find it pleasurable or terrifying, important or unimportant.

Yet many women cannot distinguish between what they've been taught about sex from what they actually believe. Our society encourages a kind of sexual schizophrenia. We're instructed to expend vast amounts of time and money to appear desirable, yet we're also told to be cool, even slightly aloof, in order to discourage unwanted and often indiscriminate male advances. We're told that we shouldn't play games in the "game of love," yet we're also told to "play hard to get." Nice girls aren't "easy," but they also aren't teases. The list of double messages we receive about our sexuality goes on and on.

It's small wonder, then, that many women would rather not bother even thinking about sex. It's too confusing; it's too much of a nuisance; it takes too much effort.

If you've ever felt similarly anxious or indifferent about sex, it may be time to analyze your own sexual beliefs and attitudes. What does sex mean to you? Is it a pleasure or a duty? Perhaps your religion considers sex sinful, or your mother made it clear that she didn't like sex. Perhaps you had very little, or no, sexual experience before you got married, and you don't feel as experienced or knowledgeable as your partner. Do you feel insecure about the way you make love? Are you uncertain about what stimulates you? Are there some acts you or your partner consider wrong or dirty? Why? Would it do you any good to let go of some of your preconceived notions?

Of course, there will always be *some* sexual activities that cross your moral boundaries. But let's see if it's possible to stretch your horizons a bit.

Sexual Drive

The amount of sex a woman wants varies greatly according to a variety of factors at any given time in her life: age (a woman's sex drive tends to increase in her thirties and forties, while a man's sex drive decreases), career pressures, children, and so on. Many of us don't realize it, but our sex drive fluctuates according to our menstrual cycle. You might assume that desire is greatest around the time of ovulation, but in fact, many women are most amorous right before or after their period, and desire tapers off toward ovulation. As a friend of mine put it, "There are times of the month when I'm indifferent, and then there are other times I could do it two or three times a day."

Of course, some women are just plain randy *all* the time, while others, perhaps anxious or fearful about sex, never feel desire. (Also, your partner may not turn you on anymore, or you might be so busy and stressed that sex is the last thing you want. "Inhibited sexual desire," as it's called, is a growing problem among stressed professionals with no downtime for relaxation or play.) Whatever your individual situation, it may be useful for you to keep a monthly record of your level of arousal, noting your sexual moods, feelings, and fantasies. Most women will see a pattern in their level of sexual interest.

Sexual Function

The variety of sexual turn-ons and turn-offs is endless. For some women sex is all about power; others can be really aroused only when there's a feeling that the sex is illicit; a lot of women feel sexiest when they're pregnant (perhaps because that's when they feel most secure and loved).

Although most women are more in tune with their emotional makeup than men are, typically women are less perceptive than men about their sexual needs. My friend Frank, a single man in his forties who's had a seemingly endless string of girlfriends, never ceases to be amazed by the number of women who don't know—or won't say—what they want in bed. When Frank *does* find a woman who knows what she wants . . . well, she is a force to be reckoned with. He's particularly fond of women who are unafraid of experimentation. "In many ways, a good sexual relationship is about creating an environment of safety," Frank says. "I love sex that seems to have an element of danger, but the operative word here is *seems.* Recently I met a woman who is not afraid to explore the darker side of sexuality. But what we do is create a place where it's safe to be dangerous. I think she can do this because she's come to terms with her own sexual nature. She's not scared of it, or ashamed, and consequently she gets more from sex than almost any woman I've known."

Remember that clothing store advertisement with the tag line, "An Educated Consumer Is Our Best Customer"? The same applies to sex. You've got to educate yourself (which I talk about a little later in this chapter). To know what you like and how you like it, you may need to do a little exploration that doesn't involve your partner—at least not until you feel confident about introducing new activities into your sexual relationship.

Reading or talking about what turns you on does not mean you have to act out your fantasies, or even that you want to. You've got to be sensitive and use your common sense. Discussing your fantasies can enhance sex, but if the timing isn't right it can also be destructive. If you think your partner will be threatened, wait until you're *not* in bed and delicately introduce the subject. See how he reacts, and proceed accordingly.

SOME CLASSIC SEXUAL "TYPES":
WHERE DO YOU FIT IN?

Sex may be very important to both you and your mate yet be important for different reasons.

The Pleaser

You take very good care of yourself. You want to be as alluring on your tenth anniversary as you were on your first. You have an extensive wardrobe of sexy lingerie, and you scan sex books in search of new erotic techniques. When he's ready for sex, so are you—never mind that the project for work is due tomorrow, and the kids are still watching television when they should have been asleep two hours ago. When he suggests a new sexual position or scenario, you always say yes, even if you'd rather be doing something else.

A desire to please and the ability to focus totally on your partner are two of *the* most important keys to a sexually satisfying relationship. Perhaps, however, you go a little overboard, letting your approval-seeking nature subsume your own feelings or needs. Sometimes you feel you *can't* say no.

The Spiritualist

Sex, for you, is primarily an expression of love. What's more important than the physical turn-on is the sense of peace and closeness you feel at the end of lovemaking. You find it hard to imagine sex outside marriage or a long-term commitment; in fact, sex and commitment are pretty much synonymous. Occasionally you may wonder why you crave more languorous, intimate lovemaking, while your partner seems to regard sex as a contact sport. What's important for you to realize and accept is that many men are biologically programmed to have sex for reasons other than intimacy. Don't worry if sometimes your mate doesn't seem as cuddly and talkative after sex as you are. He may have other ways of showing his love, like walking the dog when you're tired, or giving the kids a bath.

The Pragmatist

Joan has a problem a lot of women wish they had. Her husband, Steve, makes love to her whenever they can find a few hours of "quality time." But therein lies the problem. With three small kids, they rarely *do* have a few hours of uninterrupted time, and Joan, who describes herself as "highly sexed," would often prefer a few quickies a week to one long lovemaking session. "But somehow I just can't tell him," Joan says. "Steve thinks sex has to be some sort of great spiritual, cosmic union. There are times when I don't even care about orgasm. I just want the rough-and-tumble of physical contact with him."

No matter how much lip service we pay to our sexual freedom, many women are still uncomfortable admitting they like sex purely because it feels good, releases tension, and makes us generally less cranky. What's wrong with sex for sex's sake occasionally?

The Perfectionist

Although some women are oblivious to the trappings of romance, the perfectionist can blossom only in an environment replete with candles, dim lights, and Cole Porter in the background. What's more, you drive your partner nuts by insisting *he* be a model lover, too. You won't make love if he hasn't showered first, and you get upset if he says or does the "wrong" thing during sex.

The problem here is that if the setting has to be *perfect* before you make love, you may be missing many opportunities for satisfaction. Lack of spontaneity drives many men bonkers. On the other hand, a woman who can tune out life's little distractions—the blinking answering machine, a few crumbs on the (otherwise perfect for a rendezvous) sofa—is likely to be making love with greater frequency.

The Good Girl

So much attention is paid to the femme fatale that we forget that not everyone has to be a tigress in order to have a satisfying sex life. Certainly there are many women who do not want or need a great deal of variety in their sex life; as long as you achieve orgasm fairly regularly, you may be comfortable with a few positions and one or two different settings. For you sex may be routine, but not in a pejorative sense. It becomes part of the comfortable rhythm of your life, affording a sense of peace and security.

There's another breed of good girl, however, who is attracted to men who are powerful and dominating in bed. Maybe you don't like to take the initiative or feel the burden of responsibility for doing things that are a little out of the ordinary. You crave a man who's a leader, a teacher, a daddy, a man who shows you the way. You don't like to "own" your own sexuality; it's too frightening to you. Good girls look for men who somehow draw their desires out of them, somewhat against their will.

(Of course, let's be honest here, there are a few good girls who don't like sex, period. They feel that sex is pretty much a close-your-eyes-and-think-of-England activity.)

The biggest danger of being a good girl is passivity. If she doesn't find a sexually dominant man, she may spend years of her life in the sexual doldrums.

The Boss

Maybe you don't mind when your husband commandeers the remote control or vetoes your choice of Cheerios for his favorite Froot Loops. But in bed, do you find yourself less than thrilled that he always calls the shots? Would you prefer telling him exactly what you want, and getting it? At Cachet, we found that the men who were most aggressive at work craved a sexual situation where they didn't have to be the initiator, where they could be passive or receptive.

When it comes to taking control during lovemaking, the pleasure often lies in acting out the part of your personality that doesn't jibe with your public persona. You might be a woman who revels in the traditional role of wife and mother during the day but who is very much "the boss" in the bedroom at night.

A word of warning to the woman who enjoys being dominant: Peg Bundy of *Married with Children* should not become your role model. Being bossy *all* the time is not the same as taking charge sexually on occasion. Instead of being arousing, you become intimidating and steal from your mate the pleasure of taking the initiative.

The Adventuress

You may not need more than one man, but you still crave that little extra something: a new sex toy, the occasional adult video, maybe a few silk scarves and a feather.

The need for novelty need not be threatening; you can be

safe in a relationship and explore many options. If you introduce what you want as a *desire*, as opposed to expressing it as something that's *missing* in the relationship, you're much more likely to get the freedom to explore without threatening your man. The approach has to be, "Gee, wouldn't it be fun if . . ." or "I had this dream where we . . . ," not "Why don't we ever do . . . ?"

CAN YOU CHANGE YOUR SEXUAL PERSONALITY?

What if your day-to-day life with your partner is perfectly harmonious, but your sexual personalities are not quite in sync? To what extent is sexual personality alterable?

Some sexual personalities have diverged so widely that recapturing compatibility is virtually impossible. But before you decide your sexual relationship is in free fall, consider the possibility you may be better matched than you think, particularly if sex was explosive (or at least satisfying) at the beginning of your relationship. When was the last time you really talked to your husband about your sexual personality—and his?

If sex has been relatively unimportant or boring for a while, it will undoubtedly take some talking, some privacy, perhaps a vacation, or even some counseling to allow the two of you to get to the point where you feel comfortable reacquainting each other with your true sexual selves. So much can be changed when both partners want to change and broaden, but the operative words here are *both partners*. Sadly, if only one of you feels there's need for change, and the other doesn't see the point, the rut you're in will become wider and deeper.

But if both of you *are* committed, you're in for a pleasant surprise. Just as the trappings of a decade you thought could *never* make a comeback somehow always manage to return, so, too, can your sexual life renew itself. A better understanding of your own sexual identity and an openness to new forms of expression can bring back a richness to your love life you thought had gone the way of bell-bottoms and platform shoes.

DEVELOPING YOUR SEXUAL LITERACY

Now that you've given yourself a little time to identify your sexual personality and consider its benefits and drawbacks, it's time to become the best sexual partner you can be. The key is education. The best call girls know how to please a man not because they've had a lot of sex (with sex, practice doesn't necessarily make perfect), but because they've taken the time to learn as much about sex as they can. They've chosen to be as sexually literate as possible, which, in this culture, few women are. In short, call girls know that great lovers are made, not born.

Increasing your sexual knowledge doesn't mean becoming promiscuous or doing things that are weird or distasteful to you. (Although what seems odd one day might seem fabulous the next. Remember: No one was *born* loving sushi.) It just means that like a gourmet chef who needs lots of ingredients to prepare complex dishes, you have to have a full pantry of sexual thoughts and fantasies at your disposal— even if you never choose to act on them.

And whatever your sexual preference—and whether you have no partner, one partner, or five partners—the more you know about sex and sexuality, the more potential for joy you're bringing into your life. Sex, good sex, is ultimately about joy. And nobody can tell you what brings you joy. You've got to figure that out for yourself.

Books and Videos

For some women, books are the first place to start learning sexual basics. No one should be without two updated classics of the genre, Alex Comfort's *The Joy of Sex* and the Boston Women's Health Collective's *Our Bodies, Ourselves*. There are also several new books on the market that take a different approach. For example, Miriam Stoppard's *The Magic of Sex* explains basic and advanced sexual techniques from both the male and female perspectives. A typical entry, under the heading, "Fantasies," lists men's and women's most popular fantasies separately. (The fantasy that ranks number one with men—group sex—ranks only number six with women. On the other hand, at least one relatively common female fantasy—sexual activities involving an animal—doesn't rate anywhere in the top nineteen with men.)

For the MTV generation that would rather see than read about sex, there are dozens of instructional videos on the market. Most are billed as erotic. You may not agree—in fact, many are clinical, or somewhat distasteful—but they can be instructive all the same.

Men's Magazines

Magazines like *Playboy, Penthouse,* and their raunchier kin (*Hustler, Screw*) are an accessible and extremely useful source for gauging male turn-ons. How many pictures of shaved women licking each other can one guy stand to look at? The answer is: A LOT. You might not always like what you see—in fact, I almost guarantee you won't—but try to look at them not so much as glossy pages of naked woman, but rather as a guide to the male psyche.

If your man reads, say, the *Penthouse* erotic letters column, he probably wonders why those wild threesomes and naked hitchhiker scenarios always happen to other guys. (Never mind that those real-life adventures are almost always fantasies cooked up by staffers who rarely leave their offices.) So reading these magazines might give you a few ideas and enable a few of his fantasies to come to life! They give you an idea of what's possible. They are the building blocks that you can use to build your own sex life.

Your Local Sex Shop

Tell a woman to visit a sex shop and her first question is likely to be, "Where do I buy my sunglasses and greasy raincoat?" In fact, these days many sex shops serve average men and women who shop for sexually explicit items the way they might shop for new stereo speakers. In some cities, there are even stores that cater specifically to women. New York City, for example, has Eve's Garden, a cozy, brightly lit shop that's dedicated to creating "a safe environment for women." Men are allowed in only at certain hours, and only when accompanied by a woman. Eve's Garden is free of the male-specific sexual paraphernalia that some women find offensive—blow-up dolls, for example—but it's otherwise stuffed with books, videos, massage oils, vibrators, and other toys. (Their address: 119 West 57th Street. Call 212-757-8651 for a catalog.)

Sex Seminars

If you're looking for more direct experience, you might participate in a sexuality seminar or workshop. (Branches of adult-education schools similar to the Learning Annex or Discovery Center in your area are likely to offer such courses.) Classes may range from the most innocuous question-and-answer sessions to more hands-on contact, like Betty Dodson's masturbation workshop, where you are expected to participate, sometimes in the nude.

These days, seminars in tantric sex are extremely popular. As the saying goes, everything old is new again—and nothing could be older than tantric love. Tantra refers to the ancient Hindu books, the Kama Sutra, that taught the details of lovemaking. The emphasis is on the connection of the physical and the spiritual, and practitioners of tantric sex believe that sex is one way of achieving spiritual transcendence.

Cybersex

One relatively new method for getting information about sex is becoming extremely popular: the computer. Databases such as CompuServe have forums devoted entirely to sex and sexuality. Not only can you have mature "discussions," via the modem, with like-minded people on every subject from transvestism to public nudity to performance anxiety; you can also have your most intimate questions answered (anonymously) by a host of sexual therapists including Dr. Ruth Westheimer, Dr. Joyce Brothers, and Masters and Johnson. You simply post a question on what is essentially an electronic bulletin board, and an appropriate expert will respond.

Cloaked in anonymity, people ask questions on every subject you've ever thought about, and some you never would. One man recently wrote that he is sexually aroused by cutting women's hair and can't understand why his wife was jealous when he wanted to cut the hair of the next-door neighbor. (The therapist said that in this man's case, cutting hair really was akin to having an affair, and he should think twice before picking up those scissors.)

"But I'm Just Not in the Mood—Ever"

What if, despite your best efforts, you've simply lost all interest? For the past few years, therapists have been reporting a sharp rise in the number of cases of what they call ISD, inhibited sexual desire. And it's not only women who suffer; at least as many men are suffering from it, too.

There may be dozens of reasons why sex with your long-term partner is no longer appealing. Maybe you suspect he's cheating, and you're frightened of contracting a sexually transmitted disease, including AIDS. Maybe you're deeply angry or resentful of each other, and that anger is preventing you from seeing your partner in a sexual light. Or maybe you simply have always had different sexual styles and sexual incompatibility, which you once thought not terribly important but now can't ignore.

When sexual desire not only wanes but disappears, many couples rationalize that sex no longer *should* be an important part of their relationship: *After all, we're good companions. We get along just fine. Just because sex isn't a priority shows that we're maturing.*

Well, when sex no longer matters, you can "mature" yourself right out of a marriage. Don't fool yourself into believing the problem will go away by itself, or that sex is no longer important.

If the idea of sex is about as welcome to you or your partner as a sauna on a summer day in Texas, it's time to seek professional help. Sex therapists routinely employ a variety of fantasy and visualization techniques—even hypnosis—to help their patients revive interest in sex in general, and each other in particular.

Ultimately, you may find that a little sex education goes a long way. Adding a few choice ingredients to your sexual stew may not radically change the dish, but it can subtly and ineluctably enhance the flavor.

1

Seducing Your Man

Men who do not make advances to women are apt to become victims of women who make advances to them.

WALTER BAGEHOT

Think of the most seductive scenes you've ever seen in movies, moments that tremble with erotic tension. Lauren Bacall vamping Humphrey Bogart in *To Have and Have Not* ("You know how to whistle, don't you?"); Fred Astaire dancing with Audrey Hepburn in *Funny Face;* Kelly McGillis dancing in the stable with Harrison Ford in *Witness;* Kevin Costner painting Susan Sarandon's toes in *Bull Durham.* Seduction is spontaneous combustion—a slow buildup followed, often, by a shattering release.

Of course, familiarity is an enemy to seduction. Knowing the outcome of the seduction lessens the tension. But even longtime spouses can become masters (and mistresses) of seduction—with a little practice and a willingness to look silly every now and then. Seduction, more than anything else, is about play. It's just that you're playing a game made for adults.

One of the reasons sex gets routine and boring is that it is left to those parts of the day when you're too zonked to really appreciate it. As compared to your early dating days— when sex was the highlight of the date—it becomes the activity given least priority. The thinking is: *Let's see, Danny Bonaduce's on Letterman and that guy who can tap out "God Bless America" on his knee with a pair of spoons is on Leno. . . . I know, honey, let's have sex!*

As I said in the last chapter, sex is like anything else in life: You've got to spend the time to make it good. In the course of a week, most women probably spend more time on their hair than thinking about (or actually having) sex.

I can't emphasize enough the importance of dating in long-term relationships. Ideally, you and your husband should have one night a week all to yourself, where you can have four to six hours just to think about each other. The ground rules: You can talk about anything or *do* anything, as long as it doesn't involve your day-to-day life. (No, you cannot call the house every hour to check with the baby-sitter.)

What did the two of you do before the children came? Or before you got married? Sometimes, even if you don't want to give yourselves this alone time—if you think it feels forced and phony—*do it anyway.* You'll have a better time than you think.

You don't necessarily have to have sex. Making sex an obligation is just as dampening to the libido as not having it at all. But if you spend time together as a couple, often the sex takes care of itself. Even if it doesn't, you're still building a warm, close, loving relationship.

Remember: If you stop being lovers, you'll stop making love.

BE A SEDUCTRESS

The most important thing to remember when it comes to seduction is this: Men are basically very, very simple creatures.
Women appreciate shades of nuance in romance:

> Angela moved a step nearer to Stephen, then another,
> until their hands were touching. And all that she was,
> and all that she had been and would be again, perhaps
> even tomorrow, was fused at that moment into one
> mighty impulse, one imperative need, and that need
> was Stephen. (From *The Well of Loneliness* by Radclyff
> Hall)

Most men, on the other hand, have an approach to romance more along these lines:

> What a piece of a——! Boy, I can't wait to get her into
> bed and f——— her brains out!

I'm exaggerating, but not by much. But male simplicity
works greatly to our advantage. So if some of the things I'm
suggesting sound corny and old—say, wrapping yourself up
in Saran Wrap and greeting him at the door—well, I ask
you: How many women have actually *done* that? We've all
heard about it, and laughed, but actually going out, buying
lots and lots of Saran Wrap, and doing it? (Don't try this if
your husband is an environmentalist.) Well, he's heard about
it, too, and he probably has friends who claim some woman
did it for them. (They're probably lying.) He reads about the
fur coat with nothing underneath, for example, and wonders: *Who are the people who really do those things? Why hasn't a
woman ever done that for me?*
Why shouldn't that woman be you?
Men love stuff like this. It's not something you have to do
all that often—maybe once a month, maybe just for his
birthday and your anniversary. It's the kind of thing that
carries over, the kind of thing they remember. That kind of

stuff happens in the movies and in magazines—but it never happens to *them*. All it takes is a bottle of champagne and some bubble bath, and you and your husband can become Julia Roberts and Richard Gere in *Pretty Woman*. (Okay, so you probably won't get the shopping spree.)

As your man gets older and his performance isn't as sure a thing as it once was, remember that your seduction needs a certain amount of foreplay. Let him know ahead of time that you have "something" planned. Begin on Wednesday coyly hinting that you hope he's feeling good on Friday, because . . . and don't say anything else. Thursday feed him a high-carbo meal because he'll "need his strength for tomorrow." Friday morning give him a little note, reminding him he has to be home by seven P.M. You'll have that little brain of his working overtime to figure out what you're up to!

When you're preparing to seduce the older man, don't spring anything on him. If he comes home exhausted from a long day of work, the last thing he wants to see is you writhing in a Catwoman suit on the bed. He's supposed to feel aroused, not tested. To a man over forty, complete surprise is a good way to make him feel his manhood is on the line; you can turn fun into a duty.

And whatever kind of seduction you're planning, remember: You're going to be up close and personal. Do everything in your power to make yourself a delight to his eyes, as well as to his sense of touch and smell.

Boudoir Cosmetics

That dramatic makeup that looks fabulous across the table at a restaurant doesn't look quite so smashing at a distance of two inches. This is not the time to put on the full war paint. First of all, it's going to smudge and rub off. Second, if you're over thirty, there's a good chance you'll look much older when he's that close.

Recently I read an interview with comedian Joy Behar, who claimed she felt most comfortable around boyfriends who were myopic. Ideally, she said, she was looking for someone legally blind. But let's assume, for the moment, that your man has pretty good eyesight. If you're worried about covering up little blemishes and wrinkles, here's one trick I use. After putting on moisturizer (you can use a tinted one if you prefer), I use a loose face powder called Lucidity, made by Estée Lauder. The difference between Lucidity and most face powders is in the way the powder is ground. Most powders, if you could see them under a microscope, have jagged edges. But all the little powder particles in Lucidity are round. The effect is that when light hits your face, it sort of bounces off, instead of being absorbed. Your skin looks smoother, more even-toned, and very natural—not as smooth as if you had used foundation, but foundation up close rarely looks natural. It also reflects the light away from all the little wrinkles and lines.

If you're going to use eyeliner and blush, keep the shades muted and natural. Now's not the time to get made up as if you were headed down a fashion runway.

To avoid raccoon eyes, apply one very light coat of mascara and allow it to dry well. Then put on two coats of clear mascara (Max Factor is a good brand) to seal in the dark coat. Unless you intend to have sex in a hot tub or under the shower, do not use waterproof mascara. True, it comes off only with an oil-based makeup remover, but if you sweat during sex and you've been rolling around for a while, the natural oils from your skin will *act* like an oil-based makeup remover, and suddenly you're resembling Tammy Faye Bakker.

To avoid smeared lipstick, buy a lip liner in a color as close to your own natural lips as possible (or, for women of color, a shade a bit darker). Line your lips *and* also color them in. Then put a bit of lip gloss or Chapstick over this. It might wear off, but it won't smear. (Haven't you wondered how some women manage to eat a whole meal and still have lipstick on? That's their secret. They color in their lips with lip liner pencil and then put lipstick over it.)

LINGERIE

Because our goal was to provide our clients with a "fantasy call-girl experience," one of our trademarks at Cachet was the quality and beauty of the undergarments our women wore. Underneath their elegant, ladylike dresses they always wore matching bra, panties, garter belt, and stockings. In fact, many clients enjoyed sex even more when the girls left the underwear *on*.

Some women simply cannot see themselves flouncing around like the Victoria's Secret girls, in push-up bras and itty-bitty panties. "You know how I'd look in that, with my fat thighs sticking out and stomach roll here and no tits and . . . ?"

Well, just because call girls wear skimpy, racy things doesn't mean you have to follow suit. When you think of sexy lingerie, think of something *you* feel sexy in. If you're most comfortable in something down to the ground with long sleeves, wear it. If you're not comfortable in it, you won't feel sexy in it. Don't worry that he won't think it's sexy because you don't have a lot of skin showing. He'll think you look desirable because you've gone out of your way to wear something different and pretty just for him. Even if it's long, it can have a low neckline if you have a nice bust, or a slit up the side if you've got decent legs. Just as with clothes, look for something that shows off the best of you.

Know Your Audience

Before spending a fortune on skimpy underwear, be aware that some men are offended by the garter belt/stockings/push-up bra look. They've been taught that only sluts and hookers wear that stuff. Or they find it intimidating. It says to them, "Okay, pal, now that I've got this on, you better get it up." So make sure you buy the kind of lingerie *your* man finds appealing.

When I was writing an advice column, a reader wrote in with an interesting dilemma. One day she came home to find that her new boyfriend had bought her a present from the local lingerie boutique. Delighted, she ripped it open, and was floored when she saw a pair of men's-style pajamas. She was relieved that they didn't fit, and the next day she returned to the boutique and traded in the pajamas for a black lace teddy. Next evening, she was in bed, lounging around in her teddy, and her man came in. She couldn't help noticing the disappointment on his face. "He *wanted* me in those pajamas," she said. "They looked like something his father would wear. What do you think is wrong with him?"

I assured her there was nothing wrong with him. For some reason, the sexiest thing he could imagine was his woman in men's pajamas. Lots of men, for example, prefer the virginal little girl look—loose-flowing white cotton with lace. And others really *want* to see you in their T-shirt.

But most men will love stockings and garters—and, for *really* special occasions, a bustier or merry widow. (A bustier ends at the waist; a merry widow continues down and has garters.) Maybe it has something to do with all those old Westerns where the barmaid had her bustier-clad bosom practically popping out of her dress. Whatever the reason, bustiers and merry widows seem to be almost universally popular garments. And no matter what size you are, you're always sexy in these items. I don't want to hear that you can't find them in your size. If they make them in sizes big enough for drag queens, they make them in sizes big enough for you. The best time to get them is around Valentine's Day, when stores and catalogs (including Victoria's Secret and large-size lingerie catalogs) stock up.

The colors you wear for outerwear may not be the best colors for lingerie. Most Caucasian women look best in pastels, while bright jewel colors look very appealing on most women of color. White and bright red are not good next to most fair skins; they make pale women look drab and washed-out. And while many men think black is sexy, black underwear makes many of us look like we belong in a coffin. (Of course, these are generalities. Try on everything to determine what's best for you.)

Fabrics

Obviously, go for something that's nice and silky and soft. Not necessarily silk, because it has to be dry-cleaned, or hand-washed and ironed. Who needs that? Another problem with silk is that it's completely wrinkled after you've slept in it. It's worse than linen. Go for easy-to-care-for synthetic fibers. And although lace can be very pretty and sexy, sometimes it can also be scratchy. Beware, too, of beading. It looks beautiful, but the beads will dig into his chest when he's hugging you.

It's great to have one or two gorgeous-but-hard-to-care-for items in your boudoir wardrobe, but remember that the more difficult a garment is to take care of, the less likely you are to use it. If it's really, really beautiful, you end up "saving" it for a special occasion and wear it only once a year. Better to buy a bunch of pretty things you can wear more often and just throw in the laundry.

Here's a good gift idea for Valentine's Day or your anniversary: Send away for several sexy catalogs and let him pick out a present for you (a present that's really for *him*, too). Tell him you'll wear anything he picks out for you, no matter what it is! (While you're at it, you also might want to pick out something sexy for him, whether it's silk boxers, bikinis, G-strings, or a silk smoking jacket.)

Beyond Lingerie: Costumes

Ever hear the expression, "Clothes make the (wo)man"? Well, they can *un*make you, too. Wearing certain clothes can free you to behave in a way you normally wouldn't. And in the bedroom that freedom is a wonderful thing.

My friend Joan told me about the first time she saw a Frederick's of Hollywood catalog, some twenty years ago: "In addition to blow-up bras and padded derrieres, which

God knows I didn't need, they had this little French maid's outfit. You know: little heart-shaped top, starched apron in the front, G-string in the back, little cuffs, feather duster. Now, I can be as uptight as the next person, so don't ask me what possessed me to send away for this thing. But I'll tell you, I had more fun in that ridiculous outfit. I'd put on my French accent and start dusting my boyfriend off. . . . Just putting it on let me be a different person. And believe me, I'm not a great actress."

I have another girlfriend who bought a hula skirt while she was on her honeymoon in Hawaii. One night she was sort of in a mood. She dragged it out of her closet, put on a swimsuit top, and pretended to be a hula girl for her husband. It started out as a joke, but she tells me that she's gotten *lots* of use out of that skirt. She and her husband will pretend they're marooned on a desert island, or he's a pirate and she's his helpless captive. . . . Another friend, a horseback rider, walked into the bedroom one day wearing her riding chaps and nothing else. Her husband went bonkers.

My point is that the things that sound hokey on paper can actually be a lot of fun—and arousing—in real life.

Taking the Lead:
Creating a Sensual Ambience

When I tell women they should be more aggressive sexually, they get panicky, like I'm suggesting they suddenly come on like Vampira when she's down a quart of blood. That's a level of assertiveness most of us just aren't comfortable with. All "aggressive" means, as far as I'm concerned, is letting him know you're interested before he lets you know he is. Perhaps you could call it "premeditated"; he would probably call it "initiating." But whatever you call it, men like it.

And you can do this so easily.

Put on Something Sexy and Pretty When He Comes Home

Dorothy Parker once said, "Brevity is the soul of lingerie"—
and, indeed, lingerie is a great way to get your point across
succinctly. It needn't be anything elaborate, just something a
little flirtatious and sexy that you don't wear every day that
lets him know you've been thinking about how desirable
he is.

If you've got kids underfoot and don't want to prance
around in something obviously alluring, maybe you just
whisper for him to look in your top dresser drawer, where
you've neatly folded your most beautiful nightie—perhaps
with a pair of silk boxer shorts for him—next to a bottle of
massage oil. The very worst thing that can happen is that
he'll be too tired and beg off for the night. But he'll know
what you have in mind for tomorrow.

Special Sheets on the Bed

Crisp linen and freshly laundered cotton is as sexy to a man
as it probably is to you, although many people find satin especially sensuous. Admittedly, it's difficult to sleep on—
everything slips around, and the blankets slide off in the
middle of the night. (The simple solution: Leave your regular sheets on underneath the satin, and just whip off the
satin sheets and throw them on the floor when you're ready
to go to sleep.) Select colors that are flattering to your skin
tone (peaches, pastels, ivory, or white if you have a tan or
dark skin); avoid dark colors and green or blue (few women
have skin that's complemented by green or blue). While
some bold women enjoy animal prints, geometric prints are
generally too busy and/or masculine. The effect you're going
for? Soft and soothing—bed as a haven, not a competition.
(If you're concerned that your sheets are too "feminine" and
therefore off-putting to your mate, one recent study by a
linen manufacturer showed that although men usually won't
buy little flower prints or pastel colors, they still like to see
them on a bed—*your* bed!)

Candles

Not just one or two, but six or eight, depending on the size of the room. I had a boyfriend who lit all the candles in the bedroom as a way of telling me he was in the mood.

Scented Lights

Go into just about any New Age store these days and you can buy a fragrancing ring. It fits around a lightbulb, and you put several drops of your favorite essential oil into a grooved trough. The heat from the light makes the fragrance eventually evaporate, thus delicately perfuming the room. Scents that relax: jasmine, chamomile, geranium, marjoram, lavender, and rose. Stress relievers: vanilla tuberose, nutmeg, spruce, juniper, and orange. Scents reputed to be aphrodisiacs: sandalwood, ylang-ylang, sage. Be sure your partner isn't allergic to the scent you choose. You don't want him to spend the rest of the evening sneezing!

"Your" Special Drink

Cachet's call girls were not allowed to request a bottle of wine or champagne when a gentleman asked them what they wanted to drink. They were told to say, "Oh, some wine/champagne would be lovely," and leave it to him to decide the quantity. (Although I remember one residential client whom I had to call to demand he have *something* in the house for girls to drink when they went to his house. This was a busy young stockbroker, and the only drink he kept in his house was tap water, served in plastic cups!)

Of course, in your own home you're under no such constraints! Buy a special champagne or wine you both love, with glasses you use just for special occasions. If you don't drink, get a beautiful pitcher and make up your own nonalcoholic beverage, passion fruit juice or whatever. (For those who have had problems with alcohol, stay away from wine-glasses and wine carafes—there's too much of an association between them and booze. But look for pieces that are pretty and festive.)

Draw a Bath for Him

Some of my girls who got the biggest tips always carried little treats for the men in their briefcases: Small round candles were popular, along with packets of bubble bath. The girls would surround the bathtub with candles, pour in the bubble bath, and voilà!—instant mood.

It's easy to understand the bathtub's appeal in this stress-crazed world: Spend twenty minutes suspended in water, hearing only your own thoughts and the drip of the spigot, and you'll see what I mean.

Here's the secret to the bath's relaxing effect on the body: Water displaces weight, making you feel light, and as your capillaries dilate from the warmth, your blood pressure gently drops. (Is it any wonder so many great minds found their inspiration in the tub? Benjamin Franklin wrote many of his finest works there, and Winston Churchill liked to soak while he practiced his speeches.)

Before things get going, you might want to sensuously wash him all over with a silky sponge. A special bath like this not only removes the day's grime but can also relax and inspire him a bit for the evening ahead.

Stores like the Body Shop and Origins sell wonderful bath salts, gels, herbal mixes, and oils you can buy as a special treat. And if you *really* want to go all out, you can make your own bath recipes. All ingredients are available at herbal shops or health food stores.

To RELAX HIM

2 oz chamomile flowers
2 oz calendula petals (good for irritated skin)
2 oz lime flowers

1 oz hops (helps relax and soothe)
1 oz catnip
2 oz lemon peel (for fragrance)

To wake him up

1 oz orange blossoms
1 oz marigold flowers
2 oz chamomile flowers
2 oz lemon verbena leaves
1 oz sandalwood chips
½ oz bay leaves
½ oz sage leaves
5 drops lemongrass oil
5 drops bayberry oil
2 drops orris root oil

Place bath mixture in a cheesecloth bag. Tie the open end with a piece of string, then hang the bag under the running tap water.

In my seminar I also suggest taking a champagne bubble bath together. This is not, as one of my seminar students assumed, a bath *in* champagne (although in fact the actress Sarah Bernhardt claimed that champagne baths did wonders for her skin.) It is, simply, a bubble bath with a split of your favorite champagne for two. Sip bubbly while you blow bubbles at each other.

You might also try these variations that bathing beauties of the past found soothing to heart and soul.

Calpurnia, Julius Caesar's wife, invented the first fruit bath: 20 pounds of crushed strawberries mixed with 2 pounds of crushed raspberries. (Those who'd rather not go through the day dyed a delicate shade of pink might find apricot, orange, or papaya gels preferable. Fruit has an astringent effect on the skin.)

Although Cleopatra was famous for taking milk baths, Nero's wife, Poppei, transformed the milk bath into an art. She traveled with a train of asses to provide milk for her daily ablutions. (Lactic acids in milk leave the skin feeling smooth and silky.)

In the movie *The Barbarian*, Myrna Loy filled her tub with flower petals.

The Sensual Head Massage

Most women have their own special techniques for administering a body massage, but how many know how to make him theirs *from the neck up?*

Tell your lover to breathe deeply, while he rests his head in your lap. Press your fingertips into his scalp and move slowly in circles from his forehead toward the back of his neck. Then, with your hands still cupped around the back of his head, place your thumbs at the base of his skull and methodically move them from the center toward each ear, making little circles. Run your fingers up and down the back of his ears a few times. Press your fingertips into his cheeks and make deep circular motions.

Reclaim Your Bedroom as the Place for Amour

Of course, if you have young children, you aren't free to make love whenever, wherever in your house. So your bedroom must be sacrosanct. Is the kids' play set in your room because it's the biggest room in the house? Banish it *now*. Ditto the family laundry basket, and kids' overflow toys, the computer with their games on it, and the big TV (family TV watching should be in any room of the house but *yours*). Put a lock on the door, although you should use it only when absolutely necessary. But as soon as they're capable of understanding, teach your children that *everyone knocks*. (Set an example by knocking on their bedroom door before entering as well.) Your bedroom must remain a place for romance, not family powwows!

Recipes for Seduction:
A Baker's Dozen

Ever notice how women in movies seem capable of having an orgasm just about anyplace? Standing up against a wall, bent over a desk, under a waterfall, in a hot tub. Have you ever actually *had* sex in a hot tub? You're sweating, the chlorine is stinging your skin, and the water makes your insides feel like they're made of sandpaper, not to mention what the steam is doing to your hair . . . (And he may not even be able to get it up—the water's just too darn hot!) Yet dozens of thrashing, moaning movie scenes would have you believe that sex with Mr. Big in a hot tub is deeply (and quickly) satisfying. Why is this image of women so prevalent in movies? Because the men who make these movies *are* genuinely capable of climaxing just about anywhere.

Here's my point: When you're concocting interesting seduction scenes, personal comfort isn't always paramount. Chances are they'll be more physically satisfying to him than you—unless you're one of those interesting women who are able to have an orgasm pretty much anytime, anyplace. But you're not staging these kind of scenarios very often. In fact, you'll probably get a lot of mileage out of them if you do them only a few times a year.

The Treasure Hunt

This is great for the kind of man who enjoys little projects. You start by leaving a note in his jacket pocket or on his Voicemail at work, telling him you have a surprise for him— but he's going to have to work to get it, and he must return home by such-and-such a time. In the note, direct him first to your favorite liquor store, where you'll already have picked out a bottle of something both of you love. (The liquor store can keep it chilled and then wrap it.) Instruct the clerk at the store to hand your man another little note.

This time, perhaps, he's told to report to a nearby gourmet store, where you've selected a picnic basket of goodies for him to buy. (Of course, you can prepay for these things yourself; it depends on how generous you're feeling that day or what the occasion is.) The clerk at the gourmet store will give him a note that leads him to the lingerie store, where you've ordered something fun and fabulous—and maybe something for him, too. (Make sure the store has wrapped the gift, so he can't see it.) You can keep this game going for as long as you want. A stop at a florist's might also be a nice touch. . . .

Finally, at the last stop, make sure he's handed a little note saying something like, "Where have you been? I can't wait any longer. I need you home *now.*" When he gets to the front door, another note instructs him to come in and drop everything in the kitchen. The note in the kitchen tells him to go to the bathroom. A note attached to a wrapped box of his favorite soap tells him to take a shower, then put on whatever is hanging on the back of the door. (You might want to leave a chilled glass of his favorite aperitif on the bathroom sink.) While he's showering, you can arrange the flowers, set out the picnic basket, and slip into whatever sensuous confection he picked up earlier.

A bit of work? Sure. Something he'll remember for a long time? Definitely. (However, use common sense. Don't spring this elaborate seduction on him when he's in the middle of a work crunch, or when all of the kids in the house have come down with chicken pox.) You'll be surprised at how much fun you'll have doing it. And be imaginative. You don't have to lead him into bed. You can set the scene in a hotel, on his boat, by the pool—anywhere private.

The Sex Machine

Look in the Yellow Pages and find a car dealer that rents luxury cars by the day. Track down his dream car and lease it for a day or an entire weekend. Have the dealer drop it off at your house on Saturday morning, so it's sitting in your driveway when he wakes up. Dress for the occasion—a long cream-colored silk scarf and sunglasses are a nice touch—and spend the day cruising around to his heart's content. And when he's had enough driving . . . well, so many of these cars are sold on the basis of their sex appeal. Why not see just how interesting having sex in them can be? (I know, I know, you have to be a contortionist to actually do it in a Jaguar XJS. But as I said, comfort's not the point.)

Pick your spot carefully. A friend of mine had rented an Allante, and she and her husband had taken refuge in a nearby state park. It was beautifully peaceful and deserted—so deserted, that little bunnies and birds had begun to gather outside the car, as if she were in an X-rated version of *Snow White*. She had just climbed into the backseat, and he'd climbed on top of her, when her big toe touched off the alarm on the car door handle. A park ranger materialized from nowhere. My friend had forgotten to take the car registration with her and, well, the couple had a bit of explaining to do.

Variations on the travel theme: sailboats (that rocking motion can really fly his mast), long train rides, and, of course, airplanes. There's even an official name for people who've had sex while in flight. They're members of The Mile-High Club. The key to having sex in the bathroom of an airplane is to sit on the sink ledge and brace your legs on the walls. Your guy stands between your legs, and the two of you do it face to face. Don't try doing it doggy style, because at least one of you will injure yourself; those tiny bathrooms have many sharp edges.

Restaurant Amour

Restaurant seductions have a long and proud history. Remember the scene in *Portnoy's Complaint* where Alexander Portnoy's girlfriend drove him wild with excitement by rubbing her hand between her legs and then casually putting that hand under Portnoy's nose while he was eating dinner?

And one of the great movie seduction scenes of the 1980s took place in the silliest of movies, *Flashdance*. Here, Jennifer Beals—playing that most believable of characters, a female welder who aspires to be a professional dancer—slowly and luxuriantly scoops the sweet meat out of a lobster with her tongue, while simultaneously fondling her boyfriend's crotch under the table with her foot.

I wouldn't recommend the lobster trick. *She* made it look sexy, but the average woman would simply look like a slob with strings of very expensive food dangling from her mouth. Nevertheless, Beals had the right idea. Find a restaurant with long tablecloths (so no one can see what you're doing), and while you're talking animatedly, casually work your toes around that vulnerable part of him. (Yes, *of course* you take off your shoes first.)

Whisper what you plan to do with him later. Don't wear underwear and let him touch you—but just a little. Drop your own napkin under the table, dive down there, and sort of casually brush your hands against him—just enough to make him a little nervous, not quite knowing what you're capable of. I wouldn't do anything more than this, because being kicked out of an elegant restaurant probably wouldn't be his idea of a fun evening.

The Voyeur

This isn't for everyone. I know plenty of women who find X-rated movies too gross or boring to sit through. But if you're not one of them, surprise your man when he comes home with a selection of adult videos and a room bathed in candlelight. (If you've got some of those phallic-shaped candles around that are available in erotic boutiques, all the better.) Whatever the woman on-screen is doing to her partner, you do to yours. He probably won't be paying attention to the video for very long.

The Audiophile

Some men are as turned on by audio-erotica as by visual stuff. If your man is one of them, secretly tape one of your next lovemaking sessions with a cassette player. The next time you want to make love, tell your husband you got this wild tape through the mail, you think it was from a girlfriend of yours. You know how your voice always sounds alien to you when you hear it recorded? Well, it's the same with love-making sounds. If he's never heard himself making love on tape before, he won't immediately recognize his own sounds—or yours. At first, he'll get especially turned on, thinking he's listening in on someone else. But then, when he figures out it's the two of you, just watch how aroused it makes him. (The reason not to tell him it's you, initially? Lots of guys are a bit embarrassed to hear themselves. He'll think those moans and groans are sexy if he first thinks they're *not* from him.)

The Welcome Home

If he's been away on a trip for a few days, arrange to have the kids taken care of by relatives or a baby-sitter. Take a bottle of champagne or wine with you. Pick him up at the airport or train station wearing a long coat (preferably fur unless he's a member of PETA), thigh-high stockings, high heels—and nothing else. Toast his return at the airport. Make him a little nuts on the way home: Kiss him, untie his tie, reach your hand under his shirt, fondle him through his pants. If you're in a taxi or a limo, don't worry about whether the driver can see; believe me, he's seen worse.

The Naturalist

If he was feeling amorous in the morning, call him at work and tell him you've rigged up your tent in the backyard, and you'll be back there, waiting for him, when he gets home. Set the place up: a bottle of wine, a few candles, a CD player, a light blanket, and an air mattress if you don't want grass sticking to your back. Greet him in the tent—stark naked. (Do not do this in black fly season.)

If you don't have a tent, how about christening a hammock together? Or, if you're lucky enough to have a barn, there's always the hayloft. If you live in the city, you might want to try a rooftop that's not frequented. Wear loose clothes and a skirt that can be hiked up for easy access. So what if a few people have binoculars trained on you? That's part of the fun. Still concerned? Buy a pretty feathered mask.

Theme Night

It might be anything from a Victorian tea (you in a merry widow, with a long, supple cane) to a Mexican fiesta (margaritas, taco chips, guacamole, mariachi band, and you, naked, except for a sombrero). The idea is to transform yourself, and the mood, for one night. Halloween is a particularly good excuse for theme night. Rent a motel room and surprise each other with different costumes. The more elaborate the costume, the better. Try to keep in character for the whole evening—and, if possible, don't take off your mask.

The Water Nymph

This is so simple, and it's particularly effective if you don't have a window in your bathroom. When he comes home, tell him you're going to slip into the shower to relax. You've just bought this wonderfully fragrant new bath gel, and you're eager to try it. When you're in the shower, call him to come in for a minute; you need a place on your back rubbed, where you have this crick in your neck. Maybe he could reach it better if he took off his clothes, so he won't get them all wet. Hand him the bath gel. Now turn off the lights. You are both wet, and it is pitch black. Find each other in the dark.

The Distraction

Wait until your husband is on the phone with his boss, mother, or rabbi. Get on your knees. Unzip his pants. Give him the slowest, most luxurious tongue-lashing of his life. See how long it takes him to get off the phone.

The Food Fantasy

This is one of the most obvious seductions—and one of the most effective. Think of every aphrodisiac food cliché you've ever heard of—oysters, pomegranates, boeuf bourguignon—and prepare one of them. In fact, if he'll let you, feed it to him with your fingers. Dessert, perhaps, is liquid chocolate and whipped cream—licked off him. (For those on a diet, there's a delicious sixteen-calorie-per-serving liquid hot fudge.) Don't forget the candlelight and the Chris Isaak tapes.

The Quickie

This is not about sensuality or loving or foreplay; it's about wham-bam-thank-you-ma'am. Wait until you *know* he's horny, then get his attention, in any way possible, preferably right before the two of you are due at a party or he has to catch a plane.

The Best Seduction of All

The one that's dictated by your lover's tastes—and your imagination.

8

What Call Girls Know That You Don't:

Your Man and His Sex Life

"And then it was, like, we were kissing, and it was just like that scene in Casablanca, when Ingrid Bergman fell into Bogart's arms, and we just couldn't stop moving our bodies. Oh, God, the way our hands moved over every inch of each other . . ."

"Yeah. It was good. Real good. Y'know."

Pop quiz. Which of these sex descriptions comes from a woman and which from a man? Every woman on the planet can figure this out. In general, we find it much easier to express our feelings about our sexuality, at least among ourselves. But men? With the possible exception of English professors and seventeen-year-olds doing it for the first time, few men are loquacious when it comes to describing the act or their feelings about it. But just because they don't spend hours yakking about sex doesn't mean it's not as important, or as fulfilling, an experience for them as it is for us.

So if both of you are equally dedicated to a great sex life, why does it so often become routine and boring? As I've said before, many of us put sex low down on our list of priorities. We leave it until late at night, for example, when we're too tired to read or even watch TV. It's amazing, when you think about it. We happily work at so many other things in our lives, from tending the garden to keeping in touch with friends. But sex? A lot of us spend more time on our hair than in bed with our partners. Think about it: You make an appointment, put aside the time, and you're frantic if the colorist is on vacation. How many of us think that way about sex? The operative word here is *priority.*

Sex is like anything else you do in this world: You've got to spend the time to make it good. *Commitment, planning, enthusiasm, plus uninterrupted, attention-paying time*—all this, even more than sex, is what a high-class call girl offers.

"Please, Sir, May I Have Some More?": How to Ask for What You Want in Bed

On average, it takes a man three minutes to have an orgasm (except during oral sex—we should only be so lucky). It takes a woman eighteen minutes. Mother Nature sure has a wicked sense of humor.

So it's hardly surprising that for men who frequent call girls, one of the most appealing aspects of the whole situation is that he is free to be absolutely selfish. Even though he wants the girl to like him, he doesn't really have to worry about her orgasm. He can concentrate on his own pleasure, since presumably she gets her pleasure from receiving a great deal of money.

But when they're in a relationship, most men are *extremely* anxious to make sex good for you. Many, however, simply don't know how. Or rather, they know the mechanics: simply insert tab A into slot B. There's no need to ask the woman what she likes. He (and his penis) will just *know*.

Conversely, many women—myself included—find it difficult to say what they like, because we're brought up with the equally wacko idea that if he really loves me, he'll know. Open any romance novel, and there's a woman shuddering in ecstasy from a man's touch—a man she just met, who knows how to please her in ways she never even thought of, over and over and over. . . . (In fact, one study last year showed that, in general, men's sexual fantasies focused on reaching orgasm, with little in the way of scene setting. Women's fantasies, by contrast, emphasized the who, what, and where of the scenario—mood, ambience, his feelings, her feelings, how he caressed her, etc.)

The result? Sexual stalemate. If you work up the courage to give explicit directions, the guy sulks. You may have thought you were offering gentle hints, but he acts like you've been barking orders to him through a megaphone. And if you don't say anything? Well, many of us resort to faking it.

Now, there's nothing wrong with faking every once in a very great while, when you're tired and just want things to end, or when you want to please him but really aren't in the mood to have an orgasm. (I usually advised the girls who worked for me not to fake it, however. These men were smart enough to know that they hadn't done much to turn her on, and faking, in this situation, was an insult to a man's intelligence. However, as I said earlier, there are exceptions to every rule. If the guy had gone out of his way to make it good for the girl, or if he wasn't going to stop pounding away until she was satisfied—well, then, a girl's gotta do what a girl's gotta do.)

So there are times when it's expedient to fake it. (If this is someone you don't want to sleep with on a regular basis, then it's probably okay.) But if you fake on a continual basis, this is the message you convey: *Honey, you don't need to touch me for more than two minutes. No, sirree. What I really like is for you to get hard, ram yourself inside me, and come. Yup, that there is ecstasy.*

So for the good of both of you, you have to let him know what you want—delicately. Here are a few strategies:

Whatever It Is You Want, Act Like He's Doing It Already

You'll never see the following words spoken in a romance novel: "Darling, do you like it better when I touch you here directly, or if I sort of apply indirect pressure by rubbing the lips together?" Yet this is precisely the kind of communication we *should* be able to have with our lovers.

If you're too uncomfortable to come right out and tell him what you like, here's a little trick that works really well: Act as if he's already doing it. Let's say you find it a real turn-on when a man nibbles on your ear. Perhaps your lover has never kissed your ear; perhaps the closest he's ever gotten to your ear is your cheek, but as long as he's been in the general vicinity, you can pull this off. After you make love (or the next day if your little white lie is a real stretch), tell him how much you loved it when he nibbled your ear. How having your ear nibbled has always been such a turn-on and how you went crazy when he did it. Mention it several times before you make love the next time, and let him know that you can't wait to be with him again because he knows just the special things to do that make you feel really sexy. He may not initially remember nibbling your ear, but the more he hears that he did it and the more he hears that you loved it, the more he'll be certain that yes, he *is* the best ear-nibbler this side of the Atlantic. And as long as you let him know how much you love it, he'll keep right on doing it.

The Dream Ploy

Okay, so maybe what turns you on is a little more involved than ear nibbling. In fact, it's so far removed from anything the two of you have done together that there's no way you can pretend he's already doing it. And you're way too embarrassed to talk about it as an actual desire of yours. So you tell him that you had a dream. And in this dream he tied you up and spanked you. "That's why I pounced on you this morning; there was something very erotic about it." Either he'll pick up on it and want to talk about it some more, just to be sure he's clear about your message, or he'll ignore it. If he's clearly not interested, you can easily save face by saying, "Yeah, I thought it was a little off the wall, too."

Positive Reinforcement

If he tells you he loved it when you sucked his big toe, you remember forever, right? Or you remember, as if it were yesterday, the time he told you he didn't like something you did in bed. Somehow, with men, that memory chip is missing. Gone. Never existed.

So when he does something in bed you like, you have to belabor the point. Not once or twice, but five or ten times. Call him at the office and say, "I was just thinking about how you did X, and I got so hot and bothered." Leave a little note in his pocket. Or tell him, before he goes to work, "I don't know if you have time tonight, but last week, when you ate that Jell-O off my stomach, oh, baby. . . ." That's the kind of feedback he needs.

You don't expect the dog to remember to stay off the couch if you tell him just once, right? Well, don't expect your man to be smarter than your dog.

The Art of the Moan

Even after seeing *When Harry Met Sally,* many women believe it's unladylike to act like Meg Ryan in bed—and this is a mistake. Men love women who moan. A moan is sort of a visceral thing that you have no control over. Ergo, if you moan, he must be the most incredible lover. Or so he thinks.

It's simple. When he does something you like, moan; when he does something you don't like, be silent as the grave. Unless he has the IQ of a sand dune, he'll figure it out. And the more explicit your language is, the better. Even men who like their women demure in public love to hear lots of "oohs" and "ahs" and "Harder, harder!" In fact, men are often turned on by "dirty words" in the bedroom, since it's apparently their incredible prowess that has drawn such terrible words out of you.

When you climax, try to call out his name. Make sure you get it right.

"GIMME AN E!":
THE ENTHUSIASM FACTOR

In two separate 1994 studies of college-age women and women twenty-five to forty-six published in the *Journal of Personality and Social Psychology,* those women who described themselves as passionate, stimulating, arousable, and romantic had more partners and characterized their emotional relationships as more intimate than those who were embarrassed by sex. Women with confidence in their own sexiness rated their erotic potential as above average, *whether or not they currently had a partner.*

Make no mistake about it: *Men like women who like sex.*

This is one of the most compelling elements of the sex worker fantasy. A call girl usually doesn't initiate sex. If she is charging by the hour, she's motivated to keep her clients with her as long as possible, and sex usually signals the *end* of the evening. However, the guy knows that here is a woman who won't push him away, who won't be judgmental, who is open to everything, never has a headache, and doesn't want to wait until the kids are asleep. Intellectually, he may know she's doing it for the money, but if she's doing her job he will believe she's as thrilled by his body as by his credit card.

Many of us grow up believing men don't like women who like it or won't respect us if we let them be intimate with us. Before the days of readily available birth control and legal abortions, the biggest shame a young woman could bring upon herself and her family was to get pregnant out of wedlock. So fearful parents would terrorize their daughters into believing that no man would have respect for her if she "gave in," and that a girl who liked sex too much was a tramp. This reasoning was in itself a form of birth control, and it worked fairly well until the Pill liberated young women in the 1960s from the specter of an unwanted pregnancy. Unfortunately, in many women the old tapes still play in their heads, and what with sexually transmitted diseases so prevalent today, fearful parents continue to try to keep their daughters "safe" by telling them men won't want them if they share themselves too freely. What better way to prevent a woman from having sex than to convince her she'll end up despised and rejected by those whose love and respect she wants more than anything?

There are, of course, corollaries to this line of reasoning. If you're uninhibited in bed (so the reasoning goes), you've probably done it with *everybody*. This peculiar line of logic may be prevalent among some younger men who are still ambivalent about sex. But once men hit thirty they are more confident of themselves and their sexuality. They usually want a partner who is equally confident and who has worked out her sexual hang-ups and can be an equal.

Why do men relish your enthusiasm? First, sex is usually the way men express themselves emotionally, since they're not as adept at expressing themselves verbally as we are. If you want to show him how you feel, you might make him his favorite dinner, keep the kids out of his hair for the evening, give him a back rub, or just tell him. But when he wants to show how he feels about you, he's more likely to try and have sex with you, even if what he really wants is just to be hugged and fussed over. He often doesn't know how to ask for closeness *without* sex. This is the primary reason men love your enthusiasm: It makes them feel loved and close to you.

Second, if you're enthusiastic, you convey the idea that sex is fun. The complaint call girls hear most frequently is, "Yeah, my wife does it with me, but she just doesn't seem to be having a lot of fun." Remember when you first started going out together, when you used to laugh and play and just be silly? It's not surprising, then, that some of the best sex for both men and women is at the beginning of a relationship. It's new, which makes it exciting. But it's also *the blossoming of emotion without everyday cares*—you aren't worrying about how you're going to pay the mortgage or fix the pool filter.

Great sex is about re-creating that early feeling of excitement with a sense of playfulness.

Here are a few ways grown-ups play.

Photographer

This is a good game for a man who thinks he has a great body. Say he's undressing one night. Turn to him and say, "Oooh, look at your back! Those lats! Those biceps! Can you just put your arms up a little bit again? Okay, now turn around like this! Wow, you look fabulous! You could be on the cover of *Men's Fitness*." Pretend you have a camera—or, if you have one handy, and you're both comfortable with it, use a real one. (Remember, though, that if you're using a real camera, he might want to turn it on you. Think carefully about whether you want nude pictures of yourself floating around in this universe, especially if you're thinking about a future on the Supreme Court.)

Playing photographer fulfills many of the strategies I talked about in Chapter 2: You're making him the center of attention, you're giving him admiration and praise, plus you're just being silly and playing around.

The Jackson Pollock Fantasy

Invest in a set of washable, nontoxic body paints, available at your local erotic boutique or kids' store. Spread your lover out on a sheet you don't care about messing up and make his body into your canvas: swirls, hearts, stars, cherubs, landscapes—whatever your imagination and talent permit.

Penny for Your Thoughts

Have your lover lie on his back with his hands at his sides, palms facing down. Balance pennies on each hand, and on top of each ankle. His mission is to keep the pennies balanced while you turn him on. Your mission is to turn him on so much he forgets about the pennies. (I pretty much guarantee you'll win this one.) Whoever wins gets the remote control all to themselves for an entire weekend.

There are endless scenes you can enact together: Sheikh and Harem Girl, Strangers Who Just Met, Lady Sheriff and Outlaw, Pool Man and Housewife . . . The point here is to bring joy and novelty back into lovemaking.

Lust Is in the Eye of the Beholder

I've said that you should give X-rated movies a chance. To even the most highly sexed women, X-rated movies are at best dull and at worst downright gross, especially after the first few scenes. How many times can you watch a spray of semen whiz through the air? If you're a man, the answer is many, many, many times. Guys can sit through these movies for hundreds of hours and never get bored. (Well, that's not entirely true. This is why men are so attached to their remote controls. They can fast-forward to the good parts.)

I've talked a great deal about men's ability to be visually aroused by photographs and videos. Women, on the other hand, would much rather imagine a romantic scene for themselves in a good, trashy novel. We don't like having our fantasies spelled out for us, or being told whom we should drool over. (Is Fabio the fantasy man of anyone you know?) Men, however, are much more literal. For them, there is a much more direct connection between the eye and the one-eyed trouser snake.

Women have been bemoaning this fact of nature for years, calling men "shallow" because they respond so easily to the visual. What they don't realize is that just because men respond to visual stimuli doesn't mean that they're all expecting us to resemble Elle MacPherson. In fact, most men are less critical of our bodies than we are. If you're standing in front of him in a flimsy nightgown, he's thinking how great you look, not wondering if that new thigh cream will get rid of your cellulite. (That, of course, is what *you're* thinking.)

So let's stop whining about men being visual. With all we've learned about making ourselves appealing to their eyes, let's concentrate on making their visual responses work for us.

Sexual Positions: Spicing Up the Basics

Ask five different men what their favorite sexual position is and you're likely to get five different answers. "Missionary, obviously," said one friend of mine. "It's like vanilla ice cream. You want to try every other flavor, but you always come back to the basics."

"Doggy style, definitely," says Peter. "It sort of involves the least restriction of the guy's movement, it doesn't require much effort, and, uh, you can see the point of contact. Lots of control, little energy expended, visual stimulation—what more could a man want?"

The common theme here was penetration. Whichever way a man believes he's penetrating the farthest seems to win his vote for best position. "However you can be the farthest inside the woman, that's the best," said John. "There's just a feeling that you have *arrived*."

What can I tell you? This is why they play with guns, too. On some primitive, reptilian level, it's all about who can propel his bullets the farthest.

I don't think I need to elaborate too much on basic sexual positions here, but I do think it might be useful to give you a couple of popular tricks call girls use, every now and then, to make those basics even more enticing.

The Missionary Position

One of the most common complaints of women whose lovers favor the good ol' man-on-top missionary position is that she can't climax that way. Well, if you haven't climaxed before he climbs on top of you, why not take care of the job yourself? Many a man finds it incredibly erotic when the woman pleasures herself while he's inside her. With your other hand, you might want to squeeze his buttocks, play with his nipples (if they're sensitive), or reach underneath him and gently play with his testicles.

Woman Kneeling on All Fours

Since this position is filled with visual treats of all sorts for your man, you might as well play up the animalistic aspect of it to the hilt. If you have long hair, encourage him to gather it in his hands, like a rein, while he's inside you. Or, if you're not averse to a little extra sensation, ask him to give you a couple of light spanks. If he's very well endowed and you don't want him to go in too deeply, put a couple of pillows underneath your stomach and close your legs so that he is straddling them while he's inside you. This prevents deep penetration.

Being on all fours is particularly great if you're on the bed and your lover is standing at the edge of it. But don't confine this position to the bedroom. It works very well when you're bent over a chair, the sofa, a tabletop, and the hood of the car.

Woman on Top

Many women report that being on top is their favorite position, because they can control how deep their lover penetrates them and can move exactly the way they want to for optimal clitoral stimulation. (Having him use his thumb on your clitoris is also helpful.) A man loves to be able to play with his woman's breasts, and some men like it even more if you play with your breasts, too.

One fun call girl maneuver when the woman is on top: Wait until your partner is close to orgasm, and just as he is about to come, lift his legs toward the ceiling. This requires a bit of strength on your part, and a bit of flexibility on his—but the blood rush to the genitals, plus the stretching of the muscles in the legs, can make for a mighty powerful orgasm.

Side by Side, Facing Each Other

Usually, it takes a longish time for a man and women to climax this way, but the buildup can be terrific. You might have him give you an orgasm before he enters you by rubbing his penis between your thighs, and then on your clitoris, for a while, while you fondle his testicles.

Spooning

This is a particularly nice way to wake up in the morning, when you're still kind of sleepy, and he's raring to go. (It's also useful when you're pregnant and any position on your back or stomach is awkward.) Have him insert his penis next to the labia in such a way that its head rests against the clitoris. You then lightly squeeze your legs together and have him thrust, as if he were inside you. (You might want him to use a water-based lubricant if you're not really turned on when he starts. And if worse comes to worst, if you just can't get that aroused, he can play while you doze.)

The Aftermath

For some reason, the guys who frequented Cachet usually liked to get dressed before the girls left, but they didn't want to put their clothing on when they were still sticky. So many of the call girls developed a little geisha routine that was a huge hit with clients. They'd take a warm, damp facecloth and pat him down with it, particularly around the thighs and crotch. You might want to keep a couple of warm, wet towels handy.

Don't leave the towels in place over his genitals for more than half a minute. What first feels wonderfully warm and damp very quickly feels cold and clammy. Also keep in mind that most men, after they climax, are exquisitely sensitive to touch. A caress that felt fantastic moments before can feel agonizing moments afterward. Some men don't want to be touched at all directly afterward, while others still want to be rubbed briskly. You'll have to gauge his reaction, or simply ask him.

Safer Sex: It's Not a Job, It's an Adventure

If the era of AIDS has taught us one thing, it's this: When it comes to sex, people lie. They don't mean to, but they do. You may think you know everything about your partner's sexual history. He may have told you he's never done intravenous drugs and never slept with a man. He may have told you he used condoms religiously. Well, almost religiously. "Okay, honey, so maybe there were a coupla times . . ."

Now think: Have you revealed every bit of your own history to the person you're closest to? I don't care how intelligent, careful, and politically correct you are. Wasn't there one night—a few nights, possibly—when you were intimate with people whose names you've forgotten and whose medical histories you never asked? Weren't there a few nights when a guy you didn't know well was reluctant to use a condom, and you wanted him so badly you didn't have the heart to insist? No multimillion-dollar AIDS education program will overcome the fact that, when we're in lust, many of us believe we are immortal.

AIDS, of course, is what's given the idea of "safer sex" currency. (I speak here of safer sex, not safe sex, because the only 100 percent safe form of sex is no sex.) But there are many health reasons, other than AIDS, to practice safer sex. AIDS is the fourth leading cause of death among women aged twenty-five to forty-four, with 13 million more expected to become infected by the year 2000. This is horrific enough. But additionally, each year, about 6.5 million American women contract some other form of sexually transmitted disease. And almost all of these infections could be prevented by using condoms.

The Art of the Condom:
A User's Guide

Let's get real. Despite all the sloganeering ("Safe Sex Is Hot Sex," "Learn to Love Latex"), the sensation of intercourse with condoms is never going to be preferable to intercourse without condoms. Telling men and women otherwise is like telling them wine coolers are really so much better than a glass of Chateau Lafite 1961. But that's not to say that sex with a condom—plus the zillion other variations on sex that don't involve intercourse—can't be pretty terrific.

Here's the attitude shift you need to adopt in order to enjoy latex condoms: They're not about hindering sex. Rather, they're about liberating you and your lover from worry, worry of pregnancy and worry about STDs. (And actually, for premature ejaculators, rubbers are a boon: They cut down on sensation just enough to make sex last longer for both of you!)

Note, by the way, that I keep saying *latex* condoms. Ninety-five percent of all condoms are made of latex; the rest are made from natural fibers, usually the intestinal membranes of lambs. Although most men say that lambskin transfers heat and sensation better than latex, and both are equally effective for preventing pregnancy, latex is less porous and does a better job of blocking the viruses and bacteria that cause STDs. (However, within the next year the first polyurethane condom, Avanti, will be on the market. It too offers STD protection but is reportedly thinner and more sensitive than the standard latex condom.)

What's available now?

The Basics

No-nonsense dry, round-tipped condoms still sell, but most women prefer lubricated condoms. For added protection, many are lubricated with the spermicide Nonoxynol-9, which kills not only sperm but also the AIDS virus. If you're applying a lubricant yourself to a dry condom, use *only* lubricants that are water-based, like K-Y Jelly or AstroGlide; oil-based lubricants can weaken latex fibers. Also look for condoms with a nipplelike "reservoir tip," rather than a rounded edge: It leaves room to catch semen, lessening the chances of leakage. If there is no reservoir tip built in, leave a half inch "overhang" when you're putting the condom on.

Size Counts

A condom that's too tight is as uncomfortable as too-tight underwear that keeps creeping up on you. Fortunately, manufacturers are marketing a new, larger version that measures about 15 percent wider and 6 percent longer than the standard size.

On the other hand, a condom that's too loose is downright dangerous; it may slip off while he's still inside you. Just as some women who've been called Canoe Foot all their lives insist on wearing shoes a size too small, some men demand Magnums when they're really .22-caliber kinds of guys. (In that case, *you* might want to go out and buy his condoms. Then put the proper-size condoms in an XX-Large-size condom box.)

Condoms as Entertainment

You don't own just one pair of black shoes, do you? So why should you be limited to one generic condom?

There are condoms in bird-of-paradise colors and condoms that glow in the dark, condoms with ribs, condoms with bumps, and condoms with tentaclelike "ticklers." There are condoms in every conceivable flavor, from mint to cappuccino. Sometimes, even when the condom itself is basic, its packaging is ingenious. I particularly like the Stealth Condom, in a package that looks like a stealth bomber; the copy reads, "They'll never see you coming." The Peter Meter condom has a ruler printed on it; as you roll it down, two inches is Teeny Weeny, four inches is Average Joe, six inches is Stud, eight inches is Hero, and ten inches is Farm Animal.

Tacky? Maybe. Fun? Yes. (Read the packaging closely when buying a novelty condom; some are just for laughs and don't guard against pregnancy and STDs.)

Equal-Opportunity Condoms

You've probably read about the new female condoms, marketed to women whose men are reluctant to use regular rubbers. The female condom is a loose-fitting polyurethane sheath between two flexible rubber rings. One ring lies at the closed end of the sheath and is anchored in the vagina like a diaphragm. The other—and you can imagine how attractive this looks—hangs about an inch or two outside the body. The whole thing is lubricated, which means when you're trying to insert it, it tends to leap out of your fingers and slither across the floor. Additionally, the thing tends to scrunch up like a Hefty Bag once the guy thrusts himself inside you. Given its appearance and functional drawbacks, whoever designed it clearly did not have a grasp on reality.

Although the idea of a birth control device that's entirely under a women's control and inhibits the spread of STDs is wonderful, the actuality of the device is not. It's messy, awkward, and uncomfortable. If a woman is using a Reality condom, I think the real question she should be asking herself is, "What am I doing with a man who won't protect me by using a male condom in the first place?"

Are there any risks to condoms? The biggest risk is that you'll use one that's either past its expiration date or has been exposed to extreme weather conditions, which weakens the latex and causes microscopic holes and tears. (However, for you worrywarts, a federal government study demonstrated that latex condoms can withstand a temperature of 158° Fahrenheit for at least 100 days. They also are fine at minus 60° Fahrenheit, if you happen to enjoy bathing in dry ice.) So buy new condoms; don't go for the ones that have been sitting around in your lover's desk drawer for years.

Additionally, a tiny (1 to 2 percent) portion of the population is allergic to latex, or the spermicide in the lubricant, or both, and may experience rashes, itching, or worse if latex comes in contact with the skin. If that's the case, consult your doctor. He or she may advise the man to wear two unlubricated condoms—lambskin next to his penis and a latex rubber over it for STD protection (or vice versa, if it's the woman who's allergic).

Who Doesn't Need to Use Condoms?

You and your partner have both been tested for HIV, and you are both negative. You both have not used intravenous drugs or slept with anybody else in the last six months. (Infection may not show up on tests for six months. In other words, if you slept with someone in this six-month period, he or she might have infected you and the blood test wouldn't yet show virus antibodies.) You are absolutely 100 percent certain that neither you or your mate has other sexual partners.

Can you fulfill all these criteria? Are you sure? Are you positive? Then he can take the condom off.

Otherwise, leave it on.

He Says/She Says:
Top Ten Excuses Men Make to Weasel Out of Using a Condom

You may be lucky and have a lover who's as eager to use a condom as you are. Chances are, though, he won't be. Which is why your initial discussion about the subject—that is, agreeing to use them—should not take place in the bedroom. In the heat of passion, it's all too easy to say, the hell with it.

Instead, lay down the law before ardor flares. Remember, as I've said several times, men are comfortable with bargains and contracts. Ask what his expectations are about monogamy. What are his feelings about birth control? What kind of sexual history does he have? (As I've said, few people are *completely* truthful about their history, but you can at least get a sense of what it's been.) If using a condom is part of the bargain from the beginning, you're much more likely to get your lover to cooperate. If, on the other hand, you first have sex with him and *then* tell him you want him to use a condom, he'll probably balk. (In a study of African-American college students at the University of Miami, for example, psychologists found that both men and women sometimes view their partners' sudden suggestion of condom use as an accusation of unfaithfulness or disease.)

Here are the most common excuses men give for not wearing a condom. I want you to be ready with your reply.

IF HE SAYS: You know that saying, baby: "It's like taking a shower with a raincoat on." It just doesn't feel good.

YOU SAY: I know it's not perfect, but just give yourself a chance to get used to it. After a few times, you won't even know it's there. I'll be so much more comfortable and relaxed, and I can be *wild* when I'm relaxed.

IF HE STILL RESISTS: You don't care how I feel about it?

YOU SAY: Fine. If it's got to touch bare flesh, sweetie, there's always your hand.

IF HE SAYS: It spoils the mood. I have to stop, put it on. . . .

YOU SAY: I've got one tucked away right here, in my bra. You can search for it there. *That* won't spoil the mood, will it? (You can also volunteer to put it on, or *insist* you put it on.)

IF HE SAYS: What's wrong with you? Do you think I'm a fag or something?

YOU SAY: The incidence of AIDS among gay men is dropping, and the incidence among straight men and women is going way up. Besides, honey, *real* men use condoms.

IF HE SAYS: They're disgusting.

YOU SAY: You want to see disgusting? Let me show you some close-ups of a herpes sore.

IF HE SAYS: Don't you trust me?

YOU SAY: Of course. But I can't trust every other person you've ever slept with and, unfortunately, neither can you.

IF HE SAYS: Just this once.

YOU SAY: Once is all it takes.

IF HE SAYS: I *never* use condoms.

YOU SAY: Well, okay. By the way, I don't have any birth control, and I'm ovulating. That's not a problem, is it?

IF HE SAYS
(IN A HURT TONE): I thought you loved me.
        YOU SAY: I do. But you remember what Tina
                 Turner said, sweetheart: "What's love
                 got to do with it?" This isn't about
                 being a good person or a bad per-
                 son. It's about health.

IF HE SAYS: Don't I look clean to you?
   YOU SAY: Sure you do, and let me tell you who
            else looks clean: Magic Johnson.

IF HE SAYS: But I've never done this before.
   YOU SAY: But I have.

How to Put on His Condom—
Sexily!

If you're like me, the whole process of putting on a condom makes you feel like you have the motor coordination of a two-year-old. I think the three women on the planet who *are* adept at putting on condoms should be forced, as a community service, to give seminars to the rest of us. I've had condoms fly out of my hands like miniature Frisbees; I've bitten straight through the rubber in the process of tearing open the package with my teeth. So when it comes to putting on condoms sexily, all I can do is repeat the famous adage about how you get to Carnegie Hall: Practice, practice, practice.

Whatever kind of condoms you prefer, invest in about a dozen of them and a cucumber. (Better yet, a carrot; you don't want to be making any unfavorable boyfriend/vegetable comparisons.) First, practice opening up the package in one swift motion. If you consistently find this awkward, keep a small pair of scissors handy by the bed. Next, inspect the condom to see which direction it rolls over the head of the penis/carrot. While rolling, *always* leave a little space at the top of the condom to catch the ejaculate. Practice this rolling-down motion on the carrot with your eyes closed. Ideally, in the bedroom, you will be able to kiss your boyfriend—thus distracting him a bit—while rolling the condom down with one or both hands. This is certainly preferable to staring fixedly at his private parts while muttering, "Wait . . . wait . . . almost got it . . . did that hurt?"

Some European call girls are able to place the condom on the head of the penis and then roll it down with their lips and tongue. Many men consider this erotic; personally, I consider it kind of a novelty act. (One night, one of my girls who had worked in Europe tried to demonstrate this technique to several of the other girls, using a banana. Apparently, it's a *lot* more difficult than it sounds. Several of the girls tried and just couldn't do it.) But if you think you and your lover might enjoy this, and you can do it, go right ahead.

I have to confess to a certain prejudice here. I know the common wisdom says that putting on a condom together can be part of an intimate, bonding experience. But, quite frankly, would you want him inserting your diaphragm? So unless you're with someone who's completely inexperienced, or you've got an erotic and smooth little routine worked out, it's usually easier and quicker for him to place the condom on himself.

ORAL SEX: A FRANK DISCUSSION

*I've tried several varieties of sex. The conventional position
makes me claustrophobic. And other positions give me either
a stiff neck or lockjaw.*

TALLULAH BANKHEAD

Even though one recent sex survey said that 88 percent of
men and 87 percent of women believe oral sex is perfectly
normal, my empirical observation tells me that lots of
women still aren't comfortable with it. Which perhaps explains why most working girls say it's the single most commonly requested sexual act. Many single and married men
are still under the impression it's something nice girls don't
do. And many of those girls agree.

Perhaps your religion has said oral sex is taboo; perhaps
you simply don't think it's clean. Maybe, too, your first experience with oral sex was in high school, when you didn't
want to risk pregnancy by having intercourse. He pushed
your head "down there" and demanded your services; the
implicit threat was, "If you don't do this for me, I'll find
someone who will." There was a hostility associated with the
act that some women haven't forgotten.

But most women are ambivalent about oral sex simply because, deep down, they really don't think they know what
they're doing. They've heard some guy say, casually, "My last
girlfriend gave the best head I've ever had," and they wonder what exactly that means. Most people, when they feel incompetent in any area of life, would rather just avoid the
whole subject.

The good news is: You're probably much better than you
think. The biggest secret to great oral sex, according to the
men I ask (and I probably ask more than I should): Enthusiasm counts. A man wants a woman who genuinely seems to
enjoy doing it for herself and for him.

A lot of women don't realize just how closely men identify
with that portion of their anatomy. They really, honestly

believe that the way you feel about *it* is the way you feel about *them*. To a woman, that concept is bizarre; we don't feel that way about any part of our bodies. What women would think, *Oooh, he enjoys touching my breasts. He must really love me*? But men feel this way. If you react with a bit of distaste or revulsion, they'll never feel totally accepted or loved.

So I say: Treat that part of him with the love and respect— and maybe playfulness—you feel toward the rest of him.

A man begins to think of his penis as a separate individual around the time of puberty, when, suddenly, it seems to have a mind of its own. He could be sitting there in trigonometry class, thinking about sines and cosines when, suddenly, there it is, popping up, making its presence known. Lots of men even name it: Joe, Sam, Alexander the Great. My girlfriend Angela went out with a man who called his Hercules.

Some women like to name their men's penises. If his middle name is halfway decent, and it's not his father's name, that's a good possibility. A friend of mine called her lover's private parts the Giant Redwood. Okay, I'm not saying you *have* to give it a name. But the point I'm trying to make here is that it's difficult to make love with any kind of enthusiasm to someone you don't know, who you're intimidated by, who you're unfamiliar and unfriendly with. So you've got to make friends with it.

My friend Angela used to carry on some pretty extensive conversations with her boyfriend's private portions (she plays both roles). Say her boyfriend's name is Sam:

> ANN: "So, Hercules, I heard you and Sam had a tough day."
> HERCULES: "That boss, he's such a bastard."
> ANN: "Let me just kiss it and make it better."
> HERCULES: "Ooh, I'd really like that."

Okay, so it's not exactly Shari and Lamb Chop. But it's kind of fun. And the more friendly you become with it, the easier it's going to be to put it in your mouth.

As I said before, men are visual creatures. One of the reasons they love X-rated movies is that they like to watch the action—in particular, they like to watch *you*. So it's nice to be rather elaborate about fellatio. Don't just put it in your mouth and start moving up and down. Men like a little foreplay down there; they like a show.

First, work your way down to it, kissing down his chest, stomach, and inner thighs. Tease him a little, start to kiss it, then pull away. You might try licking his testicles and massaging them a bit. Obviously you have to test your man's individual reactions here. For some men, the moment you put your hand on their testicles, they have visions of high school hockey practice and think you're going to hurt them.

At any rate, with all this attention, *he's* probably standing at attention. Start to swirl your tongue around the head and the shaft of the penis. You might also want to take it, stroke it across your face, give it some light kisses, almost as if you're worshiping it. Some of you may be thinking, *Please, Sydney, are you serious?* Believe me, he'll love this stuff. (If you're still not sure you're doing this right, rent an X-rated movie and see how the actresses do it. They lick and they swirl. Or practice on a Popsicle.)

Here are a few other useful call girl hand-and-mouth maneuvers.

Temperature Games

The theory here is fairly simple: If you blow on a penis close, your breath feels hot; if you blow on it from six to twelve inches away, your breath feels cool. Saliva enhances both sensations. A small ice cube in your mouth can also add to the fun, particularly on a steamy summer day. Try playing around with temperature while you're playing with him.

Mint Ju-lips

Savvy call girls have always known the benefits of a little creme de menthe in the mouth during oral sex. The green liqueur dribbling down the penis and testicles, plus the alternating sensations of heat and cool on the penis (heat when your breath is close by, cool when you move away), can be a powerful orgasm enhancer.

Remember, though, most menthol products are simply too hot and irritating for use on a woman's more sensitive tissues. Don't let him use creme de menthe if he's performing oral sex on you, or you're likely to find yourself charging into the bathroom for a shower.

Hand Tricks

While you're still in the early arousal stages, remove your mouth and tease him by lightly yet firmly rubbing the (lubricated) palm of your hand over the head of his penis—top, sides, front, and rear. (This technique involves intense stimulation on the most sensitive part of his penis, so watch his face to make sure the touch isn't *too* intense.)

Blowing Bubbles

While giving him oral sex, pause for a moment, place a bit of champagne or seltzer in your mouth, and go back to what you were doing. The carbonation in your mouth will make *him* fizz.

SAT Basics

No, it's not the college prep test. What I call the SAT is the Swallowing Avoidance Technique.

All this visual stuff, and the last few little "extras," will turn him on, but it won't make him climax. The idea here—the one that all call girls perfect—is to get him sufficiently aroused so that when you start in with the main event, it won't take *too* long—otherwise you risk contracting lockjaw.

In fact, I think the one thing that makes women crazy (and prevents men from getting as much oral sex as they want) is when you've been down there for twenty minutes, and the guy finally comes, then says, "Wow, that was great. I could have come fifteen minutes ago." And you think to yourself, *Fifteen minutes ago? He could have come fifteen minutes ago? Thanks a lot, pal. I won't fall for that one again soon.*

Men who hold back and make you work your jaw to death aren't going to get oral sex often. So it behooves the both of you to let him know you'd *like* him to come quickly. You might try saying something like, "My friend Jennifer gives her boyfriend head all the time. She says he's so great, because it only takes him a couple of minutes to come." He'll put two and two together.

At any rate, once you've done your elaborate kissing and licking routine, you take your hand, put it around his penis, and, working your mouth over the head and part of the shaft, move your hand rhythmically up and down the shaft.

One little trick for extra pleasure: Occasionally on the down stroke, hold the skin of the penis really taut and then sort of work your lips over the little ridge on the head, that mushroomlike part. Move your lips on it maybe eight or ten times. Then resume the movement with your hand, up and down, up and down. You can simultaneously encircle his testicles with your other hand and pull down gently, tightening the skin on the scrotum. (Warning: Some men *adore* this technique, and some find this area too sensitive. Keep a close watch on your man's reactions.)

Another little tip: If your jaw gets sore, you can close your mouth and sort of pout your lips out and fit them around the head of his penis while your hand is still going up and down. (Think Mick Jagger.) Thus your jaw is shut and resting, but he still feels your mouth on his member.

Usually at this point, women tell me, "Okay, Sydney, I'm with you up 'til here. But I don't want to swallow. I don't care if he's my husband, I don't care how much I love him. It still makes me gag."

Swallowing was always a problem in my business. No matter how much my girls were being paid, I couldn't insist that they swallow. I remember when it first occurred to me that swallowing was going to be a dicey issue. I had been in business about three months, and of course it was the night I was working the phones. At this point, our girls cost $125 an hour, while everybody else was about $75. So the clients had reason to expect something extra.

At any rate, I sent this girl to a new client. He called me later, furious: "I'm not paying $125 an hour for her to run into the bathroom and spit it out." Well, I was shocked. I'd never give one second's thought to this problem. I said, "I'm so sorry, Mr. Jones, it'll never happen again." And I thought, *Oh, my God, what am I going to do?*

So here's the technique I developed.

First, it helps if you train him to be a moaner. Some women can tell by the feel of the penis when their man is going to climax, but they're few and far between. So you want him to make noise to alert you to when he's going to come. (Of course, some helpful guys just *tell* you.)

Okay, so there you are with your hands and mouth going up and down as fast as you can, and you hear him make his "I'm just about to come" noise. You open your mouth a little wider so that your lips are not actually touching it, but you still keep your head bobbing up and down, along with your hand, so that it *looks* like your mouth is still on it but it really isn't. When your hand is moving this fast, believe it or not he can't tell that your mouth isn't really touching it. Frankly, he's not watching you too carefully at this point anyway. His eyes are probably closed, but if he opens them, he still sees your hand and your head going up and down, and he just assumes everything is the same. This technique is especially effective if you have long hair; that makes it even harder to see what you're doing.

Now, 90 percent of men are dribblers, and about 10 percent are shooters. If he's a dribbler, all you have to do is let the semen dribble down your hand. You subtly replace the hand covered with semen with your clean hand on his penis, then wipe the semen-covered hand off on something—preferably the side of the bed or a small towel you discreetly place nearby.

If the guy is a shooter, you really do need long hair to disguise what you're doing (or make sure that room is dark). Lift your head higher so you can close your lips, but be sure to keep bobbing up and down. Then when he climaxes, let it splash off your face and fall back down. Then with your clean hand, wipe off your face first.

Not too complicated, right? And he'll never know the difference, trust me.

If, by some chance, he does notice what you're doing—or he says he doesn't really care if you swallow in the first place—at least make the effort to treat his semen as if it's some sort of elixir. Tell him you think it's sexy to smooth it all over your skin or sensuously massage it on your breasts. Let him know you love his bodily essence.

Although the chances of HIV transmission through oral sex are very slim, *if you aren't in a monogamous relationship, use a condom—even for oral sex.* Let's face it: It won't feel as good to him as fellatio without the condom, but there's one trick for making the sensation pretty darn close. Using a nonlubricated condom, put a drop or two of water-soluble lubricant, like AstroGlide, on his penis first. *Then* put on the condom. While you massage him with your hand and mouth, hold the condom down with your other hand. The slippery sensation inside the condom is pretty close to the real thing. But remember: *You can't use this method with intercourse, because the condom will come off.*

WHEN IT'S YOUR TURN: CUNNILINGUS

This book is primarily about what you can do to turn *him* on. But I want to say a few words about the ways he can orally please you, because turning you on often turns him on. Also, too many women don't have the words to tell him exactly what they like "down there," and even more women feel uncomfortable asking for his oral attentions in the first place. So you might want to Xerox the next couple of pages and place them somewhere where you know he'll read them (although you should probably avoid the In box of his office desk!)

Why is cunnilingus such a, um, touchy subject? First, many women believe they are innately unpleasant-smelling and unattractive. Nothing could be farther from the truth. As long as you always wash before your man goes down on you, the taste, smell, and look of your genitals will almost invariably be erotic to him. (You'd be amazed how many of our clients at Cachet enjoyed giving oral sex to our ladies, which is surprising, in a sense, when you consider that a working girl may have been with other men only the day before. Still, it didn't matter to them; they just loved the sensation of being enveloped, in a way, by a woman's most intimate parts.)

Second, a lot of women find the experience of oral sex somewhat cold and lonely. I mean, he's all the way down at one end of the bed, attending to your pleasure, and you can't really see or hold him. For women who find cunnilingus somewhat alienating in this way, I recommend the 69 position—performing oral sex on him simultaneously. The disadvantage here, of course, is that it's easier for him to lose his concentration on you and your pleasure, but if you feel cunnilingus is too "selfish"—although it isn't!—the 69 position may quell your uneasiness. (Sometimes, too, cunnilingus can be *physically* cold, because the sheets are somewhere around your ankles! You might do well to turn the heat up in your bedroom beforehand.)

Performing oral sex on a man is a cakewalk compared to a man performing oral sex on a woman. We are more complicated creatures in that area, and every woman likes something different. (When you're with someone new, you can always tell the way his last girlfriend liked it the first time he does it to you.) Do you like his tongue soft or hard? Do you like direct clitoral stimulation or indirect? If direct, do you like to be licked on the sides of your clitoris or on the top? (Most women report that the very top of the clitoris is too sensitive, until they're so aroused they're almost at the point of orgasm.) Do you like him to use the flat of his tongue or the tip on your clitoris? (Most women prefer the flat of the tongue, but most men naturally use the tip.) How will he know any of this stuff if you don't tell him?

Here are a few little tricks you can ask for:

- When his lips and tongue are over your clitoris, tell him to shake his head from side to side a few times.
- Alternately, when he's positioned in this way, tell him to hum; the vibrations can be incredible.
- Have him insert a finger or two into your vagina, or one finger into or *against* your anus, while he's going down on you. (Even if you don't like the idea of anything inserted inside your anus, just the pressure of his thumb there can be tantalizing.)
- Suggest that he put a small ice cube in his mouth. (The ice shouldn't be in constant contact with your genitals; it's the variation between his hot mouth and the melting ice cube that's exciting.) Obviously, this one is better on a steamy hot night.

Of course, proficiency at fellatio is really just Sex 101, vanilla sex. In the next chapter, we'll try a few more exotic flavors.

9

Fantasy Sex: Beyond Vanilla

*One should try everything once, except incest
and folk dancing.*

SIR ARNOLD BAX

You may know your favorite
ice cream flavor is vanilla—has been, always will be. But
when you go to a Häagen-Dazs ice cream store and are faced
with a dazzling array of choices, do you *always* opt for the
vanilla? Don't you want to try the Caramel Cone Explosion
just this once? You'll always come back to your favorite, simple flavor, but the caramel or the rum raisin provides an occasional diversion.

And so it is with sex. Why limit yourself to the basics, wonderful though they may be? True, when I opened Cachet, I made a conscious decision to run a business that focused on straight "vanilla" activities, intercourse and oral sex. But I did so because at the time, those were the only activities my partner and I were familiar with and the only activities we believed we could expect a "nice" girl to do!

But as our business grew, we found that we had girls who were a little more adventurous than my partner and I: A few actively liked light bondage and domination, threesomes, or other mildly exotic activities. Interested clients were told that such-and-such a girl was available for, say, a threesome, but these clients were not allowed to ask just *any* girl to participate in this activity. I was very careful not to put anyone who worked for me in an uncomfortable position.

Clearly, then, in my business, the element of variety usually came in the form of the many different girls the client saw, not from what he did with them. However, between you and your long-term partner, variation in activity is what we're talking about.

I can't emphasize enough the need to be nonjudgmental and open to your lover's fantasies and desires. You may not want to make every idea a reality, but everything—literally *everything*—should be open to discussion.

The most important thing is to understand and accept your partner's fantasies. He had them long before you were on the scene. You are not a replacement for them, and they are not a replacement for you. With your support, they will become a part of your life together.

And that's where our first "alternative" sexual diversion comes in.

TELEPHONE SEX

Telephone sex didn't exist when I operated my call girl service, but now it's one of the fastest-growing parts of the sex industry. And why not? In this age of AIDS, it's safe, it's clean, it's anonymous, and men can convince themselves they haven't broken any vows of fidelity.

So why not learn the gift of sexual gab? Maybe your lover is regularly on the road, or maybe he's horny while he's at work and wants to lock his door, pick up the phone, and make you his "lunch break." "We're all connected," say those ubiquitous telephone company ads, and phone sex may be his way of staying connected to you.

Sexual boredom stems, in part, from an inability to fantasize together. One great way to get out of the doldrums is through telephone sex. What does being a phone sex diva take? The gift of gab, a certain lack of verbal inhibition, and the ability to lose yourself in whatever fantasy you spin. (If men and women had the ability to talk to each other about their innermost fantasies, telephone sex wouldn't be the multimillion-dollar industry it is today!)

For some women, phone sex comes easily. All it takes is for him to ask, "What are you wearing?" and you're off and running. (Possible answer: *Why, a T-shirt and shorts, and underneath, only a G-string, darling . . . and I'm thinking about what you're doing to yourself right now. . . .*)

But those of you who are among the verbally challenged, who think, *My God, what am I going to say next?*, should write down some miniscripts for the stories you want playact with him. You probably know some of his fantasies already, and you certainly know your own. So don't be afraid to weave scenarios that suit the two of you. For example:

He is Michael Jordan, and you are an adoring groupie who just wandered by mistake into the locker room. . . .

You are applying for a very important position at a major corporation, and he is the man interviewing you—imposing, impressive, formal, and seemingly incorruptible. But as you're talking, you notice he's distracted by your short, short skirt. You decide it's time to clear those knickknacks off his desk and *really* do business. . . .

You are the youngest and most luscious prostitute in the world's most exclusive brothel, and he is the favored client, whom the madam has called on to "break you in." (The next time you see your lover in person, demand payment!)

He is Santa, and you're a mischievous elf. . . . He's a priest, you're a novitiate, and the two of you are alone in the rectory late one night. . . . He's making love to your beautiful sister, and you're there to watch. . . .

In telephone sex, you can throw out all ideas of what's "right" or appropriate and indulge yourself in whatever idea gives you pleasure. A man can play a woman, a woman can play a man, and either of you can be the prisoner or the captor, whichever you wish.

(Many women become frightened when their fantasies include an element of violence. In fact, fantasizing about being raped has nothing to do with actually *wanting* to be raped, which is horrific. Rather, rape fantasies are a way of exploring the idea of completely letting go, having someone else take control safely. Because you, after all, are completely in control of your own fantasies.)

Don't worry if the talk between you and your lover seems stilted at first. With a bit of practice, the conversation—and your mutual arousal—will flow more and more easily. You also might want to have a few props on hand that will allow for realistic sounds: a riding crop to smack on the table, if he's been a "bad boy," or a carrot that you can suck on loudly, to simulate what you'd *really* like to be sucking on.

BONDAGE AND DOMINATION

Is everybody really jumping out of their business suits at the end of the day and getting decked out in leather and chain mail, caning and being caned in the name of good clean fun? Hardly. But the fact that sex and power are inextricably linked is undeniable. The urge to control or, more commonly, to lose control, to dominate or be dominated, exists to some extent within all of us.

Sexual researchers at the Kinsey Institute estimate that 5 to 10 percent of the U.S. population engages in dominance and submission fantasies for sexual pleasure at least occasionally, with most incidents being either mild or staged activities involving no real pain or violence. As compared to S&M, where the participants get aroused by pain, bondage and domination (B&D) is about control; it's a head game. According to Gloria Brame, author of *Different Loving: An Exploration of the World of Sexual Dominance and Submission,* dominance and submission is "an overt expression of a primal need, which exists in us all, for a power hierarchy, creating leaders and followers. The dominant is excited or even exhilarated by exerting power and control over another, and seeing the submissive respond exactly as the dominant wishes. The submissive derives a similarly exciting and fulfilling emotion from the act of surrendering to another." The submissive, says Brame, can then enjoy sex without guilt; it is an authority figure who compels the submissive to experience pleasure. The dominant, meanwhile, can experience a feeling of superiority without guilt, since this is what the submissive wants and expects.

Many more people prefer playing the submissive role than the dominant. And men are more likely to prefer B&D activities than females, which means that if you happen to be a woman who enjoys dominating men sexually, you'll never lack for willing partners who want to kiss your feet.

(Incidentally, although prostitution is clearly illegal, being a dominatrix is a more shadowy area of the law, because the sex is, for the most part, in the mind: The "dominant" and the "submissive" never have intercourse and rarely touch each other sexually. Generally, the man derives his pleasure from being treated like a slave, and then the dominatrix might "allow" him to masturbate.)

Occasionally at Cachet we let our girls indulge some of our clients' light bondage-and-domination fantasies—if we knew the client very well and if the girl knew what she was doing and was comfortable in that role. Mostly these fantasies were requested by powerful businessmen who wanted to relinquish the role of decision maker for a little while; they enjoyed a strong woman who would tell them they had been naughty and now they'd have to pay the price. The "price" rarely involved more than verbal humiliation, a couple of whacks, and admonitions about being a very naughty boy—just like when Mommy spanked him.

In B&D sex games, it's really the submissive partner who's in charge of the proceedings. He (or she) sets the limits on how much "punishment" he can take. Usually a couple agrees beforehand on a word or gesture that will signal that the "submissive" partner has had enough. ("No" and "Stop" aren't useful words, because they're often used within the context of the fantasy when the submissive really *doesn't* want the dominant to stop. You're better off with words like "Red" or "Yellow" for "Stop" or "Slow Down.")

If you've never tried these games, start with something light and playful. First, tie your partner up. If handcuffs or leather contraptions seem a bit too harsh to you, lots of stores now sell gentler alternatives. For example, there are fuzzy handcuffs with Velcro, and long satin strings you can tie to your bedposts. There is also something called Sportsheet, a soft fitted bedsheet, plus hand and foot cuffs mounted on Velcro pads that attach to the sheet and thus can be moved around. (The company motto is: "For the couple too bold for boredom and yet too bashful for bondage.") Scarves and neckties are fine, too, but if pulled too tightly they can bite. They can also be hard to untie.

Once your partner is secured, you might blindfold him. The key here is never to tell him what's coming next. When a person is blindfolded, his sense of touch is really heightened, which can be deliciously sensual. You might want to start off by rubbing a piece of fur all over him, or a long feather, or perhaps just your hair, sweeping it back and forth over his chest, belly, and groin. Then start kissing him slowly, languorously, over every inch of his body—until he's begging you to put him out of his misery. Tell him you'll do that only when you're good and ready. . . .

You can tease him like this for a half hour or more, until he's ready to explode (and vice versa, if he wants to turn the tables).

From this kind of light game playing, you might choose to move on to a bit more "stinging" play. Then again, you might not. It's important to realize that for the most part, people interested in these sex games do not want pain. They want pleasure, a particular kind of pleasure that comes from these little mind games.

A word of warning: NEVER LEAVE A PERSON BOUND UP AND UNABLE TO ESCAPE. Even if, in the context of the game, you say, "I'm just going to leave you here to suffer for a little while," only *pretend* to leave. Whenever you hear about some disastrous B&D scene, it's almost invariably because someone was tied up and alone, some natural disaster happened (fire, earthquake), and the person was killed or injured. Also, you might want to keep a pair of heavy-duty scissors next to the bed so ties can be cut in a hurry in case of an emergency.

SPANKING AND TICKLING

I'm all for bringing back the birch, but only between consenting adults.

GORE VIDAL

Spanking is a variation on bondage and domination; the thrill for spanking aficionados probably originated in childhood, when being spanked by a parent or teacher aroused some nebulous sexual feelings (perhaps from the genitals rubbing against the teacher's knee). Usually, there's a whole mental fantasy involved: teacher/pupil, parent/naughty child, and so on. You would be amazed at how many CEOs of major companies would call Cachet and let me know, subtly, that what they needed was a good spanking.

Erotic stores sell not only an extraordinary assortment of canes and whips—which can be really, truly painful—but also things like fuzzy mitts. Your "spanker" can alternate between a few stinging smacks on your bottom and the caress of a piece of fur. Many people report achieving orgasm just from the act of being spanked.

Tickling, too, is a pretty common turn-on; there are magazines and X-rated movies devoted entirely to this diversion. A lot of tickling fans remember first being aroused by tickling as kids when being held down and tickled by an older, stronger friend. If you think about it, tickling is really about power. You're putting the "ticklee" in a position of helplessness. He or she is laughing, but it's involuntary. Maybe you enjoy it because on some level you like being disarmed by your lover—you like the momentary feeling of control he has over you, the way the laughter breaks down your defenses. Everyone's erotic sensors are wired differently. If tickling's your thing, buy yourself a great big feather, often sold at erotic boutiques.

Anal Sex

When a client called us and asked, "Do you speak Greek?" we knew what he meant. "Greek" was the insider code for anal sex, and that's obviously something we didn't permit our girls to do. It just didn't make sense, either from a health or comfort standpoint.

Still, you may find that your partner is keenly interested in anal sex. Why? "Let's put it this way. When you're in there, there's no limit on *depth*," says my friend Bob. Some cite the pleasure of the tightness of the anal sphincter muscle as compared to the vagina (although my friend Sam suggested that men who need that much tightness "must be kind of tiny"). Some enjoy the rareness of it; they're pushing the envelope sexually, and thus anal sex is somehow more of a conquest than "everyday" sex. More often men simply relish the sheer illicitness of the act—after all, anal sex is still illegal in some states (so is oral sex, for that matter). "Have you seen any porno movies lately?" asks my friend Martin. "Most have at least one anal sex scene. There's this sense of power involved. At first, the guy kind of forces her to do it, and then she ends up loving it." (Yes, Martin, and that's why these films are called *fantasies*.) Adds another friend, somewhat wistfully, "Well, most women I know have already slept with lots of people, but not that many have had anal sex. So if you're the first person to do it with them, well, you're the *first*. That makes it kind of special, doesn't it?"

I probably don't need to tell you that anal sex is one of the primary ways of transmitting the AIDS virus, since it can rupture tiny blood vessels in the anus, thus making the transmission of the virus from his semen to your blood more likely. (We often associate anal sex and AIDS with homosexuality, but AIDS is very much a heterosexual disease, especially in many African countries. The reason? Condoms are expensive, and men and women have anal sex in lieu of using birth control.) So if you are going to have anal sex, make *sure* he's using a condom (or even two).

With those caveats in mind, anal sex can be extremely pleasurable for the woman as well as the man. There are many sensitive nerve endings around the entrance to the anus, and stimulation can heighten orgasm. The key to enjoying anal sex is taking your time . . . and using a lot of lubrication (invest in a tube of K-Y jelly).

When beginning the proceedings, no matter how many adult movies your boyfriend has seen, don't let him just ram himself inside you; that will hurt. Instead, when you're already very aroused, have him start with a well-lubricated finger or two, moving *veerrry* slowly in and out while he massages your clitoris. You might choose to limit your pleasures to his finger; it's possible that no matter how gentle he is, his penis will be too painful. But if you feel comfortable at this point, you might have him introduce his penis—again, slowly and carefully. You might even want to back up onto it (this is easiest in the spoon, rather than doggy, position). The buildup of sensation can be wonderful. And you'll never be able to watch that butter scene in *Last Tango in Paris* in quite the same way again.

CROSS-DRESSING

Nobody knows exactly why Tarzan sometimes wants to play Jane, but the best clinical guess is that roughly 1 percent of men have some interest in cross-dressing. Interestingly, the majority of cross-dressers (about 90 percent) are heterosexual, and many are in jobs that demand a lot of macho (read: stressful) posturing. Most of them wear the garments under their clothes to work. (Think about that the next time you meet a Wall Street trader.) Women's clothing is a way of getting them in touch with their feminine, softer selves. For some men, it's infinitely soothing, and for many more, it's a powerful aphrodisiac. These men who want to don women's clothing don't necessarily want to assume a more feminine role in bed; it's just that they find the clothing arousing.

Some men like to go even further than wearing women's underwear or clothing; they want a complete transformation. This was an activity that a number of men engaged in with our girls, rather than alarm their girlfriends or wives. A girl would go over to the client's house and do his hair, makeup, etc.—all the while telling him how pretty he is. We always had one or two girls at Cachet who enjoyed this sort of thing, since they often didn't have to have sex with the client at all. Although for other men, the cross-dressing was a prelude to sex, where he and she would pretend they were "lesbian lovers."

At any rate, if your lover has more than a passing interest in women's attire, you might find it somewhat of a turn-off initially. But why not let him make love in woman's clothes and see how the two of you feel? Essentially, you have nothing to lose. If the clothing is just an occasional kick for him that's confined to the bedroom, fine. Perhaps it won't bother you and may even become a bit of a turn-on. If, however, the male-to-female transformation is an integral part of his sexuality, you'll have to figure out if you can accept the situation. Repeated studies show that a cross-dresser is both unable and unwilling to give up this form of arousal. All your disapproval will do is drive him into the closet—probably with his own extensive collection of dresses and wigs.

Vibrators and Other Sex Toys

There are literally dozens of vibrators on the market; even Dr. Ruth Westheimer has lent her name to one brand, called the Eroscillator. They used to seem unnecessary, almost a bit scary to me. After all, they're big, they're noisy, and they don't send flowers. Why not hands, tongues, fingers? But as one friend sensibly replied: "If you love Paris, does that mean you won't also love London?"

The sensations of the vibrator are very different from other forms of stimulation. With a finger or tongue, there's generally a gradual, slow buildup of sensation, finally leading to an explosive conclusion. With a vibrator, you're happily buzzing along, and suddenly—*boom*—you have, so to speak, come and gone.

This is why, I think, vibrators are so strongly recommended for women who have problems achieving orgasms. If you have difficulty, a vibrator will almost certainly get you there. If you *don't* have trouble using more conventional means, however, you're likely to climax too quickly. As a friend once told me, a vibrator is the Chinese food of sex:

immediately satisfying, but after an hour you're hungry again.

Nevertheless, many women have sworn loyalty to them and keep an extra supply of batteries handy. (Battery-operated models tend to be lighter and easier to handle; plug-in electric models tend to give off stronger, more intense vibrations.) Many vibrators come with instructions on how and why to use them. (Eve's Garden, an erotic boutique in New York City designed especially for women, suggests that you repeat to yourself a loving self-affirmation: "I have a right to pleasure. . . . I give myself permission to enjoy my own body. . . .")

Many men also find vibrators erotic. But at first they may be put off by a large phallic object that guarantees you pleasure—but is not attached to them. So when introducing a vibrator into your lovemaking, proceed with good humor and tenderness. If he already knows he can give you an orgasm without the vibrator, he's less likely to be threatened by it. He'll look at it as a supplemental toy for increasing your pleasure. If, on the other hand, you don't usually climax with him, hand him the vibrator and explain that this is the way *he* can make you come.

The vibrator can become his playmate as well as yours. Try using it to massage and tickle his shoulders, neck, chest, and buttocks. Then position it on the perineum, the area between the testicles and the anus, or the frenulum, the tiny band of skin on the underside of his penis that is, for many men, exquisitely sensitive. Although some guys find the vibrations too intense, others love it and quickly climax.

Dildos are made of everything from plastic to ivory to solid gold. These penis-shaped objects have been used by women (and men) for centuries to provide that pleasurable, filled-up feeling that even an orgasm can't provide. Use one during masturbation, or when your man has had enough and you still want something inside you. There are even some small ones that are meant to be inserted inside *him*. If you're really into this sex-role reversal fantasy and want that dildo to fit you like a man, you might want to invest in a harness, which is an adjustable black leather garment device designed to hold the dildo in place.

(A warning: There's some evidence that HIV can be spread via sex toys. If you have more than one partner, or you don't know your partner's HIV status, routinely clean all toys with bleach after each use.)

MASSAGE OILS AND OTHER BODY BALMS

Baby oil or coconut oil are just fine for full-body rubdowns, but you might want to try some more exotic unguents. Rachel Perry makes a series of scented oils that heat slightly when rubbed in, and Pleasure Balm, which becomes cool on contact, is great for those hot summer evenings. Or try Kama Sutra Honey Dust, a powder packaged in a pretty little urn, which feels like an oil when rubbed into the skin. (Make sure that he's not allergic or sensitive to any smells before buying scented products; you don't want him to spend your entire lovemaking session sneezing.) A few girls at Cachet always carried some massage oil in their purses (in spill-proof containers, of course).

Virtually every oil on the market stains all but 100 percent cotton sheets. So if you're using oils, you might want to make love on top of some large towels.

SEXY NONSEX

Outercourse refers to every kind of sex that doesn't involve the exchange of bodily fluids, everything from cybersex to mutual masturbation. It's useful not only for protecting you from disease but also for pleasing yourself and your partner sexually when it's not a good time for good ol' fashioned in-and-out sex: You have cramps, your lover is away on business, it's your most fertile time of the month and you've run out of spermicidal jelly. Here are a few variations of outercourse.

Making Out

When's the last time you just kissed and fondled your partner for hours without the possibility of sex? Probably junior high school. Just kissing, without the prospect of sex, can make you pay attention to the nuances of foreplay like never before. (In fact, lips are very sensitive because they're one of the most nerve-rich areas on the body.)

Reading Erotica to Each Other

As you've undoubtedly heard before, the biggest erogenous zone on a man's body is his brain. So why not play his brain for all it's worth? Buy a few of the most lascivious books available—Anaïs Nin's diaries, *The Pearl* (a collection of Victorian erotica), *The Story of O*, or whatever strikes your fancy—and read the best bits to each other out loud.

Watching Adult Movies Together

Even if you're not particularly turned on by his pornographic movies, you might ask him if he'd like to watch one of the films geared to women produced by Femme Productions (popular titles: *Three Daughters, Urban Heat, Sensual Escape*). Not only are they not violent, they also tend to have a plot and feature safe sex.

Eating off Each Other

That's right. Remember Mickey Rourke eating Jell-O off Kim Basinger's stomach in *9 1/2 Weeks*? Also consider liquid chocolate, whipped cream, peanut butter (smooth, not chunky), and butterscotch topping. (Leave time for a shower after this one.)

Massage

When's the last time you got—or gave—a really long, generous, body-liquefying massage? Preferably in candlelight with soft New Age music in the background. Or you might want to cover yourselves with oil, then rock and roll and slip and slide all over a king-sized bed. Or, for a bit of variation, massage him with a specially formulated oil that heats up with rubbing (Rachel Perry is one brand). Then simply blow on him all over. . . .

Flying Solo

Many men get very turned on watching a woman touch herself. You could slowly and sensuously caress yourself all over (use of body lotion or oil optional) and, if you're comfortable with it, bring yourself to climax.

Most men are so accustomed to photos and videos of guys masturbating onto a woman's breasts or stomach that encouraging him to do this with you would not only be easy, he'd really enjoy it. (Don't forget to massage his sperm all over yourself afterward.)

When His Fantasies Are Your Nightmares: How to Say No and Still Keep Him Happy

What if you discover your man has needs you're simply not interested in fulfilling? Needs that, not to put too fine a point on it, gross you out? Do you:

A. Go through with it anyway?
B. Tell him to get over it?
C. Suggest he go see a call girl?

I know I'm going to get a lot of flak here, but to me, the correct response is clearly C.

Let's say that at times he enjoys dressing up in women's clothing when he makes love, a fetish shared by about 1 percent of heterosexual men. The woman's clothing is arousing yet somehow soothing to him at the same time. (Hey, I don't say I understand it, either.)

Let's also say you find the sight of your beloved in a French silk bra and stockings kind of repulsive. Dedicated cross-dressers say that no amount of cajoling or threatening will ever make them give up this habit. It's part of their sexual nature, and criticism will only drive them farther into the closet (probably yours).

Under circumstances likes these, assuming you're happy in the rest of your marriage, I think there's nothing wrong with accommodating your partner's need—provided it's with a professional. (Some of the more common fetishes don't even involve sexual intercourse.) This is one of the most useful services the sex industry can provide. The call girl is in effect keeping your relationship together by allowing the man to fulfill his need *without emotional entanglement* while staying with you.

Some men really are compelled to act out their fantasies.

For many others, however, there is an alternative. In fact, for the vast majority of men, talking about their "forbidden" activities is almost as satisfying as acting out the fantasy—maybe more so. Whatever he wants can be talked about in lieu of doing it.

For example, what if your lover is interested in "golden showers," the practice of urinating on a lover for sexual pleasure? He wants you to pee on him, and there's not a chance in hell you'll do it. Well, let him talk about it. Let him talk about the first time he saw a girl pee and how it gave him an erection; let him talk about how good your urine would feel coursing down his chest, onto his genitals, into his mouth. He's probably never met a woman who would simply be open enough to let him explore his fantasy out loud. *He'll be infinitely grateful.* And you won't have to do anything more difficult than maybe moan a bit at the appropriate moments.

Whether you can be comfortable and your partner can be satisfied just talking out his fantasies, or whether his need to act them out is so strong a professional is the only realistic answer, it's vitally important that you try to be as understanding and nonjudgmental as possible. And it should go without saying that if he trusted you enough to be honest about something so personal, it must never be repeated or used against him in a future quarrel or argument.

So now you're a sexual diva. You know what to do and when to do it. Embarrassing or difficult sexual moments are a thing of the past.

Well, maybe for you. But what about him? Is your lover having sexual difficulties? If so, you won't want to skip the next chapter.

10

Sexual Problems,

Sexual Solutions

No matter how comfortable you are with your sexuality, no matter how educated you consider yourself, you and your partner are bound to encounter some bumps on the road to your own sexual Shangri-La.

Working girls are not doctors or sex therapists, but inadvertently they often find they've helped some clients conquer their fears and frustrations. I remember in particular one gentleman in his seventies who came to us after having had prostate surgery. He was terribly worried that he wouldn't be able to perform anymore with his wife. So he wanted to "try out the equipment," as it were, with someone who would not be emotionally affected if it didn't work. As it turns out, it *did* work, and that's the last time we saw him. He was one satisfied customer!

A large percentage of men's sexual difficulties are physical and can be easily treated medically. A smaller, but nevertheless significant, portion of sexual problems are psychological in origin, and these are the more difficult to solve. In this chapter, I explore the most common sexual problems couples encounter and what they can do about them.

What He's Afraid to Tell You

Men often hide from their lovers what they most need to tell them, fearing rejection, ridicule, or simple misunderstanding. Whether the problems you're encountering in bed are chronic or occasional, many of them may disappear if you have a better understanding of what your partner may not be telling you about his own sexual needs.

His Penis Needs More Attention

When he was sixteen years old, all he had to do was think about a girl—no, never mind the girl, just her *underwear*—and he would get an erection. In his early twenties, he could probably have sex twice a day and still be ready for more. He needed very little in the way of stimulation: a whiff of your perfume, the sight of you bending over the sink . . . and he'd be there, hard and ready.

Well, time marches on, and with it, those instant erections. The vast majority of men produce well above the minimum amount of testosterone needed to enjoy sex well into advanced age. But aging increases the length of time between orgasms. This interval lengthens from a few minutes at the age of seventeen, to as much as forty-eight hours by age fifty or sixty.

So although he is every bit as turned on to you as he was back then, he needs more foreplay—kissing, hugging, caressing—as well as more stimulation from your hands and/or mouth in order to become hard. He also might need a slightly different kind of stimulation: a firmer grip, or more concentration on the head of his penis. (A number of men have told me that their wives' "manual maneuvers" would be *sooo* much better if they just moved their hands a half inch higher up toward the tip. Also, many complain that their partners are too gentle. Ever watch a man masturbate? Most of them look like they're going to rip it out of its socket.

Of course, for women, a man's natural aging process provides many benefits. After all, he's no longer two-minute Harry, and the fact that it takes longer for him to reach orgasm means his sexual responses are becoming more in sync with yours.

What's painful is that lots of men expect their penises to behave as they did when they were younger—and if they don't, the insecure guy panics. Then he has to find fault: If only she weren't so heavy, if only she would wear a sexy negligee, if only she would . . . Since it *can't* be his fault, it *must* be hers. Unfortunately, many women are all too quick to blame themselves as well.

This is why the older man finds himself in the arms of a twenty-year-old. He's desperate for the reassurance that his little soldier will still stand at attention at a moment's notice. He just cannot comprehend that his libido is *never* going to be the way it was when he was twenty. He searches for that magical person who will make him (and his penis) feel the way they did thirty years ago.

So not only do you need to pay more attention to that portion of his anatomy during lovemaking, you also need to reassure him that this is what *every* guy is like. No need to lecture him about the aging process, though (I wouldn't even mention it). If he comments on how it takes longer than it used to reach orgasm, you might say something like, "Of course it does, and thank goodness. Don't you know that's great for me?" Or "The longer we do it, honey, the better." (Obviously you might not be so thrilled if he's pumping away for a half hour or more. That's when it may be time to take him in hand, so to speak.)

He Wants to Be Able to Tell You He's Not in the Mood

Ever notice how guys from the Pentagon are always getting on television and talking about America's "state of preparedness"? They are obsessed with the notion that America must have its finger forever poised on the button, ready to meet the challenge of war.

Men's thinking about sex is not so different. Every American male has grown up with the myth that in order to qualify as a Real Guy, he has to be ready for sex at a moment's notice. Just as these guys grew up thinking it was a sin not to clean their plates, so it was a sin to turn down a woman who offered herself sexually. After all, this might be the last meal or girl *ever*. A Real Guy never says no.

The problem is, as a man gets older, a stressful day at the office or an extra-hard workout at the gym may make him *want* to say no—but he's ashamed and worried you'll think him less of a man. Rather than being able to say, "Gee, I'd love to hold you tonight, but I don't want to do anything else," he might brush you off with, "I have an early day tomorrow," and avoid touching you altogether. Then you become a bit anxious because you also feed into the he-should-always-be-ready theory of male sexuality. You feel even more desperate for reassurance that you're still attractive and appealing. You either withdraw in hurt and/or panic or try to turn him on anyway, to prove you've still "got it." What happens? He retreats farther. And pretty soon the two of you are at a sexual standoff.

A younger guy, who doesn't worry about his ability to have

sex physically, may just not want it for a myriad of reasons: He's tired, he's tense, he's got other things on his mind. In some ways he feels more pressured to have sex than you ever could. (Nobody ever says a woman is not a "real woman" if she doesn't want to make love for some reason.) He needs to know you won't think less of him if he just doesn't want to make love.

So this means if he says no on occasion, there can't be weeping ("Is there something wrong with me?)", irritation, or derision. Instead, you might ask, "Can you just put your arm around me?" You probably don't even have to say anything. Just smile, say "Fine," and hold his hand. He'll get the picture.

Older Guys May Not Like to Be Surprised

Younger men love a sexual surprise. If they're between the ages of twenty and thirty-five (maybe up to forty), you will get just the reaction you want if he comes home and finds you lounging in bed, wearing only a strand of pearls and a smile. His hormones will carry the day.

But after a certain age, that element of surprise can actually be upsetting. If you go to great lengths to create a romantic scenario and just *spring* it on him as he walks through the door, he'll feel the pressure to perform, NOW—and if he doesn't (so he thinks), you'll be disappointed and less inclined to be romantic in the future. Even worse, he'll be disappointed in himself. He'll worry that you will think there's something wrong with him. He may even be subconsciously angry at you for putting him in that situation.

With the over-forty man, it's better to tell him ahead of time (say, in the morning, or the day before) that you're planning a special evening and give him time to think about you and look forward to your rendezvous. The older man's mind needs to be more engaged during lovemaking than the younger man's—and, really, this is a boon to most of us women.

Here's a method a client at Cachet used with his ex-wife

(their marriage had foundered, but not because of sex!). When she was in the mood, she'd chill a bottle of champagne and set out two glasses on the kitchen counter. When he came home and saw the glasses sitting there, he knew she was interested. It was their little signal to each other. If he was in the mood, they would enjoy their champagne—and everything else—that night. If he was exhausted, he could say to her, "I see you have some champagne. Would you mind if we saved it until tomorrow?"

"We've never even discussed our little game," the client told me. "It was kind of an understood thing. It was great, though, because I could say no without having to feel like I was rejecting my wife. It's not like I was saying, 'I don't think you're sexy,' and pushing her away."

You can come up with your own signals. My friend's lover would lay out sexy lingerie for her if he was in the mood to make love that night. She'd put them on if she was, too. She would reciprocate by putting out his silk boxer shorts when she wanted to make love. Another couple I know used candles: Whichever one of them wanted to make love put candles around the room, and if the other was also amorous, he or she would light them!

Sometimes He Just Wants to Lie Back and Enjoy It

Many couples struggle with the question of who is "responsible" for the sexual relationship. Who creates the romantic ambience? Who makes the first move? (In the recent Janus Report surveying the sexual habits of 3,000 Americans, 54 percent of men and a surprising 67 percent of women reported they like to initiate lovemaking. Yet a related study showed that it was the men who actually *did* initiate sex 91 percent of the time.) The question of sexual responsibility can become as big a source of friction as who does the dishes or who takes out the trash.

At Cachet, many of our older clients loved just to lie back and have the women take care of *them*. At first, many of the young women were upset when a client just lay there and didn't pounce on them. Because they were accustomed to dating men their own age who were constantly pressuring them for sex, they assumed these clients didn't find them attractive. I had to reassure them that was not the case at all.

Rather, these guys came of age in the generation when women weren't supposed to enjoy sex that much, or were expected to have orgasms strictly through intercourse. But then during the 1960s, women began demanding orgasms, too. All of a sudden the rules of sex had changed, and the men now felt pressured to be great lovers. So when they came to a call girl, they were pleased to have the chance to be totally selfish. They were absolved from the responsibility of "making it good for her" because they were giving her cash instead.

I had to make the girls see that passivity was actually an advantage of sorts. After all, with these clients the girls were entirely in control of the situation. They could do whatever they felt most comfortable doing.

So in your relationship with your partner, you may want the occasional lovemaking session where all the attention is on him. (Of course, he may also want to give you the very same kind of undivided attention sometimes. Let him.)

He'll Always Be Attracted to Other Women

The two of you are out for a weekend stroll, and you notice his eyes glance furtively to the left, where a Cindy Crawford look-alike with the legs of a gazelle is striding down the street. You:

A. snap, "See something you want?"
B. whine, "You notice everyone but *me*."
C. comment, "Boy, she's gorgeous, isn't she?"

Most American women choose A or B—and they're making one heck of a mistake.

To notice other women—to admire them, to be attracted to them—is human. It's what makes him vital and sexy. If he didn't notice women—if he didn't fantasize about them occasionally—*then* you should worry.

Yet most women decide that the day their lover becomes involved with them he should cease to notice the rest of the female species. If he so much as looks or ventures an admiring comment, she makes him feel guilty. And she starts to play something I call Test the Relationship, where the object of the game is to correctly answer the question: What's wrong? Aren't I good enough for you??

Obviously, a guy who's constantly gawking at or commenting on the vital statistics of every women he sees has a problem, but that problem has nothing to do with you. He probably needs to prove to you, himself, and the rest of the world that he's "all man." One of my girlfriends was engaged to a man who simply could not take his eyes off the breasts of any woman he met. It was as if all these women were dangling a hypnotist's watch fob right at bust height, and intoning, "You must have these . . ." One day, my friend introduced Karl to a particularly stunning, bosomy woman, who happened to be gay and was not appreciative of that sort of behavior. As they were introduced and she noticed where his eyes were resting, she waved her arms near her face and loudly announced. "Hello, yoo-hoo, I'm up here." (Not surprisingly, this fiancé is now an ex.)

But the average faithful, loving man does look and does admire. It certainly doesn't mean that he wants a *relationship* with every bombshell he sees.

The savviest thing you can do is use his sex drive to your advantage. For example, say you're going to a party where there are bound to be women younger, prettier, and thinner than you. Are you going to spend an hour before the party fishing for compliments, insisting he tell you how uninterested he is in every other member of the opposite sex? No. What you're going to do is tell him how fabulous he looks, and how every pretty girl in the room is going to be jealous of you, being with this gorgeous hunk of manhood. When you get to the party, you might say, "Hey, I saw how Lola over there was making eyes at you." Doesn't matter if Lola wasn't making eyes; most men are so egotistical they'll believe you. Then, when you get home: "I'll bet Lola would give anything to be unbuttoning your shirt like I am right now," etc.

What have you accomplished? You've made him feel that other woman are attracted to him (who doesn't want to be attractive to the opposite sex?); you've let him know *you* know other women are attracted to him; you've let him know you think he's gorgeous; and you've told him how lucky you are that he's yours.

It's only the rare psycho-hound who'll think, *Hey, I am great. I can do better than the chick I'm with.* (And what do you need with a guy like this, anyway?) The vast majority of men will see that you appreciate them and will admire and respect you for your unerring good taste.

He Desperately Wants to Satisfy You but Is Afraid to Ask You What You Want

Consider this: In the mid-1960s, the sex researchers Masters and Johnson refuted claims that most women climaxed through vaginal intercourse alone. Since that time, many more sex researchers have argued that clitoral stimulation is usually necessary, and I think most of us would heartily agree. Yet as recently as last year, *Playboy* surveyed the sexual habits of readers in eleven countries and found that most men throughout the world (90 percent of men in Brazil, 75 percent in the United States) are convinced that their partners regularly climax by vaginal intercourse alone (even though the latest research shows that only about 25 percent of women can climax this way).

My point here is that despite all the blatant displays of sex that surround us, misinformation is still rampant. And many men are intimidated to ask us what works for us sexually and what doesn't. Just as you've been conned into believing that a man who loves you will know exactly what you want, he's grown up with the same expectation of himself. Therefore, to ask you what feels good in bed is to admit that he doesn't know everything about you. If they can't ask for directions in a car when they're lost, for crying out loud, they're hardly going to be able to ask about *this!*

This simple inability to ask for information and receive it—nonjudgmentally—is at the core of many couples' sexual difficulties.

He Wants to Explore His Sexuality with You

Men look at movies and magazines and they see a sexual smorgasbord, a land where everyone is doing everything all the time. Then they think about their own life. Your man may adore you, but if he's doing the same old things with you, month after month, and if he feels that mentioning anything new will distress you . . . well, it's sort of like watching reruns of *Gilligan's Island.* I mean, no matter how fond you are of the show, after the millionth episode it dawns on you: These people are going to be on that island forever.

Occasionally, everyone's got to get off the island—at least in their imagination.

You may be saying to yourself, *But I've asked him a hundred times if there's something missing in our sex life, and all he ever says is, "Honey, I love everything you do to me."* That's what most loving men say, and it may very well be true. But you must make sure you're not sending out a double message. You say you're open to sexual exploration, but are you sure your actions aren't perhaps telling him that if he actually broached the subject, you'd tell him it was gross, perverted, or not the sort of thing you do?

Many men go to call girls because they want to try something they feel uncomfortable or ashamed to ask of their wives. And as I've said, if he has urges that you really don't want to fulfill (you just can't see yourself making love with another woman, or tying him by the wrists and ankles and scolding him, or whatever), maybe seeing a call girl periodically isn't such a bad thing.

But if you think there's any chance you might enjoy his fantasy, try to be open to it. Women fear that if they even dare to discuss a subject they find distasteful, their lovers will assume they're keenly interested and try to make them act out the scenario. This is often not true at all.

For the vast majority of men, talking about the fantasy with the women they love is as erotic as doing it. (Maybe more so, since a fantasy that's in your own head is completely under your control: It's his play, and he's the director, star, and audience all rolled into one!)

Now that you've had a chance to think about these fears and desires, let's talk about those times when they translate into real sexual difficulties.

PREMATURE EJACULATION

A friend told me this story: "I was dating this guy who came—no kidding—about ten seconds after he was inside me. *If* he lasted until he was inside me. I complained about it to everybody, I couldn't help it. I even told my sister. Finally, I wanted to introduce Stan to my parents. Just as he rang our doorbell, my sister, who has a rather warped sense of humor, turned to me and said, 'Gee, Emily, do you think I should shake Stan's hand? I mean, it might be too much for him. . . .' We couldn't stop giggling. It was awful."

Of course, call girls do not see premature ejaculation as a problem. After all, the quicker he climaxes, the easier it is for her! But they may be the only people on the planet who actually like it. For men and women in loving relationships, premature ejaculation, the most common sexual dysfunction, is a serious problem. It's certainly frustrating for a woman (particularly if she's with a man whose next words after orgasm are "Zzzzzzzz . . .") and deeply humiliating for a man. The good news is that it's probably the easiest sexual problem to solve.

First of all, as men age, most grow out of this difficulty—the aging process simply slows them down. But even those for whom the problem persists in the late twenties, thirties, and beyond can usually solve it.

Men who can control when they ejaculate recognize the signs that they're about to come: the additional swelling of the penis, tightness of the testicles, feeling of urgency, and so forth. Men who can't control their ejaculation fail to recognize these signs. The climax just sort of sneaks up on them. They don't get to enjoy long periods of arousal, as other men do.

Premature ejaculation tends to be worse with a partner than when masturbating, because of the added pressure and anxiety: Is it going to happen again? Am I going to disappoint her? Oh, God, let me just think about baseball for a moment here. . . . AAAAH, damn, I rounded too many bases. . . .

So the trick is for your partner to recognize the signs of approaching orgasm and to slow down in time.

If your man has a chronic problem with premature ejaculation, it may be time to see a sex therapist. Reassure him that this won't be expensive, long-term therapy. The majority of premature ejaculation cases can be solved in a matter of a few months, or even weeks. You and your partner will probably go through a series of exercises that address his particular needs; generally, they're designed to let him sense ejaculation and control it before it's too late.

One common technique: Do not have intercourse for a while. Practice masturbating him until he tells you to STOP—or, when you sense he's about to come—then squeeze firmly right behind the head of the penis. Wait anywhere from ten seconds to a minute—long enough for him to gain control, but not long enough for him to lose his erection—and repeat the exercise. Chances are the first few times you try this he'll climax immediately anyway. But if you practice these techniques for a few weeks, he'll soon begin to recognize the feelings of arousal for himself and gain more and more control.

When He Can't . . .

If American men today were told, "You have a choice. You can lose your right eye, or you can lose your ability to have an erection. Which will it be?" we would suddenly have a country of one-eyed men. It doesn't matter how many times you tell him that there are other ways he can please you. His self-respect, power, and dignity are inextricably linked to his ability to rise to the occasion. As one male friend who'd suffered a temporary bout of impotence told me, "It was as if someone had robbed me of my personhood. Everything around me seemed as lifeless and limp as my dick."

At certain points in history, impotence was actually seen as a kind of crime. For example, during the seventeenth century, impotence used to be the only excuse for dissolving a marriage in the Catholic church, because the husband could not follow God's commandment to procreate. Church officials of the time actually conducted erection tests for prospective husbands. (Wives had to undergo virginity checks.)

Causing impotence was also seen as the penultimate act of revenge (right after murder). During the Renaissance, a forsaken mistress believed she could make her man impotent if she secretly removed the front band of his underclothes and tied knots in it. Or if a groom was lying in bed with his bride, one of her spurned lovers could knock on the door and call out the groom's name while implanting a knife in the door. If the groom responded, the malcontent would break off the tip of the knife, leave it in the wooden door, and silently depart. Many a new husband lived in dread of this sort of treatment.

When you stop to think how complex an erection truly is, you marvel that it ever works at all! It's an intricate choreography of nerve endings, hormones, brain chemicals, and blood flow. When a man is excited, blood (about eight times the normal amount) flows through the penile arteries into the corpora cavernosa, two cylinder-shaped, spongy chambers located in the shaft of the penis. These chambers become engorged with blood, and valves in thousands of tiny blood vessels trap the blood, preventing it from flowing out of the penis and causing it to become rigid and erect. Any interference with this mechanism, either physical or mental, can prevent a man from having an erection.

These days, according to the Erectile Dysfunction Unit at Cornell Medical Center in New York, up to 30 million men are affected by varying degrees of erectile dysfunction. But how many of them actually acknowledge the problem to themselves, never mind to anyone else? (A few years ago an ad for Impotence Anonymous explained the problem like this: "You can tell your best friend that you have cancer. But who can you talk to about impotence?")

Only a few years ago, doctors believed that about 90 percent of impotence was psychological. But more recent studies reveal that 50 to 75 percent of impotence is caused by physical problems.

To determine the difference, doctors often recommend a simple "stamp test." A row of stamps is placed snugly around the base of the flaccid penis before the man goes to sleep. Because the average man has several automatic erections during the night, a man with no physical impairment will rip apart the strip of stamps by morning. If this man is having problems getting an erection with his lover, it can be assumed that the problem is psychological.

If, however, the stamps remain attached, the man is not experiencing erections in his sleep and therefore probably has a physical problem.

Many men don't realize that orgasm and erectile ability are two separate entities. Just because a man can't have an erection doesn't mean he can't have an orgasm. But because erection and orgasm are so closely linked in most men's minds, those who are unable to achieve an erection *believe* they can't have an orgasm, and therefore they don't. They are so devastated when their equipment doesn't work that it's very difficult to get them to a doctor: Only one in twenty actually seeks medical treatment. Instead, they'd rather blame you, or decide "It's just not that important to me."

Often, the problem can be traced to alcohol or drugs.

We all know that a glass or two of wine will relax us, perhaps allowing us to be less inhibited sexually. But a moderate or large amount of alcohol impedes sexual function. Essentially, alcohol dilates the blood vessels, which makes it more difficult for a man to maintain an erection (the penis is kept hard by the *constriction* of blood vessels).

Cocaine often results in a condition called "coke dick." The guy either can't achieve or cannot maintain an erection.

A number of prescription drugs impede sexual function. Drugs that control high blood pressure, such as thiazide diuretics or beta blockers (which might also be prescribed for migraines) can reduce desire and impair erection in men (and, incidentally, lubrication and orgasm in women). Other libido dampeners: antihistamines, certain ulcer medications, and drugs used to treat depression. The biggest offender is the newest class of antidepressants, the selective serotonin reuptake inhibitors such as Prozac, Paxil, and Zoloft, which dampen sexual response in 30 percent or more of their users. In fact, the drugs are so effective in delaying orgasm that they're beginning to be used as an antidote to premature ejaculation.

What about the man whose problems with the little head stem from problems in the big head, in other words, men whose impotence stems from stress, pressures at work, negative emotions and attitudes toward sex, financial difficulties, or even a new sexual partner? Scores of men have discussed the subject with me, and the pain they experience merely *talking about* the subject is palpable. Here, according to the men I've talked to, are a few of the best ways for a woman to deal with the problem—what you might call Impotence Etiquette.

When it first happens, don't launch into a whole dialogue about it. Talking may be comforting to you, but it's generally not comforting to a man.

A lot of women pay attention to their man's penis only when they want to have sex, or know he wants it. But for a man with occasional erectile difficulties, this tendency can be alarming and somewhat defeating. He knows that every time you approach his penis, you're expecting to have sex. On the other hand, if he feels you're already on friendly terms with it—you play with it, kiss it, touch it, lick it, and so forth when you're *not* going to have sex—he won't feel so intimidated and nervous when you do go down there and try to get things going. It really helps if you're on such good terms with it that when you're down there kissing and stroking it, he can think, *Well, she's just down there playing around again. Nothing* has *to happen.*

After fifteen to twenty minutes of foreplay (or five to ten minutes longer than the norm for you), if you notice no response from that particular portion of his anatomy, casually make your way down there and begin gently, possibly playfully, to use your mouth and hands.

Every once in a while one of our girls would have a client who confessed to having some difficulties with his wife, and very often a playful approach with this sort of guy worked. He knew the girl wouldn't be personally offended if he couldn't get it up. Usually, for these guys, sex with their regular partners had become an emotional minefield. So if the call girl was simply sweet and nonchalant about sex, more often than not the "problem" client was perfectly able to perform.

My point here is that you can't seem to be trying *frantically* to make his wiener work. You know how anxious you feel when he's practically doing a tap dance on your clitoris and you just aren't responding. Well, to him, your attitude of "hard-on or bust" makes him feel equally pressured and is almost always counterproductive. Suddenly his erection is all about *your* ego. You're telling it, *C'mon, Big Boy, show me I'm a real woman, prove you love me, c'mon, fella* . . .

If, after five to ten minutes, you are still not getting a response, don't do an obvious "enough is enough" or "that's it, I've had it" routine. Rather than suddenly giving up and moving away from that area, slowly wind down your "efforts" and kiss, stroke, and nibble your way back up his tummy, chest, and neck.

If he's still feeling amorous and cuddly (and he may be so upset that he won't be), play kissy-face and stroke his chest, shoulders, back, whatever, and then perhaps say something like, "You know, I had a really rough day and I'll bet you did, too. Why don't we just turn off the lights and go to sleep?" Do *not* refer to the fact that he was having problems.

Don't even *think* about trying to make light of the situation or think that maybe a little joke might help. It won't.

The next time you're together, realize that he is probably anxious that it might happen again (terrified is more like it). If it happens several times, during the next couple of lovemaking sessions you might want just to kiss and touch without expecting or trying to make anything happen—so he knows you enjoy being with him whether or not he can "perform."

I hardly need to tell you the effect of ridicule or criticism in a situation like this. "What happened to my big, strong man?" "Funny, this never happened with any of my other lovers," and "Wow, I never knew anything could just shrivel up that fast" are not going to get you the desired results, unless the results you desire are skid marks in the place your lover once stood.

Women who criticize or make fun of impotence truly don't understand the pressure that sex entails for a man. Just imagine, for a moment, all the times you've wanted sex and enjoyed it, but for one reason or another haven't necessarily wanted or needed an orgasm that day. Now imagine that you *must* have an orgasm. That's the way a man feels about his erection.

Do not take his problem personally. This is the most common female trap. They do not criticize him; instead, they criticize themselves: I'm too fat. I'm too old. My skin's not soft enough. I'm not doing it right. . . .

This is not the time to whine and whimper about how he must not find you sexy anymore or fish for positive comments about your looks or sexual attractiveness. In other words, it's not the time to focus on you. First of all, even if you could lose a few years or pounds, the chances are *exceedingly* remote that his problems have anything to do with your looks. Not to be indelicate about this, but the average guy could close his eyes and have sex with anything that's breathing (and a few things that aren't). So while all along I've emphasized that men are visual creatures, their ability to have an erection exists apart from their need to be visually stimulated.

As to the fear that he no longer loves you, well, look at this poem about impotence, penned in the seventeenth century by John Wilmot, Earl of Rochester:

> Thou treacherous, base deserter of my flame,
> False to my passion, fatal to my fame,
> Through what mistaken magic dost thou prove
> So true to lewdness, so untrue to love?

As call girls everywhere know, for most men sex with a stranger is easy—no uncomfortable intimacy to deal with. It's *closeness* that can be tough. So, far from being a sign that he doesn't love you, impotence—especially early on in a relationship—can be a sign that he cares a great deal.

If he thinks that you are blaming yourself for his inability to get an erection, he'll be doubly pained. He has to worry not only about his own sinking self-esteem but also about yours. (I had one friend who, when her husband failed to get an erection, burst into tears. Weeping: now *there's* a reaction guaranteed to add levity to the situation.)

Of course, there's little you can do for someone with chronic psychological problems that cause impotence other than encourage him to see a therapist. Here are a few things the therapist may prescribe.

Stop Having Intercourse

One of the most common treatments is abstinence. The idea here is to remove all pressure from the sexual experience, because the more you try to force the issue, the more pressured he feels to perform, and the less likely it is that his little hydraulic system is actually going to work. So instead of trying ceaselessly, like you have in the past, you just don't try at all.

This doesn't mean that you stop being sexual with each other. For the first week, you might take a couple of showers together, giving each other long massages with lotion or oil, or perhaps fantasizing together—but not to orgasm. The next week, you might progress to kissing, caressing each other all over the body—but still making sure neither of you tries to climax. After another week, you could masturbate together—but don't try to make each other come. By the fourth week most couples have a renewal of desire and a better understanding of what gives the other pleasure.

Call a Cease-Fire

If the two of you have a particular ongoing argument—your child's poor performance in school, visiting his mother every other weekend—make a pact to not discuss it at all for two weeks. This is an arbitrary amount of time, but that doesn't matter. It's an artificial way to end a disagreement, even though the problem probably won't go away. Often resentments festering outside the bedroom are brought into the sexual arena, so the very act of trying to be agreeable to each other makes you more receptive to each other in bed. And once the two of you are making love again, the feeling of closeness may go a long way toward helping you bridge those minor squabbles that can assume major importance when you're not getting your sexual needs met.

Relaxation Therapy

If he's having a particularly difficult time at work, you may have to face the fact that his problems in bed will abate only when his problems at the office do. After all, the only area of his life that's as linked with his sense of self-worth as his penis is his job. Consider experimenting with therapeutic forms of relaxation: a quiet hour when he comes home from work where he's guaranteed no interruptions; if he's not exhausted, a brisk walk, bike ride, or game of catch with the kids to help him unwind and release endorphins; a gift certificate to the local masseuse; soothing relaxation tapes or tapes of his favorite music; even some time by himself with some X-rated videos or magazines you've thoughtfully provided! (Few things are more relaxing than an occasional masturbation session. Knowing he can "do it" himself helps restore his confidence.) At Cachet, our ladies often found that what a man required sexually was in some way an antidote to what was going on in the workplace. In other words, the guy who felt constantly under the gun or powerless because of a tyrannical boss wanted to feel dominant and all-powerful in bed; while a man who *was* the boss, who had the pressure of making decisions and being "Yes sirred" all day long wanted someone else to take control! You might want to keep this in mind if he does show some interest in sex. Let him be the boss or let him submit to your will, depending on what's going on at work.

Encourage Him to Cut Back on His Drinking

Even if excessive drinking causes only occasional bouts of impotence, the psychological effects of that failure carry over into your intimate life as a whole, causing a vicious cycle. You feel resentful and critical when he drinks and isn't interested in satisfying you; you complain to him; he pours another, telling himself he just needs to escape from you for a while; and then he can't get an erection. . . . If he's an alcoholic, he may deny that his drinking has anything to do with erectile problems, or he may not even care. But if his drinking is sporadic and noncompulsive, he may care enough to forgo a glass of wine or two when he knows you're in the mood. (However, it won't help his morale if you pour him one glass of wine and drink the rest of the bottle yourself.)

Let Him Know He Can Satisfy You in Other Ways

There's such a thing as *healthy* selfishness in a sexual relationship, and it's most definitely needed when your man is having erectile problems. Since half of his worry revolves around you ("My God, I won't be able to satisfy her"), encourage him to satisfy you with his hands and/or tongue. Let him know in no uncertain terms that although you love his penis, and you like it very much when it's big and hard, there are other parts of his body you also love, and these parts can make you very, very happy.

He'll still be upset, but at least he won't start obsessing about *your* sexual dissatisfaction and fearing you're going to run away with the postman unless his problem gets fixed, pronto.

Sexual CPR for the Man Who's Not Impotent, Only Tired

These techniques are appropriate when your man just needs some additional encouragement (perhaps you've made love once, and he'd like to try for round two).

- When his penis is really small, you can just put it in your mouth, letting it rest on the top of your tongue. Just like a baby sucks a bottle (apologies for this unsavory analogy), you can very slowly, gently, and calmly suck on it.
- There's an extremely sensitive place called the perineum, between his testicles and anus. You

don't want to push it or rub it hard, but just gently massage it while you're stroking his penis.

- For many men, massaging the prostate works wonders. Using a bit of lubricant, insert your finger into his anus and feel for a walnut-sized gland toward his belly. (Incidentally, unless he's constipated, your finger is not going in far enough to touch anything other than skin.) A very gentle massaging motion can be highly erotic and cause a quick erection. (Wash your hands thoroughly soon afterward. Bacteria that are harmless in the gastrointestinal area can cause infection if they enter your vagina.) Of course, not every man (or woman) is comfortable with this technique. Even if it feels great, he may think that any fooling around with that portion of his anatomy is too threatening to his sense of heterosexuality. You might have to introduce the subject gently: "Wouldn't it feel good if I put my finger . . ." If he looks uncomfortable, don't insist. If he looks interested but also seems afraid you'll be turned off, you might add, "I'd just love to try this. . . ."

Above all, keep your sense of humor about any challenges the two of you face in the bedroom. It's sex, for goodness' sake, not the cure for cancer! Remember, too, that although you're always there to offer support and empathy to help him overcome any difficulty, it's nobody's "fault." Certainly not yours.

11

Understanding the Male Mind: What Matters to Him and What He Can Do Without

These days, finding and maintaining a good relationship seems to be right up there on the national agenda with welfare reform and reducing the national debt. In our quest for love, we spend our lives trying to answer the eternal question, What do men want?

Many of us leap to the conclusion that men and women want very different things. She wants commitment; he wants Pamela Anderson from *Baywatch*. She wants love, respect, and intimacy, witty repartee, bottles of Dom Perignon shared in front of a roaring fire; he wants Pamela Anderson from *Baywatch*. Yet research shows that the sexes actually have similar yearnings.

Take a recent study at Pepperdine University in California, where men and women were asked to rate the twenty-five most desirable characteristics in a mate. For men, attractiveness was at the top of the list; but personality was a close second. The men's top five were attractiveness, personality, age, interests/activities, weight. For women, the top five were personality, interests/activities, attitudes, attractiveness, age. Although earlier studies showed more dramatic gaps, with men placing much greater emphasis on a date's attractiveness and women stressing a man's economic status, those gaps have narrowed.

At any rate, here's what your man most wants from you—and for himself.

Relationship Turn-Ons

The Kind of Attention He Got from Mom

I like men to behave like men—strong and childish.

FRANÇOISE SAGAN

My friend Renee came home from work one afternoon to see her husband, Sam, admiring himself in front of the mirror. He had just returned from his weekly basketball game, which was just about as thrill-packed as you'd imagine a team of middle-aged dentists would be. Sam looked himself up and down, sucking in his sagging abs, checking out his expanding love handles, and flexing his none-too-bodacious arms. He turned to Renee with a big grin on his face. "Not bad for a forty-year-old guy, huh?" he said. "I still look as good as I did in college."

"He would not give up until I told him how fabulous he looked," Renee told me. "I work out in aerobics class four times a week, and I've *never* liked my body that much."

(It's not just that women are more forgiving of men's bodies than they are of ours; it's that men are actually more forgiving of their *own* bodies. In a recent study of 146 students at the University of North Texas, both men and women tended to overestimate their intelligence, but only men overestimated their attractiveness.)

I think about this incident between Renee and Sam whenever I stop to consider just how much attention men want and need from us, and how even a little goes a long way. "I can live for two months on a good compliment," Mark Twain once said. Little did he know he was speaking for men everywhere.

Whereas women innately have a keenly calibrated bullshit detector ("He told me my earrings looked wonderful. He must want an extra night out with his friends this week"), most men have no such radar. They soak up praise like sponges. It's virtually impossible to overdo telling them how wonderful they are.

I'm not saying all men are looking for their moms, not by a long shot. What they do want, however, is the kind of uncritical, unconditional love they got from their mothers as children, with the faith in their judgment they believe is their due as men. Difficult, I know.

Here, for example, is mom-like behavior they love:

PRAISE, PRAISE, PRAISE Marla Maples may be America's shrewdest woman. When news of her affair with Donald Trump broke, the headlines in the *New York Post* screamed Marla's assessment of The Donald: BEST SEX I EVER HAD. Now, there were some rumors that Trump actually planted that story himself, but it's just as likely that Marla whispered this "confidentially" to a reporter at the paper. Can you imagine how an egotist like Donald Trump must have felt when he saw his sexual prowess praised in 100-point type? I'm not sure if that headline was a turning point in their relationship. Undoubtedly Marla has more than one trick for keeping Donald in line (not the least of which is his reported phobia about disease; he always knew, with her, he was 100 percent *safe*). But certainly that public praise didn't hurt.

Smart mates, like smart moms, offer praise when their partners least expect it (the way he bites his lip when he's concentrating at the computer keyboard is so *cute*) and when they really deserve it (he took out the garbage for the fifth consecutive evening and remembered to put a rock on the garbage can lid so the raccoons couldn't invade).

Dog trainers (and child psychologists) will tell you that the best way to train your pets is to praise lavishly when they do what you want and gently and firmly correct them when they do something wrong. When they're bent on getting attention by purposely being obnoxious, you ignore them.

Men are not all that different. Constantly calling attention to their deficits rarely gets results. Making a huge fuss over things they do that you love gets them to repeat that activity endlessly. (Keep this in mind the next time he surprises you by bringing home a bouquet of flowers. Don't just accept it as your due; get excited over it. My personal guarantee: more flowers.)

GENUINE INTEREST IN HIS LIFE Genuine interest, like orgasms, is something that can't be faked over the long term. You really have to care about what the guy does. In other words, if you fall in love with a bond trader, you'd better know *something* about munis, because that's how the guy spends eight to ten hours of his day. You can't just say, "Oh, I love Jim, but what he does for a living is so dull," because chances are, if you ask him his opinion, he'll say what he does for a living is *who he is*. Similarly, if Jim is, say, an amateur botanist, you don't have to know the difference between hooded pitcher plants and horned bladderworts, but it wouldn't kill you to know the difference between an oak and an elm.

ABILITY TO LISTEN TO BOASTING WITH RAPT ATTENTION "The advantage of doing one's praising for oneself is that one can lay it on so thick and exactly in the right places," Samuel Butler once said. Indeed, there are few people in his life to whom your man can express his pride in himself without seeming like a pompous boor. Just as his mom, eyes sparkling, would listen to him tell all about his big moment sliding into home plate at the bottom of the ninth, so you would do well to take in every detail of how he fixed the trash compactor, or dashed off a memo so impressive the boss dropped by his office to discuss it.

ABILITY TO LISTEN TO BORING STORIES The one quality any call girl has all over any spouse is the ability and motivation to give this kind of undivided, mom-like attention, even when she's not terribly fascinated. Think about all the times your mother had to listen to you natter on about what happened in math, or how you did on Mr. Kenner's typing test. She was bored silly, but she didn't let on, did she? That's because she knew the important thing was not the content of the conversation but the spirit in which you and she exchanged information. It was a spirit of intimacy. Call girls understand this principle, too, and many use it to their advantage.

My friend Joan complains that her husband, John, calls her at work every day to discuss lunch, specifically, what she's eating and what he plans to eat. "Sometimes," Joan says, "I will hang up the phone and think, *I'm fifteen minutes closer to death, and I've just spent that fifteen minutes discussing an avocado stuffed with tuna.*" Sometimes Joan feels pressured to make up exciting, elaborate lunches she hasn't actually eaten, in order to satisfy her husband's gustatory curiosity. "Last week I told him I'd just eaten salmon teriyaki, watercress and celery salad, rice and green chili pilaf, and banana walnut upside-down cake for dessert. He was delighted. Actually, I'd had a bagel. But when he called I happened to have a copy of *Gourmet* sitting on my desk. . . ."

Joan understands what's going on. In some peculiar way, knowing what she eats makes John feel connected to her throughout the day. (There may be a tiny element of the male desire to possess his wife here, too. Not that he wants to control her eating habits, but he just doesn't like to think that *anything* goes on in her life that he doesn't know about.) So as annoying as it may be to recite her lunchtime menu, Joan does it, and she listens to his recitation, too. "I don't feel any closer to my husband, knowing he just consumed a salami sandwich. But, hey, if it makes him happy . . ."

Confidence and a Sense of Self-Worth

For the most part, women in our society are almost pathologically frightened to celebrate their self-worth. We're trained from childhood to dilute self-confidence with feminine modesty. If a woman is not appropriately self-effacing, society tells us, she's a self-aggrandizing bitch. There is no middle ground, no room for self-confidence and assertiveness that are uniquely female. (Think Barbara Bush, not Roseanne.) We may have come a long way, baby, but not long enough to realize that having the courage of our convictions does not mean being pushy, arrogant, and "male."

Confidence is sexy. Self-respect is sexier still. A woman who doesn't shilly-shally or play games, who says what's on her mind, who follows through on her word, who doesn't make idle threats ("I'm leaving!") and then renege ("I'll give you one last chance")—this is a woman who's going to gain her man's respect. Men understand bargains and contracts better than they understand raw emotion. If you make some sort of contract together and he doesn't hold up his end of the bargain, he expects repercussions. If there are no repercussions, you will lose his respect, possibly forever.

Many women confuse respect with respectability—a great mistake, I think. *Respect* is what you earn from your character and your behavior; you must respect yourself before others can respect you. *Respectability* is other people's judgment of you; you gain respectability by conducting your life according to convention. A call girl's business, for example, might prevent her from having respectability, but she can certainly be a deeply moral woman and can respect herself if she's honest, kind, loyal to her principles, and so forth.

If you are proud of who you are, if you believe your standards and values are well thought out and meaningful, if you go to bed every night knowing you have done very little that you are ashamed of, then it is not important what "they" say. Remember, the people who are the quickest and harshest judges of others are almost always rigid, sanctimonious, small-minded people you wouldn't want to know anyway. As Oscar Wilde said, "Any preoccupation with ideas of what is right and wrong in conduct shows an arrested intellectual development."

Optimism, Enthusiasm About Life, Warm Personality

A surprising number of people believe that the only way to avoid disaster is to anticipate it. My friend Joan explains it this way: "Whenever I'm traveling by airplane I know, beyond any doubt, that it's my responsibility to keep that plane aloft. If I relax for one second—stop thinking about the engine whirring, say, and concentrate on my cocktail peanuts—the plane will burst into flames and two hundred and fifty people will plummet to their deaths."

Joan has some perspective on her own angst. But normally, going through life anticipating the worst is an ordeal—not only for you, but for your mate. Your husband gets a raise? Yes, you say, but was it as big as his colleague Dave's? The two of you are planning a minivacation? But you can afford to go away for only three days, and then not very far—what good is that?

Nobody expects you to be relentlessly upbeat all the time. But the next time something unpleasant happens to you or your partner, ask yourself if there is another way you could be looking at this that might make the unpleasantness easier on everyone involved.

Genuine warmth, which springs from an optimistic outlook, is also eminently desirable. Ice queens are sexy only in Hitchcock movies, and only if they happen to look like Grace Kelly. In real life, men much prefer the woman who is obviously happy to be with them: good-natured, easygoing, gregarious, forthright, flirtatious (*selectively* flirtatious, that is), with a genuine smile on her face.

True, men enjoy the chase. They like having hurdles to climb in the pursuit of their goal. But for most guys the climb better be more along the lines of a grassy hillock in the English countryside than the rocky cliffs of Mt. Everest.

Honesty, Openness, Trustworthiness

Those Boy Scout qualities count. Of course we all have our little secrets, pockets of privacy we're entitled to hold onto even after we're married. So by open and honest I don't mean you've got to reveal every little escapade you've ever lived through. (Things like, "I'll never forget how scary it was having wild sex with a forest ranger I'd just met when a grizzly started making like he wanted to join us," are better left unsaid.) But a man has got to feel he knows pretty well what's going on with you. One of the most damaging things you can do to your relationship is somehow to give your mate the impression you're leading a life apart from him. Even if you have perfectly innocent explanations, an observant guy is easily spooked if he starts seeing matchbooks around the house from places you didn't go together (that business lunch you didn't mention) or letters to old boyfriends stuffed in your desk drawer (*he* doesn't know the letter was written years ago).

One friend of mine almost got divorced after her new husband found an alarming bill addressed to her—from a sperm bank. "Before I met Jerry I was involved with a married man. The whole thing sounds ridiculous now, but, well, I was madly in love with him. I knew we'd never end up together, but I thought that at one point I might want to have his child. So I got him to make a few 'donations' to this sperm bank, and even after we broke up I continued to pay the storage fees. I had those usual weird girl-fears that maybe I'd never meet anyone I cared for so much again. Then I met Jerry, and the sperm became like . . . an old memento. This sounds so lame. Anyway, when Jerry saw the bill, he thought I was hiding a *horrible* secret from him. You can imagine. It took a few weeks to straighten it out. Obviously this was one memento from a past relationship I couldn't keep."

Similarly, many women tell little white lies just to avoid a hassle. If your man is constantly catching you in these lies, however trivial they are, they will breed suspicion. My friend Nancy discovered this recently when she told her husband that she was going to an early morning business meeting, so would he please take their daughter to school that day? "Actually, I just wanted to have breakfast with a girlfriend, and I knew Steve would give me a hard time," Nancy told me. "So I told this little white lie."

That little white lie backfired when Steve, on his way to school with his daughter, ran into Nancy's friend Laura. "Oh, I've got a date with your wife in fifteen minutes!" Laura chirped.

"Three weeks have passed, and even though the whole thing was completely harmless Steve still hasn't let me forget it," Nancy says ruefully. "I hardly ever fib. But now he's wondering what else I've been lying about. . . ."

Try to keep the lines of communication as open and honest as possible, even if that means having the occasional confrontation you'd rather avoid.

Sense of Adventure

I've already discussed how important a sense of adventure is to a relationship, even if your own man is not exactly a thrill seeker. Being adventurous can take many forms, from trying out exotic foods and cuisines to exploring a part of the city or a neighboring town you've never been to. Why not take a cruise or an escorted tour of a foreign country instead of spending a week at the same hotel you always go to in Hawaii? Research a faraway place that has always fascinated you like Egypt, Morocco, or Tahiti, and put away ten dollars a week until you've saved up enough to go there, even if it takes five years. Being adventurous means opening up and expanding your experiences, trying new things, and going to new places. It might be a little uncomfortable at first if you're not used to it, but it's a wonderful way to build a shared history, and it keeps both your relationship and your life from getting monotonous and stale.

(Are men just naturally more interested in adventure than women? A researcher at New York City's Museum of Natural History recently discovered that male cockroaches stay out later at night than female cockroaches. If that's not proof of biological determinism, what is?)

Competence

I admit it: Sometimes, I feel intimidated by women who are good at too many things. I have one acquaintance who has made Martha Stewart her God. I'm always afraid to ask Erica what she's up to because the answer is invariably something like, "Oh, I'm just going outside to slaughter an old horse, to make the glue to attach my hand-designed labels on the brandied cherries I've been canning. Why?"

Nevertheless, to most men competence is definitely a turn-on. No man wants to feel responsible for every detail of his mate's life; he doesn't want her running to him over every little thing like a child. If you're capable, he can relax. The only men who want us to be helpless are control freaks. Of course men want to be needed—don't we all?—but a woman who is adept at a wide variety of tasks, whether it's petit point or engine tune-ups, is a woman men admire. (Although I've never met a guy who didn't enjoy showing off his masculine prowess by opening a reluctant jar lid, firing up the barbecue, or squashing a water bug.)

Sense of Humor and Easy Laughter

Anyone who's been out on a bad date knows how excruciating it is to spend one evening—let alone a lifetime!—with someone who doesn't share your sense of humor. On my list of Top Ten Great Things About Marriage is going to a stuffy, pretentious party with your mate and laughing about some of the people there afterward. As one wit observed, "To appreciate nonsense requires a serious interest in life."

Intelligence and Intellectual Stimulation

Some men want to sit down to breakfast with the female equivalent of George Will; some men don't. But any guy with more than two brain cells is thrilled to be with a woman who is interesting and who challenges him (at least a little bit) intellectually. Perhaps she's informed on issues that he hasn't had time to learn about, so being with her is an education. Perhaps she sees an issue in a different light and he comes to realize that his position was rather ill-considered (even though he'd never admit it).

After all, we're all put on this earth to learn and share that learning with others, which is why, if you feel that your own mind has been on the shelf too long, you might consider trotting down to your local college and checking out the adult continuing-ed courses.

Eventually, even the most beautiful, well-tended body wilts. The well-tended brain never does.

Home-Cooked Meals and a Full Refrigerator

There is no spectacle on earth more appealing than that of a beautiful woman in the act of cooking dinner for someone she loves.

THOMAS WOLFE

Girls, I'm afraid it's true: To your man, after the first few years of your relationship, his penis is only his second most precious organ. His stomach is definitely first.

You're saying to yourself: *All this and I've got to be a gourmet chef, too?!* Of course not. I myself am kitchen-averse; it's all I can do to get up and make tea in the morning. Most of us simply don't have the time to devote to preparing elaborate meals. (Some of us—the lucky ones—have discovered that our mates like to cook more than we do.) But every man on the planet has a few simple dishes he loves, recipes so basic that even *you* are capable of preparing them a couple of times a month. Or maybe your task is even simpler: Keep the refrigerator stocked with all the foods he loves and, with any luck, can prepare himself.

We all know food is not just food. It's thoughtfulness, generosity, and, yes, love. It's a way of showing that you care for him that he will understand even better than words.

But what about me? I hear your asking yourself. *Why can't he cook for me every once in a while?*

A comedian I heard recently suggested that the best way to get a man to cook for you is to get him to associate cooking with danger. Men who don't like to fuss with sauces and muffin pans nevertheless can get pretty excited about grilling meats or chopping just about anything. If cooking involves fire or large knives or a whole fish—preferably all three—he's there.

(However, *I* say: Forget about it. If he doesn't cook, make him take you out.)

Very few of us have mates who expect us to cook like Julia Child; that's the expectation we impose on ourselves. In fact, most guys would be just as happy if we knew how to flip burgers and fry onions with the finesse of the chef at Denny's.

RELATIONSHIP TURN-OFFS

Overmothering

I've said men crave the kind of attention they once got from their mothers. But I don't want to create confusion here: In most circumstances men do not like to be treated as children. Here again, a call girl has every advantage over a wife or mother. She can be attentive without overwhelming a man with concern, advice, judgments, opinions, and an endless need to fix things he wants to solve for himself. In other words, she keeps a healthy distance while still conveying her interest and caring. His life is not a reflection on *her.*

Why do some women overmother? We enjoy creating for ourselves a double illusion. First, there's the illusion that our lovers, like our children, are under our control. We feel powerful and needed—after all, what would the darlings do without us? Second, there's the opposite illusion: If men are children, when they do something that hurts us they "just can't help themselves." Thus we not only absolve them from taking responsibility for their behavior, we absolve *ourselves* from taking any action that might prove unsettling or uncomfortable. Conveniently, the man-as-child paradigm lets us feel a sense of power and control when we want it yet allows us to comfort ourselves with the knowledge we have no control when they've done something we'd rather ignore. It's all part of this country's strange cult of the victim: Nobody is responsible for his or her behavior anymore. Women let themselves be abused and mistreated, losing men's respect in the process. Why? Because they can't help themselves (they're untrustworthy and incompetent) and *we* can't help ourselves (we have to stay with them, no matter how they treat us, because they're still children).

By putting yourself in the role of mom, you are effectively guaranteeing that your husband will resent you and desexualize you, just as he had to do with his own mother in order to break away from her during adolescence. You are also making it likely that he will take you for granted and therefore lose respect for you. You're *not* his mother, and you won't be, no matter how hard you try.

Here's the kind of mothering your man *doesn't* want or need.

DOING SOMETHING FOR HIM BECAUSE YOU ASSUME HE CAN'T DO IT HIMSELF Want to know a sure way to get your husband to do absolutely nothing around the house? Ask him to, say, wash the kitchen floor and then monitor him to make sure he does it as thoroughly as you do. If he's not living up to your standards, grab the mop away from him and mutter something about "the only way to get something done is to do it yourself." Repeat this with everything from doing the laundry to making dinner reservations, and you're sure to have a garden slug sitting in the backyard, watching *you* skim the slime off the pool.

In other words: Don't worry about whether he's doing something the way you'd do it. Let him do it his own way, praise him for it, and watch him get better at whatever the task is all on his own.

REMINDING HIM ENDLESSLY OF THINGS YOU'RE SURE HE'LL FORGET "Where are the house keys? Did you remember to turn off the iron? Did you feed the dog? If I've told you once, I've told you a thousand times . . ."

Well, you probably *have* told him a thousand times, which is why, around the fifth or sixth time, he tuned you out. Thoughtlessness therefore becomes a self-fulfilling prophecy. The woman who's constantly checking up on her husband (and reinforcing his helplessness) is the same woman who's always "taking care" of the problem for him and therefore making sure there are no consequences to his actions—or inaction. He becomes more sullen and more recalcitrant the more you expect him to be irresponsible.

BEING OVERLY SOLICITOUS Ever go out to dinner with a woman who practically spoon-feeds her husband? Usually, it begins with a guessing game: "What would you like to eat tonight? Does rack of lamb sound good? No? How about some yummy pasta? But get it without the cream sauce. You know you have a lactose sensitivity. . . ."

This behavior (besides being kind of nauseating) suggests a desperate need to control. It makes me want to ask, "Just what does this guy do that's so threatening when he's not in your company that you need to turn him into an infant when he *is* with you?"

PICKING LINT OFF A JACKET (OR OTHER TERRITORIAL GROOMING ACTIVITIES) Remember how our mothers used to "fix" our hair after we'd gotten it exactly right? In addition to being annoying, attention to your mate's appearance in public is sending the message, "Private Territory. Do Not Trespass." Usually, it comes across as galloping insecurity. If you *must* straighten his tie and comb his hair, do it privately.

SCOLDING OR NAGGING, ESPECIALLY IN PUBLIC Scolding is really the flip side of being overly solicitous. You're still desperately looking for ways to keep your man in his place (and that place seems to be a high chair). Any man with a backbone will, at the very least, learn to ignore you. Or he'll quickly learn to resent your very presence—and then avoid it.

Indeed, avoidance is the usual male tactic for defeating the nag. As my friend Jim told me about his ex-wife, "What Sheena most enjoyed was an audience in front of which to expound upon my many, many flaws. She particularly liked to wait until we were among my friends to bug me about, say, not attending my daughter's last dance recital—which, she happily explained, would probably traumatize our child for life. (Never mind the other seven recitals I *had* attended.) She rejoiced in being the Perfect Parent, and I the Absentee Father. And eventually, I became exactly that."

Conversely, the woman who is appreciative when her man does follow through ("Honey, thanks so much! That's such a load off my mind") has a man whose memory is likely just to keep getting better and better.

Falling in Love Not with Him but with His Potential

Here's a typical conversation I have with my friend Connie, who consistently falls for hyphenates—actor-waiters or novelist–word-processing temps.

> ME: So, Tyler's been a proofreader for how long now?
>
> CONNIE: He's not a proofreader. He's a musician. His band, the Consenting Adults, is on the verge of signing with a big label. Oh, my God, he's so beautiful!

ME: Wait. How long has he been proofreading?

CONNIE: Twelve years. I'm worried that the strain of life on the road will take its toll on our relationship.

ME: You say he's just about to sign with a big label?

CONNIE: Well, not *tomorrow*. But he thinks he saw a scout from Elektra at a wedding he was playing last week . . . the guy was probably there to see him. Anyway, I'm helping the guys get a little money together to make a video, and . . .

Connie has fallen for a rock star, but what she has on her hands is a proofreader. He may be the most gorgeous, intelligent, soulful proofreader ever born, and he may be the perfect man for Connie. But she has projected onto him a life that she's planning to share, which may never be the life he lives.

Some women project dreams onto their men that the men don't even share. Jean always tells me what a brilliant trial attorney her husband would make. He is, undeniably, an incredible showman: intelligent, articulate, persuasive, charismatic. Unfortunately for Jean, Norm prefers exercising his talents on a class of five-year-olds. He loves teaching kindergarten. For some reason, when they married Jean thought teaching kids was "a phase." She set herself up for disappointment and in the process made her husband (now, not surprisingly, her ex), feel there was something wrong with him for wanting to "play" all day.

Why do women fall in love with a man's potential, instead of with the man himself? Most of us are desperate to be perceived as "good," which, in womanspeak, means helpful, self-sacrificing, generous, noble. If we support a man through those difficult periods of his life, he'll love us all the more when he's become a success, and he'll take us along for the ride. (Well. Tell *that* to all the Hollywood first wives who were dumped after their husbands made it big.)

The problem with this line of thought is that women often begin to resent all those sacrifices before their investment (i.e., their man) bears fruit. And the man is all too aware that he's resented and cast in the role of burden. Essentially, falling in love with a man's potential is setting the two of you up for failure. And he knows it.

This desire to shape and mold our mates to our ideal image is almost universal, yet it should be almost universally avoided. Because however much we believe we are "helping" and "improving" him, every day we are giving him the message: You are not living up to my standards. You are a disappointment. You are not good enough. Soon he will feel guilty; then he will feel defensive; finally he will resent you— and look for someone who thinks he's fine just the way he is.

"Whom the Gods wish to destroy," Cyril Connolly once wrote, "they first call promising."

Preoccupation with Money

It's one of life's little ironies that men pay call girls for sex in order to be in the company of women who are not overly concerned with money. Well, that's not quite accurate. The call girl does not confuse money and love. She wants something simple, something he can understand: payment for a job well done. But the wife or girlfriend? For many couples, money is an area fraught with peril.

Times, of course, are changing. But men and women still grow up receiving very different messages about money. Women expect that someone will care for them, and a man who loves them will show how much by providing money. Men are taught that it's their role to be good providers. If they're not, they're less desirable; but if they are, women probably want them because of their money.

Men worry: Does she love me for myself or for my money? Women worry: If he really loved me, he'd be working harder and trying to get ahead for our future.

We're all concerned with money: getting enough, keeping enough, getting ahead. But I think most men have the same relationship to money as women have to their weight: It's a source of chronic concern and emotional turmoil, engendering feelings of envy, power, powerlessness, and fear. So a woman whose main concern is her husband's earning power is as damaging as a man who's preoccupied with his wife's weight.

Money is closely connected to a man's self-worth. So it is crucial for you to be a team player in this arena of your relationship. A man desperately craves a woman who is a supporter and contributor to the family unit's financial well-being. You don't necessarily have to earn a penny yourself. But you do have to be willing to cut back during hard times and to cheer him on during good times, appreciate him when he can spend and not resent him when he can't. Money is not love. But it may be closely aligned with his feelings of success or failure as a human being.

No Life of Your Own

Kay is a successful lawyer in her mid-thirties, attractive, intelligent, and one of the most deeply unhappy people I know. Her professional success means little to her, because she comes from a family that told her, since she was a little girl, that the highest goal she could aspire to was to be the wife of a powerful man. She has not yet found that man. Therefore she is miserable.

Worse, I suspect she'll *never* find that man, because whenever she gets involved with someone, she abandons her own life. Literally *abandons*. If he likes to go to jazz concerts, she decides she likes jazz; if he's an opera buff, she's boning up on Wagnerian librettos. When she took up with her last boyfriend, a photographer, she suddenly decided her own work was "meaningless paper pushing"; she actually quit her job and spent several months working as a videomaker's assistant. His friends become her friends, and her friends become memories. Kay also makes herself available day and night. If he can't see her until two A.M. and then just wants a quickie, well, that's okay by her.

Generally, after a few months, the guy either relegates her to the position of occasional lay or runs away. He's terrified.

And why shouldn't he be? Few things are scarier than a woman who wants all her needs met by one person. This woman isn't a partner, she's a succubus, leeching the life out of her victims. And this is how most men perceive her.

It's one thing to be deeply interested in your partner's life; it's quite another to make his life your own. The message you give him, loud and clear, is: My life is really not very interesting or worth living. I don't think I can sustain myself. I need your air to breathe.

You don't need to have a high-powered career in order to have your own life. Your world may revolve around friends and family. But no matter what, make sure you have pockets of satisfaction and happiness that you yourself can control, that are not dependent on the whims of anyone else, including your partner.

Jealousy

Poets and prophets have written volumes on the "the green-eyed monster which doth mock the meat it feeds on," as Shakespeare wrote. But my friend Erica summed up the emotion quite nicely: "You understand jealousy at the same moment you understand that everyone, under the right circumstances, is capable of murder."

This combination of craziness, yearning, malice, and despair is the most human of emotions and is common to virtually all societies. But I'm not talking about jealousy that has a basis in fact. I'm talking about unfounded jealousy, which almost inevitably wreaks havoc on a relationship. At the root of jealousy is usually a person's fear of being abandoned or unloved. But it manifests itself as being critical and controlling.

If you can't get a handle on your jealousy, your mate will feel constantly harassed and controlled. It's only a matter of time before he acts out his anger in some way. Thus unjust accusations of infidelity sometimes can become self-fulfilling prophecies: When you already stand accused of something, you're more likely actually to *do* it.

Perhaps the most destructive form of jealousy is that directed not toward other women but toward other people your husband needs in his life—particularly his children. Even if he loves you, pitting yourself against his kids may well be a battle you can't (and don't deserve to) win.

Incidentally, remember that little nugget of wisdom your mother gave you, the one about keeping your man a tiny bit jealous for the good of the relationship? Forget it. It may work at the *very* beginning of a romance, since most men like some challenge, that primal triumph of winning you from the affections of others. But once you've declared that you're serious about each other, making a man jealous is destructive. He needs to trust you just as much as you need to trust him.

Incessant Need to Discuss the Relationship

For you, discussion is part of the ongoing flow of a relationship, a way of assuring yourself everything is okay. In other words, it's vital and necessary. But your man is working on a different set of assumptions, the old, "If it ain't broke, don't fix it" theory.

Talking about a relationship that—to him—is just fine, thank you, is at best unnecessary and at worst destructive, because his *perception* of the discussion is totally different. He associates talking with solving a problem, so if you keep wanting to talk about your relationship, he assumes you're subtly trying to tell him there are lots of problems. His level of frustration and worry will rise as he tries to figure out just what those problems are. If he can't, he'll give up and tune you out.

I'm not telling you to forget about those relationship discussions. But don't force them on him all the time. Keep your discussion of issues specific and concrete—more along the lines of "I'd like us to make time for each other at least one night a week," not "You never want to spend time with me anymore."

Constantly Testing His Love

Many women pose little questions to their men and tell themselves, *If he really knows me, he'll answer X* or, worse, *If he really loves me, he'll say Y.*

Men *hate* this stuff. Most men are pretty straightforward creatures, so when they ask us a question, it's easy for us to figure out the thing *they* want to hear. (Actually, they want to hear only two things: "It's not falling out" and "Darling, if it were any bigger, it would hurt.") But women's questions are considerably more complicated than men's, and men know there are no right answers.

As soon as you ask him whether you should wear the red dress or the black dress, he knows he's in trouble. If he says red, you think that means you looked fat the last time you wore the black one. (Vice versa if he says to wear the black dress.) If he says both dresses are fine, you'll accuse him of not paying attention or not caring how you look.

At this point you're feeling unloved. He's annoyed because it's late and you're still not dressed. And he's wondering why he has to talk about your clothes, hairstyle, etc. That's what your girlfriends are for.

Although it's difficult, keep your testing to a minimum. As my friend Dan said, "Living with my ex-wife was like taking the SATs every day of my life. And I was always sure I wasn't going to pass." What you're unconsciously doing is looking for ways to be a little hurt, which will then make him guilty, which will then, you think, make him easier to control.

Most men who feel they're on the verge of failing all the time won't try harder. They will stop trying at all.

Unending Drama

High drama—screeching fights, then making up passion-ately—can be cute for, oh, the first month of a relationship. Then it gets tiresome. Remember: Most men shrink from emotional conflict. You might find it cathartic to have a tear-ful scene, but he finds it disturbing and uncomfortable. Also, drama queens eventually find themselves in the same posi-tion as the boy who cried wolf. After a few months of hyster-ics, your partner will tune you out.

Ill Health and "Female Plumbing Problems"

All I can tell you is, if you're going to play invalid, you'd bet-ter genuinely *be* an invalid. Nothing is more annoying than a mate who's conveniently sick when presented with things she doesn't want to do but mysteriously gets better when an opportunity for pleasure comes along.

And most men are still uncomfortable with talk about your menstrual cycle. Save those fascinating discussions about water retention and cramps for your girlfriends.

The Ultimate Appeal of the Call Girl: She's a Great Communicator

At forty-five, Christopher is the son every mother dreams of: kind, thoughtful, intelligent, *and* a millionaire lawyer who's not too busy to call home every day. But there's one thing he hasn't dared tell his mom. He's divorcing his wife. For a call girl.

There were, of course, a myriad of problems in Christo-pher's marriage. As his career soared, his wife, Barbara, felt more and more resentful of the time and attention Chris spent on his business. They had one child, and Chris desperately wanted more. But Barbara, who wasn't interested in having more children, told Chris she had "female problems"—and secretly stayed on the Pill. Even more disturbing, over the course of several years she'd pilfered about $50,000 out of their savings account to pay for her addictions to Valium, alcohol, and shopping.

Chris may have had less time to devote to his wife, but he still wanted Barbara's attention when he was available. Increasingly resentful and angry, Barbara was less willing to give it. Chris felt that frequenting call girls would make it easier to stay in his marriage, which he wanted to keep for the sake of his child. This way, he could still get some of the attention he craved without emotional involvement. "Actually, it cost about as much as therapy, and it was more satisfying," he said, laughing. "I could have gone on indefinitely, seeing girl after girl. But then I met Sandra."

Sandra had never worked for me when I was running Cachet, but I met her through one of my former girls. A coltish brunette with lush lips and menthol-blue eyes, she looks more like a cheerleader than a lady of the evening. Forthright in her language and manner, there's nevertheless a sweetness and earnestness about her. She doesn't want to be perceived as a "home wrecker." In fact, after four years in the business, Chris is only her second real boyfriend.

Sandra's story is sad and troubling. "My mother abandoned us, and my father raised me and my brothers. He was kind of a disturbed man. He was also a strict Catholic who never taught me anything about sex," she said. "I remember when I was fifteen and got my period, I didn't know what it was, and I was sent home from school covered in blood. I was crying. My father took one look at me, decided I was a sinner, and locked me out of the house. I haven't been home since."

Sandra got on a bus to Miami, where she took a job in the only place nobody checked her age: a local strip club. She was a waitress for a while, before graduating to stripper. She was making a decent living, but out of sheer loneliness she often found herself going home with some of the more attractive club clients, just to have a bit of company. "I didn't even particularly like sex at that point in my life," she told me. "I never had an orgasm. But I wanted to be touched, I wanted to be hugged and held. Sex seemed a pretty small price to pay."

One night, Sandra visited a local music club, where a famous rocker and his band were playing. Her wholesome, fresh beauty caught his eye, and he sent for her after their gig was over. They went back to his hotel, the most luxurious in Miami. In the morning, as she was leaving, he tucked $500 into her pocket. "He thought I was a hooker. At first I was shocked, then insulted. But then I thought, *Wait a second. I'm doing this stuff anyway for free.*" Sandra began crisscrossing the country as one of the stripper "circuit girls" who are sent from one city to another, fulfilling the clubs' perpetual demand for new bodies. When she went home with someone, she made it clear that she expected money. Drugs were a big part of the scene, too. "A lot of guys would like us to keep them company while they did coke. The sex was secondary," Sandy says. "Many of these guys were high, wide awake, and frightened of being alone. They wanted more than one girl around at a time, but mostly for companionship." Although Sandy did her share of experimenting, she never became addicted to anything, so, unlike a lot of girls, she was able to save money during her working years.

Somehow, Sandy never became jaded about the business, and she was a favorite wherever she went. "I know the old stereotype is that Jewish men make the best husbands. But for some reason my clientele was about ninety percent married Jewish guys," she laughs. "Maybe they thought of me as the shiksa they couldn't get in high school, I don't know. Most of them craved oral sex—it was something they thought wasn't 'proper' to ask their wives to do.

"I'd recently arrived in New York City when I met Chris," she continues. "I knew he couldn't be just another client. He was gentle, sweet, and talked to me like I was a human being, not just a new piece of meat. And he was such a soft touch—

too soft, actually. He threw around one hundred dollar tips as if they were nothing. A lot of girls took advantage of him."

What most moved Sandra about Chris was his tremendous need to talk. "He'd stay with me a couple of hours, and we'd have sex for maybe five or ten minutes. Nothing unusual. Then he'd stay *another* couple of hours," Sandra recalls. "He talked as if no one else in his life ever listened to him."

And that, in fact, was the truth. Chris frequented call girls not because his wife wouldn't have sex with him, but because he was desperately lonely. She no longer showed the slightest interest in his life. "Even when she was with me, she was *absent*," Chris says. "I never really understood what was going on in her mind, and God knows she had no interest in what was happening in mine. I would sit down at the end of the day to talk to her about something that happened at the office, and within seconds I'd see her eyes glaze over."

Despite the chasm of difference in their ages and backgrounds, something between Chris and Sandra clicked. "She's had very little education, but Sandy's smart about people in a way lots of Ivy League women I've dated can't come close to," Chris says. "She's gorgeous and sensual, sure, but she makes me feel special and appreciated like no other woman I've known. I can talk to her about anything. If she doesn't understand what I am talking about, she won't pretend, or change the subject, or lose interest; she'll *ask*. Whenever we have a disagreement about things, she has this uncanny ability to resolve problems without either of us ending up feeling like the loser."

Of course Sandy, for her part, is thrilled that the man who fell for her has money, but this is hardly the first time a wealthy man lavished her with gifts. It is, however, the first time she has reciprocated a client's affections. "When I began to have orgasms with Chris," she said, "I knew I couldn't keep the relationship professional."

Sandy and Chris have problems, big problems. Chris is still not sure if he's going to tell his friends and family how he met his fiancée and what she's done for a living. "In the past she's just told everyone I know she was a bartender or a waitress," Chris says. "It's horrible living a lie, and I don't want Sandy to have to do that for the rest of her life. On the other hand, I come from a very traditional Catholic family, and as much as I love her I find it very hard to face my mother and say, 'By the way, your daughter-in-law was a hooker.'"

Since Sandy doesn't want to take even the slightest risk with Chris's health, she has quit having sex with clients. But she still occasionally plays the dominatrix for a few regular clients, which doesn't involve sexual contact. "Chris is so generous. But we're still not married, and I don't want to be entirely dependent on him for money," she explains. "Besides, as liberal as he is about sexual issues, I don't think he'll ever quite understand that I *enjoyed* my work. I loved being the special 'treat' of so many powerful and attractive men."

At thirty, Sandy has gotten her high school equivalency degree and would like to go to college to study psychology. "If I have any talent at all, it's not for sex per se," she tells me. "It's knowing how to make people feel better about themselves."

The chances of a love relationship developing between a call girl and a client are remote at best. But Sandy and Chris's unusual situation illustrates the power of good communication between even the most unlikely of couples.

Communication is a term you hear so frequently that it's become almost meaningless. Yet the ability really, truly to "reach out and touch someone," as the AT&T commercials put it, is sorely lacking between many couples today.

Perhaps because we're all so inundated with information—much of it junk—from magazines, newspapers, and television, we've become adept at tuning out. Tuning out has become a tool for survival. Can you imagine how overwhelmed you'd feel if you actually *paid attention* to every single thing you were told in the course of the week?

The unfortunate effect of needing to tune out in order to survive is that we also reflexively tune out the things we most need to pay attention to: our friends, family, and most particularly our partners. I honestly believe there's a "listening crisis" in America. We are exposed to too much trivia, and therefore we have slowly lost the ability to hear and respond to what's important.

Here's something every call girl and mistress knows that you should know, too: You can put on sexy lingerie, play your entire Sade collection, and take champagne bubble baths together until you have a major case of prune-skin. But if you really don't understand the fundamental differences in the way you and your man think, if you don't find ways to communicate despite those differences, if you can't hear him (and, as a result, he begins to pay less and less attention to you), your relationship will founder.

THE ART OF LISTENING

Being a good listener is second nature to an experienced call girl. Obviously she has an advantage when it comes to paying attention to her clients: She can be extremely empathetic and also neutral because the problems don't involve her. She can always keep an ear out for what he wants to hear, too, since it's obvious what he wants her to say. A wife or a girlfriend needs to be more honest. But it certainly doesn't hurt to see which way the wind is blowing.

These are the key qualities of a good listener.

Be Attentive

A lot of men don't understand that we can fold laundry *and* listen, or straighten up the living room *and* listen. In other words, we can do two (or more) things at once. They can't. If two men talk to each other, that's the only thing they're doing. So when they see us doing anything besides sitting and watching them when they talk, they feel we're really not interested.

Even if it's only for ten minutes twice a week, sit down and listen to him without doing anything else. Don't let your mind wander to the clogged shower drain that needs to be snaked out. I want you to practically put a bowl underneath his mouth to catch every pearl of wisdom.

Don't Judge Him

Even if you think he's done something to bring on his problems, it's inappropriate to tell him when he's unburdening himself to you. If he's got a problem, he doesn't need to feel any worse about it at that moment than he already does.

Don't Offer Advice

Eventually, if he's upset enough, he'll ask your opinion. And that's the time to say, "Well, next time, you might want to consider . . ." But don't offer your opinion unless it's asked for. Men believe that it's insulting for the one without the problem to offer advice. Women don't understand that, since we usually welcome advice, even if we don't always take it.

Be Discreet

He needs to know that whatever he tells you will be held in confidence. Most men hate the thought that their innermost secrets will be discussed and dissected with your friends (and probably passed on to their boyfriends or husbands).

Men also want to believe that you're the kind of person who won't remind them of these confidences in a moment of anger. Nothing guarantees a man's losing his faith in you more than a whispered intimacy later used as artillery during an argument.

Don't Be Overly Sympathetic

Don't make whatever's bothering him into an even bigger deal than he already thinks it is: "Oh, my God! You mean Charlie said that to you? And you just stood there and took it? You poor, poor thing!" It's one thing to be understanding; it's quite another to ooze so much sympathy the guy feels pathetic.

GETTING HIM TO GIVE:
THE KEY IS COMMUNICATING

Listening, of course, is only half the job of communicating well. Knowing how to express your own wants and needs is the other half.

Former president Ronald Reagan was called the Great Communicator for good reason: He was perceived as a man who conveyed his vision for the country without inciting personal animosity and resentment. You might think Reagan was a simpleton, you might vehemently disagree with him, but he was a supremely effective salesman. He knew how to get his message across to the public.

How do *you* become a great communicator? You develop the ability to convey what you want and need without making your man feel defensive or resentful. In other words, it's getting what you want without whining, threatening, pleading, or inflicting guilt.

Subtlety Will Get You Nowhere

If you have a problem with a female friend and you subtly tell her what's wrong, she'll pick up on the nuance quickly and try to clean up her act.

Subtlety doesn't work with most men. If you go to a party with a girlfriend and say, "Boy, that onion dip is strong," she knows you mean, "Girlfriend! Run to the bathroom and brush those teeth immediately if you plan to chat up Mr. Sugarlips over there." If you say the same thing to your husband, he'll probably think, *Really? I like onions. Let me go over there and have some more.*

If you have a complaint, it's always better to be direct, funny, humorous—and *noncritical*. Go back to the onion dip scenario for a moment. Don't say to your husband, "Are you using your breath as a human shield?" A better approach is, "Oh, honey, we'll both have to brush our teeth for ten minutes tonight before we go to bed. That onion dip is a killer."

Men Need to Know What's Expected of Them

One of the great fallacies a woman labors under is the notion that a man who loves her knows exactly what she wants. He doesn't. He hasn't a clue.

He needs to be told what you want—not with anger, not timidly, not with accusations or judgments. Simply. Matter-of-factly. "Honey, I didn't have time to put new sheets on the bed this morning. Would you do it while I finish up these dishes?" is much more likely to get results than, "I never get a chance to sit down and relax. After I finish these dishes I *still* have to put clean sheets on the bed."

Follow up your requests with endless doses of praise when he does what you ask.

And what if he doesn't do what you request? What if he sort of tries but screws up? Praise him anyway. That is, if he's done something close to what you wanted in the first place, act like he's already done exactly what you wanted.

Say you're having a dinner party and you want a centerpiece for the table but have no time to run out and get it yourself. You give him a general description of the flowers you want; after all, he's looked at the table setting himself, so he should know what would match. Your table setting is in shades of blue and white. He comes back with an autumnal arrangement of oranges, crimsons, and yellow.

Do you criticize him for having no eye for color? Of course not. You make a big fuss about how beautiful the arrangement is, how tasteful, how the guests will love it. Then you put the flowers on the mantelpiece and say, "Sweetheart, I think these would look so much better over here. But we still need something for the table. You know, candles would be really nice." Then you get out the candles. He may know that he kind of screwed up, but he'll appreciate the fact that you didn't rub his nose in it. (Later, be sure to point out *his* flowers to guests—he chose them, aren't they beautiful, etc.)

Next time, you know you have to be more specific about the flowers. But you've made him feel pleased about accomplishing a task he would have been reluctant to take on otherwise. All of us are naturally drawn toward what we do well and shun what we believe we don't do well. The more competent your man feels, the more likely he is to take on jobs and responsibilities that would otherwise be left in your hands.

Phrase Requests with "Would You . . . ?" Not "Could You . . . ?"

Most women are intimidated when it comes to asking for what they want. "Oh please, please, please, could you do me a huge favor?" works well with women, because women see humility and gratitude as politeness. Men, on the other hand, see humility and gratitude as weakness. And being creatures who are more attuned to hierarchy than we are, they don't respond well to weakness.

Instead, we need to make our requests from a position of strength. "Would you throw the clothes that are in the washer into the dryer for me?" Not "I'll be so indebted to you . . ." but "Here's what I expect of you, being the great human being you are." Never be afraid to be quietly commanding.

Men Are Geared Toward Action and Conquest

There was a story in the local papers recently that caught my attention, about a polar bear in the Central Park Zoo. This bear was worrying his zoo handlers because all he did all day, every day, was swim back and forth in his pool. He'd dog paddle to one end of the pool, do a back flip, dog paddle to the other end, flip over, and repeat. *All day.* Was it an obsessive-compulsive disorder? Was the bear just neurotic, like the rest of us New Yorkers? He wasn't eating well, he wasn't playing, and he wasn't mating with his lady friend, who was herself getting a little testy over her beau's inattention.

An animal psychiatrist was brought in as a consultant on the case. After a few days, the shrink zeroed in on the problem: The bear had nothing to challenge him. He was bored out of his little bear mind. Bears need to hunt. So if the handlers couldn't provide live food for the bear, they at least had to make him work for his dinner. The handlers had to *hide* the food and hide the bear's toys. They had to come up with ingenious ways to get him out of the pool and reengaged with his life.

So they did. And within a few weeks, the polar bear was spending more and more time out of the pool, looking for his food, playing with his toys, entertaining the crowd, and, most important, mating with the female polar bear.

I think of the polar bear every time a woman complains about how easy she's made life for her husband: She does everything for him, and still, all he does is complain.

These women are not taking into account men's basic need to be challenged. They need to do things for you and themselves, or they get bored. If you are, in a sense, your man's favorite "possession," it is in his best interest, as well as yours, to take care of you to the best of his ability.

This is why, I think, men have throughout history paid for female companionship but women haven't paid for men. Feminism has shown us the importance of being able to pay our own way and made women overly sensitive to being accused of relying on men for their money. But feminism has ignored a basic tenet of human nature: Men need to pay.

Not all the time, of course, and not necessarily with money. If you make a lot more money than he does, you might find that you take him out to dinner more than he treats you. But he needs to treat you sometimes, or he needs to find other ways to take care of you: running errands, baby-sitting the children and giving you time off, making love to you where *all* the focus is on your body. And you have to let him. You also have to let him know, in no uncertain terms, that this is what you expect on occasion. If he doesn't have money, he can "work for" you in other respects, just as you are giving and generous to him.

Call girls instinctively understand this pay-to-play rule. Paying makes the visit something special, something he had to earn. If we lived in a utopian society where government health care policy covered two visits a month to a working girl, I don't think very many men would go!

When Men Fall in Love, They're Falling in Love with Themselves as Well as with You

I want you to permanently etch in your mind Othello's exquisitely beautiful explanation of how he and Desdemona fell in love (the italics are mine).

> She gave me for my pains a world of sighs;
> She swore, in faith, 'twas strange, 'twas passing
>   strange;
> 'Twas pitiful, 'twas wondrous pitiful.
> She wish'd she had not heard it; yet she wish'd

That heaven had made her such a man. She
   thank'd me;
And bade me, if I had a friend that lov'd her,
I should but teach him how to tell my story,
And that would woo her. Upon this hint I spake:
She lov'd me for the dangers I had pass'd;
And I lov'd her that she did pity them.

Othello fell in love with Desdemona because he saw his own greatness reflected in her eyes. I'm not saying this is the noblest reason to fall in love, nor, in Othello's case, was it the wisest. But even with the most humble among us, isn't there a large element of self-love involved in falling in love with someone else? When you fall for a man, you may think he is handsome, intelligent, funny, brave, kind. But don't you also think, *Gee, he makes me feel great about being me?*

Each of us has traits or abilities that we are proud of, and nothing makes us feel as loved and accepted and understood as a partner who both recognizes and likes those things in us that we like about ourselves.

Neither men nor women tire of hearing other people—whether it be family, friends, or especially our partner—talk about how terrific we are and how much they like and appreciate something we said or did. If that "something" is something we're particularly proud of ourselves, the attention is even more meaningful.

Epilogue

A few weeks ago, I received the following letter from a woman named Mona who had attended my Just Between Us Girls seminar:

Dear Sydney:

When a friend of mine dragged me, kicking and screaming, to your class six months ago, I never imagined in a million years I'd be writing to express my thanks. The week before I attended, I found out my husband had been having an affair with another woman for about a year. Of course, some part of me knew about the affair without actually *knowing*. My husband was absent more than he had been; but then, we'd been married twelve years, and I wasn't paying much attention to whether he was around or not. It was as if we had been shouting to each other from opposite ends of a long tunnel. Sometimes, our messages reached each other; more often, they were drowned in the noise of everyday living: the children, the responsibilities, the bills, work, work, work. Over the last few years, the fabric that holds a marriage together had begun to unravel—and instead of patching the thing up, I just decided I would become used to the tattered edges.

After discovering the cache of credit card bills he'd been hiding from me (the most devastating? He bought her THE SAME PERFUME as he had bought me on our honeymoon), I sobbed. I screamed, I ranted—and I immediately went to call our lawyer. I made my husband move out of the house (probably, I realize, right into the arms of his girlfriend). I obsessed about how beautiful she must be (I imagined something along the lines of Uma Thurman), and I spent three days lying in bed, eating chocolates and watching daytime talk shows—particularly the shows where the theme of the day was "Men Who Cheat on Their Wives." I found myself driving by her home late at night, just to catch a glimpse of her. And I was in for a surprise: she was attractive, yes, and perhaps a couple of years younger than me, but she was hardly the bombshell I imagined. In fact, the real shocker was: She looked like *me*.

It was about that point that my girlfriend saw an advertisement for your seminar and suggested we go. I refused. What was the point? My marriage, and my life, were over. Even after I finally agreed to go, I *still* didn't cancel the appointment with my lawyer.

What you said about men straying—and what women could do about it—really opened my eyes. I began to realize that he had been sending me signals of his unhappiness for a long time. Not in the way a woman would do—he never came out and *told* me he was unhappy. Instead, he would ask me to do things with him—boring stuff that I never had time for. Once he asked me if I loved him, and I laughed—*of course* I loved him. Who cooked for him? Who bore his children? If I didn't love him, would I do these things? What a childish question!

He would buy me skimpy underthings—and I'd laugh, saying only a pervert would want to see a woman in that sort of stuff. I usually felt exhausted by life with three small children . . . but when he volunteered to help me, I always found that *I* could do the work (whatever it was) better. Eventually he stopped volunteering, and slowly but surely, he became little more than a shadow moving through his own house.

I left your seminar and immediately went home and canceled my appointment with the lawyer. I picked up the phone and called a marriage therapist—before I even knew if my husband would go with me. (As it turned out, he agreed to go, reluctantly—there are a lot of things he's been afraid to tell me.)

I'm not saying our problems are over, or even that our marriage will be saved. I'm still devastated, and although he says he has broken up with the girlfriend, I'm not ready to have him move back home. But for the first time in years, it seems, we're talking. I feel like I'm seeing him again—he's always been there—the Husband—but I don't feel like I've really *seen* him for a long time. And when we made love last night (for the first time in over a year—it had been a while since we'd made love, even when we were still together), the touch was familiar, but the emotion behind it seemed utterly new.

If I'd not gone to your seminar, I know that by now I would have been another divorce statistic. There are moments when I still hate my husband for what he did to me, and I still don't feel I can trust him 100 percent. But at least his affair made me realize I had lost something precious, and I may be lucky enough to find it again.

Mona loved her husband and was faithful, and her husband rewarded her by having an affair with another woman. So it's clear who's the good guy and who's the bad guy here, isn't it?

Well, maybe not.

After reading this letter, I began to think about the sometimes enormous gap between the way women think they treat the men in their lives and the way they actually treat them. We say we love them, but we don't spend enough time showing them we *like* them.

For most men, the feeling of being liked is in some ways just as important as being loved. Liking is demonstrated by the little acts of kindness and generosity. A note left in his pocket telling him you look foward to seeing him at the end of the day. Flowers of his favorite color on the dinner table. Getting up at three A.M. to feed the baby, even though it's his turn, because he's got an important meeting tomorrow.

This certainly is a book about kindling passion. But a slow simmer usually cooks a dish more deliciously than a blowtorch. Think about creating bonds of mutual liking, affection, and understanding. The more you show your *liking* and *appreciation* of your man, the more he'll be able to show his *love* and *respect* for you.

It's that complicated. It's also that simple.

Recommended Reading

Laura Schlessinger, *Ten Stupid Things Women Do to Mess Up Their Lives* (New York: Random House, 1994).

Barbara De Angelis, Ph.D., *Are You the One for Me?* (New York: Delacorte, 1992). Primarily for singles.

———. *How to Make Love All the Time* (New York: Dell, 1988).

———. *Secrets About Men Every Woman Should Know* (New York: Dell, 1991).

John Gray, Ph.D., *Men Are from Mars, Women Are from Venus* (New York: Harper, 1993).

———. *Men, Women and Relationships* (Hillsboro, OR: Beyond Words, 1990).

Barry Lubetkin, Ph.D., and Elena Oumano, Ph.D., *Bailing Out* (New York: Fireside, 1993).

———. *Why Do I Need You to Love Me in Order to Like Myself?* (Stamford, CT: Longmeadow, 1992).

A. Justin Sterling, *What Really Works with Men* (New York: Warner, 1992). Primarily for singles.

Boston Women's Health Book Collective, *The New Our Bodies, Ourselves* (New York: Simon & Schuster, 1992).

Alex Comfort, *The New Joy of Sex* (New York: Crown, 1991).

Miriam Stoppard, M.D., *The Magic of Sex* (New York: Dorling Kindersley, 1992).

Bernie Zilbergeld, Ph.D., *The New Male Sexuality* (New York: Bantam, 1984).

A Note From the Author

The Just Between Us Girls seminar has been given to thousands of women across America since 1989. It has been used as a spouse program at business conferences and conventions, as the featured event at fund-raisers, or just for fun at private ladies' luncheons, bridal showers, or birthday parties. For information on the Just Between Us Girls seminars or any of the other presentations I give, please write:

Sydney Biddle Barrows
210 West 70th Street
Suite 209
New York, NY 10023

When you call my relationship advice line, you can speak to me or one of my colleagues personally about specific problems or questions you may have about men or your relationships.

1-900-745-1234

My first book, *Mayflower Madam* (Ivy Books), is still in print in paperback. If your local bookstore is temporarily out of stock, they can easily order it for you.

As we go to press, I am in the process of developing a radio call-in show and reviving my newspaper advice column.

Of course, I have to make sure that I don't get so busy that I ignore my own advice and don't leave enough time to spend with my wonderful husband, Darnay Hoffman, who is a hard-working New York attorney.